THE POLITICAL THEORY OF ROBERT NOZICK

THE POLITICAL THEORY OF ROBERT NOZICK

Santosh Bakaya

Publications

KALPAZ PUBLICATIONS

DELHI-110052

The Political Theory of Robert Nozick

Rs. 750

ISBN: 81-7835-481-0

Published in 2006 in India by
Kalpaz Publications
C-30, Satyawati Nagar, Delhi-110052
E-mail : Kalpaz@hotmail.com

Laser Typesetting at : Master Computers, Delhi
Printed at : Salasar Imaging System, Delhi

Contents

Preface

Liberalism, which has spanned a long period of more than three hundred years, has been a very complex and intricate ideology. In this period, it has undergone a lot of changes–right from the natural rights libertarianism of John Locke to the of Robert Nozick.

The present book is an attempt to evaluate the political theory of Robert Nozick, whose path-breaking book, 'Anarchy, State and Utopia' (1974) sowed the seeds for a resurgence of Libertarian political theory.

With the publication of John Rawls' *A Theory of Justice* (1971), two things became crystal clear to philosophers and political theorists alike–firstly, that liberalism had found a new and able defender in the economic contractarian based system of Rawls, and secondly, reaction against 'A Theory of Justice' was diverse, coming from different variants of liberalism, and one of the most appealing, lasting and influential attacks on Rawls, came in the form of Nozick's 'Anarchy, State and Utopia' (1974), which, holding a plea for the 'Minimal State' and the 'Entitlement Theory of Justice', revived the classical liberal ideology of Locke's—Absolute property rights and self-ownership–under a new name 'Libertarianism'.

Central to libertarianism is the claim that individuals should be free from the interference of others. Personal liberty is the supreme moral good. Hence one's liberty can justifiably be restricted only if one consents to the restriction–Any other restriction, including taxing incomes for redistribution—as Rawls wants—is considered unjust by Nozick, who holds it at par with robbery.

Couching his theory in the language of rights, in the Lockean spirit–Nozick emphatically maintains that no individual or organization can violate the rights of another individual, thus only a Minimal state—the night-watchman state of classical liberalism limited to the narrow functions of protecting all its citizens "against violence, theft and fraud and to the enforcement of contracts, and so on ..." (ASU, p. 26) is justified, and any other extensive state, by attempting the task of social engineering and redistribution is a blatant assault on an individual's rights of self-ownership.

In the post-communism world, there have been enormous socio-economic changes, and we find more and more nations adopting the capitalist mode of development, the welfare rhetoric has begun to waver, putting a question mark against welfare statism. It is against this backdrop, that Robert Nozick's views become relevant. With his emphasis on the minimal state, he has given voice to the debate regarding the nature of the state—whether it should be an agency of redistribution of wealth and services from the rich to the least advantaged, or merely a safety net establishing a minimal level of welfare, beneath which no one should be allowed to fall.

The present book tries to prove that Nozick, has revived the Lockean state of nature in the contemporary setting, and it is from this Lockean state of nature that the minimal state voluntarily emerges, without violating individuals' rights—hence, is moral, legitimate, just and inspiring, unlike the Rawlsian state, which, with its emphasis on welfarism and redistribution, violates individual rights–hence according to Nozick is unjust.

A true libertarian, he has revived the classical liberal–individualistic theory of the state, and toeing the line of Locke, has revived the inalienable rights of an individual, which he possesses independent of society.

The book has been divided into six chapters. The first chapter introduces the political theory of Robert Nozick, giving a brief summary of his major works.

The second chapter expatiates on the progress of liberalism, right from the ideas of John Locke to Robert Nozick. It also throws light on the Libertarianism/ Communitarianism debate.

Robert Nozick's Entitlement Theory of Justice is dealt with in the third chapter, which also attempts a comparison of his theory with other popular theories of justice–Plato's Theory of Justice, the Marxist Theory of Justice, the Anarchist Theory of Justice, and Rawls' Theory of Justice.

The fourth chapter focuses on Robert Nozick's theory of the minimal state which is limited to the narrow function of protection against force, theft, fraud and enforcement of contracts—It also tries to explain the rationale and utility of the minimal state in the contemporary world.

Both Rawls and Nozick represent two dominant ideologies of our time. While Rawls' represents the Keynesian tradition of liberal egalitarianism, Nozick represents the classical liberal view of the free market and the minimal state. The fifth chapter tackles this great debate between Rawls and Nozick.

The sixth and final chapter highlights the level of abstraction of Nozick's libertarianism, and tries to place his theory in the current liberal tradition.

Santosh Bakaya

Acknowledgements

It was Keynes who said long back. "It is astonishing what foolish things one can temporarily believe in if one thinks too long alone". I shudder to think of the follies and the blunders I would have committed, had I vainly believed in the efficacy of single handed effort. Thankfully, I did not think too long alone.

This book which is the result of doctoral research, needless to say, is not the product of alienated labour, hence I have many to thank in this endeavour.

At the very outset, I would like to thank Dr. Dadhich, Professor in the Political Science Department of Rajasthan University, Jaipur and also my Ph.D. supervisor, for his intellectually stimulating lecture on Ralws/Nozick at a refresher course in Ajmer, which shoved me into the Nozickean world, where everything was new for me–and of course, mind-boggling! Through his incisive and apt comments, he not only enriched my knowledge of Nozick, but also put me on the right track, helping me in making the desired changes and additions, and giving it the present form.

There has been an Invisible Hand, quite different from the Invisible Hand that Adam Smith talks of, and that Invisible Hand has always goaded me forward in all my endeavours—the Invisible Hand of my late father Dr. Kashinah Bakaya. I indeed owe a colossal debt of gratitude to that Invisible Hand.

Thanks are also due to my husband Lalit Magazine, whose moral support has always proved more eloquent than action. His small, encouraging words have indeed gone a big way in the completion of this project.

A love-filled thanks to my daughter Iha, who has waited these three years with an exemplary patience and an incredible stoic calm, so that she could be the sole focus of my time, after I had completed what she innocently thought was my home assignment!

I owe a special debt of gratitude to my student Paritosh Goyal of Day Time Cyber Cafe, Bharatpur for giving me the most generous access to the internet and helping me in gathering a lot of online material, over hot and sometimes not so hot cups of tea!

A special thanks to Dr. (Mrs.) Rita Dadhich for her warm hospitality on my Jaipur visits, and also to Shruti and Archa fo their effervescent warmth, when I desperately needed it.

I also wish to record my gratitude to the following libraries which facilitated the task of collecting the required material:

Rajasthan University, Library, Jaipur
The American Library, New Delhi
The British Library, New Delhi
The Central Library, JNU, New Delhi
Jammu University Library, Jammu
M.S.J. College, Library, Bharatpur
The Departmental Library, Political Science Dept., Jammu University

I would also like to say a word of thanks to my students Ajay Saini, Vishnu Saini, Deepak Khatri, Amit Khatri, who, taking a strong personal interest in this endeavour, put in days and nights of hard labour and succeeded in giving the handwritten chaos, a systematically and neatly typed form.

Last, but far from the least, there have been many more who have helped me in their own small ways—Deepak Gera and Hema Gera, Deepak Agarwal, Vipin Sharma, Prem Prakash, Narendra Sharma, Ram Kumar Kaushik, Rinkesh and Nripesh of Royal Forex, Bharatpur.

And to these, in the words of Shakespeare:

"I can no other answer make but thanks and thanks and ever thanks."

Santosh Bakaya

1

Introduction

Liberalism has been the most complex and intricate of ideologies, spanning a long period of more than three hundred years.

Liberal values developed gradually from the seventeenth century, and this ideology which has strands jutting out in the social, political, moral and economic sphere crystallised in the early 1800s as a way of thinking.

A synoptic view of liberalism reveals that right from the natural rights liberalism of Locke to the libertarianism of Robert Nozick, there has been a common strand which runs through the different shades of liberalism–and that strand is the principle of individual liberty.

It emerged in Great Britain in the middle and late seventeenth century and later spread to Europe and America. In the middle of the twentieth century, communism and fascism threatened the very existence of liberalism but then it reemerged with a new vigour and enthusiasm, specially in the USA and U.K.

Liberalism is a concept and attitude whose definition and meaning has changed over the centuries, but whatever language the liberals speak—the idea of liberty, tolerance, diversity have been eloquently expressed by most of the liberals—right from John Locke to John Stuart Mill to Isaiah Berlin to John Rawls to Robert Nozick.

Although, it is indeed a hazardous task to isolate the key liberal thinkers, as the most representative of the liberal creed, it is not hazardous to maintain that human rights, human freedom remain central to the liberal creed, whatever the specific nature of the political-economic arrangements of a liberal–democratic society.

As a writer puts it :

'Liberalism is preoccupied with the creation and defence of a world in which free and equal individuals can flourish. This is the position maintained alike, by for example, Locke, J.S. Mill and Nozick."[1]

Liberalism has been characterised by a shifting emphasis, having undergone a change from its classical form as represented by John Locke and Adam Smith, through the revisionist liberalism of Bentham and Mill, to the modern liberalism, as represented by John Dewey, Milton Friedman, Frierich Hayek, C.B. MacPherson and Isaiah Berlin, and finally to contemporary liberalism, as represented by John Rawls and Robert Nozick.

Classical Liberalism

All varieties of classical liberalism believed that individual liberty must be maximised, and the chief threat to it comes from the state, Locke emphasised the three primordial rights of life, liberty and property, strongly believing that the individual needs to be freed from the shackles of an authoritarian state.

Revisionist Liberalism

In the hands of Bentham and Mill, liberalism was revised in the context of utility, which meant the greatest happiness of the greatest number. Both thinkers represent what can be labelled as revisionist liberalism–Mills' ideas represent a type of liberalism that gives up the Lockean baggage of state of nature, natural law and social contract.

In Mills' defense of liberty, we find an interplay between the rights of the individual and social utility.

Modern Liberalism

At the turn of the twentieth century, the fortunes of 'classical liberalism', and its laissez faire prescriptions began to change for the worse. Instead of delivering prosperity and universal freedom, vast inequalities became rampant, as seen in the growth of powerful monopolies and trusts, and moreover with the onset of 'great depression', in the 1930s, classical liberalism seemed a faith whose day had come and gone.

Although no liberal society has succeeded in removing government totally from the economy, yet, the nineteenth century was a period when the classical liberal formula of free market and limited government, as represented by Locke and Adam Smith was clearly ascendant, but at the turn of the twentieth century, questions were raised regarding the efficacy of the limited government, and the market that had caused the depression–and thus, in this scenario, the redistributing welfare state became firmly entrenched and institutionalized.

During F.D. Roosevelt's new deal programmes and even later, it was accepted as part of their policy by the Republicans during the Eisenhower period, and Lyndon Johnson's great society in the 1960s, but after the Second World War, we see that an important contribution was made to the theory of liberalism, by theorists whose allegiance lay with classical, rather than welfare liberalism, which had held sway in the preceding years. Theorists like Hayek, Friedman held a plea for the free market and limited state, and Berlin with his emphasis on negative liberty gave a new impetus to the liberal individualist tradition, sharpening it by his insistence that negative liberty 'leaves more paths for individuals or groups to pursue.....' and that freedom... 'is coterminous with the absence of bullying or domination.'

The great American pragmatist philosopher John Dewey (1859-1952) tried to bring liberalism up-to-date, by plunging the individual deeply into the social firmament. He believed that individual can realise his potential only within the social firmament.

Milton Friedman was a great believer in the power of the free-market and held that political freedom cannot exist without economic freedom.

Similarly, Friedrich Hayek (1899-1992) was also a free-market oriented economist who strongly opposed extensive government intervention in economic life–'The Road to serfdom', published in 1944, was a strenuous objection to the escalating departure from the classical liberal creed, in the form of the entrenchment of the welfare state–he raised his voice against the redistributive welfare state, and a planned economy, stating that this would inevitably lead to totalitarianism.

When published, it was treated as the 'last theoretical gasp of an obsolete and reactionary ideology',[2] but the 1980s and the 1990s saw this allegedly dying gasp, gaining a whole new life, in the form of the revival and resurgence of libertarianism and a number of books were published which sought to articulate libertarian ideals within a contemporary setting. One such book was Robert Nozick's *Anarchy, State and Utopia* (1974), which was one of the most appealing and influential attacks on Rawls' 'A Theory of Justice' which was published in 1971.

Contemporary Liberalism

Contemporary liberalism is permeated with the views of John Rawls and Nozick who gave a new tenor to liberalism.

When John Rawls' 'A Theory of Justice' was published in 1971, it was not only acclaimed for having revived normative political theory, but also because, of the fact that through it, liberalism had found a new and able defender in the economic contractarian based system that it upheld.

Reaction against 'A Theory of Justice' was diverse, both the communitarians like Charles Taylor and libertarians, like Nozick criticised it vehemently.

To John Rawls, goes the credit of single-handedly reestablishing liberalism as the political ideology of the world, and also the credit for the revival of political theory in recent times.

Pointing out the limitations of utilitarianism, which was undoubtedly very popular in the nineteenth and early twentieth century, he tried to put forth a reasonable alternative to it.

As the 'Dictionary of Important Ideas and Thinkers' states :

"Rawls' Theory of Justice has been called the most influential contemporary contribution to political philosophy and has been credited with revitalising the discipline".[3] The theory's most notable critic is Robert Nozick, who had denounced it as advocating a redistribution of wealth and property in 'Anarchy, State and Utopia' (1974). He countered Rawls' conception with a libertarian theory of social equity based preeminently on individual rights–which were inalienable 'and there are things no person or group may do to them.'

John Rawls (1921-2002)

This American social-political thinker and philosopher was born in February 1921, and died on 24th November, 2002 in Baltimore. An instructor at Princeton in 1950, a Fulbright scholar at Oxford in 1952, a professor at Cornell in 1955, he moved to Harvard in 1962, and since then he had been a professor of philosophy there. He indeed carved a niche for himself in the field of political theory by his path-breaking and trail-blazing book. 'A Theory of Justice" (1971), which has been translated into every major European language as well as into Chinese, Japanese, Korean.

'A Theory of Justice', which reached its culmination in the year 1971, was actually the result of more than a decade's labour.

What started with an article 'Justice As Fairness' (1958) in the Philosophical Review, culminated in a full-fledged text in the form of 'A Theory of Justice', which was critically acclaimed. In this book, he has tried to 'create a logically interrelated structure of a liberal state which can provide equality without sacrificing liberty. The thrust of his argument was, that by borrowing Kantian contractualism, it is logically possible for a liberal state to be just and caring for the 'least advantageous person' without sacrificing liberty. He was hailed as a saviour of liberalism, who gave a moral justification of American hegemony. The interest that this book ignited, resulted in the publication of a lot of books on political theory revolving around the ideas of Rawls.

Nozick's 'Anarchy State and Utopia' (1974) was a critical rejoinder to Rawlsian arguments. It resulted in the division of the whole movement of liberalism, into liberals and libertarianists.

Roughly two decades after the publication of his first book 'A Theory of Justice', Rawls' second book 'Political Liberalism' was published in 1992, by Columbia University Press–New York–It had a less extended but more complex period of development–Beginning with the 1980 Dewey Lectures at Columbia University, and extending through a series of papers written during that decade.

'Political Liberalism' represents a distinctive form of liberalism, resting on an idea of free public reason that yields new insights into the questions of justice facing us today in our pluralistic society.

In 'A Theory of Justice', he had tried to offer an alternative to Utilitarianism. As he says in the introduction of 'Political Liberalism' :

"....during much of the modern period of moral philosophy the predominant systematic view in the English speaking world had been some form of utilitarianism."[4]

'Political Liberalism' a more mature work, incorporates all the thought processes of Rawls after 1971, and in this work, Rawls admits, that there were certain inconsistencies in A Theory of Justice, which he tries to remove in 'Political Liberalism.'

As the front flap of 'Political Liberalism' points out :

"Rawls ... asks how can a stable and just society of free and equal citizens live in concord when deeply divided by ...... reasonable though incompatible doctrines?"

His answer is based on a redefinition of a "well-ordered society". It is no longer a society united in its basic moral beliefs, but in its political conception of justice.... Understood as a political conception, it can be endorsed by the main religious, philosophical, and moral doctrines that endure over time in a well-ordered society.

Such an overlapping consensus of reasonable doctrines, Rawls believes, represents the most likely basis of social unity available in a constitutional democratic regime.

On the basis of his two path-breaking books, we see that Rawls has indeed given liberalism a new lease of life, his 'A Theory of Justice' being hailed as probably the most important work of political philosophy written in English since the Second World War.

Right from the time of John Locke to the present, we see that the conceptual, socio-economic political elements of liberalism are interconnected, and form a single historical process permeating the discursive universe of political theory.

In the recent years, some of the literature that has had the greatest impact on the field has been devoted to attempts, such as those of John Rawls and Robert Nozick to provide new foundations for liberal theory.

In simple terms, liberalism, as mentioned earlier, is the belief in, and commitment to a set of methods and policies that have as their common aim greater freedom for individuals–A bird's eye-view of the representative liberal thinkers shows that their aims have been the same, although the means have differed from time to time.

Although there were times when apprehensions and misgivings were expressed regarding the demise of political theory, yet the fact remains, that it resurfaced at the beginning of 1970's, with a new found gusto and vigour as reflected in the theories of Rawls and Nozick.

Similarly, some critics had also sounded the death-knell of liberalism, forecasting that liberalism was likely to disappear after having performed its negative role, and that whatever virtues it boasted of, were no longer useful or safe. Critics of all hues and shades used all shades of adjectives for it, some derogatory, some not so derogatory, yet despite allegations levelled against liberalism, and its coherence, the fact is that there "has been a remarkable revival of liberal theorising all of which seeks to portray liberalism as offering a neutral framework for resolving the division of the modern world."[5]

With the shift of liberalism from negative to positive– the state acquired its all-pervasive form. But still the fight for the classical liberal laissez faire perspective of the state was not given up. After the Second World War, there was a noteworthy contribution to the theory of liberalism–this contribution was made by theorists like Robert Nozick. After 1960s this movement became popular in USA and England and came to be known as libertarianism. Etymologically, libertarianism means free will or free advocacy of liberty.

The Great Depression which began in 1929 in North America, Europe and other industrialised areas of the world, lasted until about 1939, which culminated in the stock market crash of October 1929. This was followed by a decline in economic activity, and as a result, until 1932 one out of every four U.S. workers was unemployed. Other industrial countries like Germany and Great Britain were also adversely affected rendering millions of workers job less. As the Encyclopaedia Brittanica (Vol. V, Page 443) observes:

"The Depression had important consequences in the political sphere strengthening extremist forces and lowering the prestige of liberal democracy. In the countries that did not succumb to totalitarianism in the 1930s, mass unemployment and economic stagnation persisted until the outbreak of World War II in 1939, which its demand for men and munitions and its spur to technological advance opened a new economic era."

When Franklin D. Roosevelt accepted the Democratic nomination for the Presidency on July 2. 1932, he gave a speech wherein he promised a new deal for the forgotten man, and in reaction to the ineffective administration of President Herbert Hoover in tackling the problems unleashed by the Great Depression, the American voters voted overwhelmingly favour of the Democratic promise of a new deal.

So, in accordance with his promise, Roosevelt's domestic programme between 1933 and 1939 focussed on bringing economic relief with immediate effect, as well as reforms in industry, finance water power, labour and housing. Needless to say, this greatly enhanced the scope of the federal government's activities dealing a blow to the American political philosophy of Laissez-faire as The New Deal was based on the concept of a government regulated economy.

Harry S. Truman's (1945-1953) Fair deal largely followed The New Deal of his predecessor.

It was against this backdrop of increased government activities that a movement opposing such massive state interference re-emerged in the name of libertarianism.

Here, it would not be out of place to throw some light on libertarianism, because of Robert Nozick's immense contribution to it. It was with his path-breaking book 'Anarchy State and Utopia' in 1974, that the libertarian movement received large scale academic attention, and it was through this book, that for the first time, in atleast a century, some one made a serious, sustained and vigorous attempt to refute philosophic anarchism and defended the libertarian doctrine that the minimal or night-watchman state is the most powerful state morally justifiable.

In the preface of his book 'Anarchy, State and Utopia', he wrote "A minimal state, limited to the narrow functions of protection against force, theft fraud, enforcement of contracts, and so on, is justified; that any more extensive state will violate persons' rights not to be forced to do certain things, and is unjustified; and that the minimal state is inspiring as well as right."[6]

These lines amply demonstrate his libertarian leanings, and as, he himself admits. "I found myself becoming convinced of (as they are now often called) libertarian views due to various considerations and arguments."[7]

In the light of his libertarian views, it is essential to know what libertarianism actually stands for.

According to the Harper Collins' Dictionary of Thought. Libertarianism is :

"The doctrine that no state can be legitimate which sets out to do more than enforce individuals rights; extreme libertarians hold that no state whatever can be legitimate and that we are not obliged to obey any authority to which we have not given our actual, and not merely our hypothetical, consent. Libertarians differ from 20th century liberals in disbelieving in social justice and in thinking the welfare state is simply robbery under the cover of law."[8]

Similarly, Murray N. Rothbard says that libertarianism is "a movement in political philosophy based on the doctrine of the rights of the individual. It holds that each individual possesses the absolute right of self-ownership–that is the right to own and control one's own person without molestation ..... The libertarian opposes interference with the rights of person and property and sees the state as the major source of such interference. The government receives its revenue by taxation, which the libertarian sees as the institutionalised theft of private property."[9]

Hugh Lafollette opines : "Libertarianism has experienced a noticeable reemergence in the past few years F.A. Hayek, Milton Friedman and Robert Nozick have given new intellectual impetus to the movement, while a growing concern for personal autonomy has provided personal ground for the sowing of the idea. Central to libertarianism is the claim that individuals should be free from the interference of others. Personal liberty is the supreme moral good. Hence, one's liberty can justifiably be restricted only if he consents to the restriction. Any other restriction, including taxing incomes for purposes of redistribution is unjust or the libertarian may couch his theory in the language of rights : each individual has natural negative rights, or at least life, liberty and property. No one can justifiably harm him, restrict his freedom, or take his property–that is no one can violate his rights .... without his consent ....."[10]

Libertarianism owes much to classical liberalism. Its core value is liberty, and liberty can be safeguarded only when a society has :

(a) Strong Private Property Rights

(b) A Free Market

(c) Minimal Government

Arising as a reaction against the social welfare and collectivist state, libertarianism is an attempt to revive the liberal–individualistic theory of the state. It has a very strong doctrine of individual rights–particularly the right to hold property, and it believes that an unrestricted system of laissez faire capitalism is the most desirable social system.

While the Liberal Welfare notion believes, that the rights of the people can only be guaranteed by an interventionist state, the libertarians, on the other hand, believe that any sort of state–intervention is an attack on fundamental freedoms and the sacrosanct rights of the individual.

David Miller[11] believes that the liberal welfare theory of state is different from the libertarian view because of two reasons :

(a) Libertarianism upholds an extremely strong doctrine of individual rights–specially the right to property.

(b) People unfettered by state compulsions would very likely establish the economic system of laissez faire capitalism.

Another writer, also gives his views about libertarianism in the following words :

"While the libertarian ideal of individualism has certain family resemblances with the neo-classical defense of capitalism, anarcho-individualism and classic liberalism, it is reducible to none of these. Libertarianism can only be fully understood against the backdrop of totalitarianism and the modern welfare state since the 1930s."[12]

So, we can say that libertarianism is a highly distinctive version of what is termed as 'Neo Individualism'. Although it has its roots in the classical liberalism of the past-which emphasised–Negative Liberty–or the absence of restraints, it has taken a new meaning in the 1960s and 1970s, challenging 'the reigning assumptions of western countries, if not the whole world.'

Another writer talks about the dual arguments of libertarianism one, which is the moral argument, emphasising self-ownership. Second, the practical argument regarding the benefits accruing from reliance on private property/free market system. These twin arguments provide a 'consolidated justification of liberty'[13] which emphasises that it is 'morally opprobirous' if the state infringes upon the self-ownership rights of individuals.

The West was facing a severe crisis of the welfare state, which lead to protracted economic and political difficulties, and this crisis prompted a search for new policies, new institutions and new strategies. There was a renewed concern about the sphere of individual freedom, about limiting the possible uses of state power, about the proper sphere of state activity–and this concern gave rise to some new theories on both the right and the left of the political spectrum–libertarianism was one such theory which received large scale academic attention with the publication of Nozick's 'Anarchy, State and Utopia' in 1974.

Of late there has been a global trend towards a state which is so obsessed with security that it has whipped up a frenzy of fear, resulting in a form of state which is all inclusive, and more intrusive exactly the form of state which libertarians like Nozik had warned against.

George Bush II got reelected on an agenda that played on the security fears of the American voters similarly in Britain there is an all pervasive concern that prime minister Tony Blair's policies are also toeing the line of Bush specially after his II term as Prime Minister. Ironically enough, George Orwells' Big Brother seems to have shifted from his alleged original habit to countries like USA and Britain thus pushing the state into an increasingly anti-libertarian direction.

Although such a trend started before 9/11, the great of terrorism has made there governments create a bugbear of terrorism and in the name of terrorism, the state is becoming omnipotent and intruding even in the moral sphere of the individual. Such an all-inclusive state had also come into existence in the wake of the Economic Depression and it was this sort of all-powerful state that Nozik had raised his voice against.

And, now so many years later, more and more people are raising their voices against this trend, which has gained precariously reckless momentum. Tony Blair's own MPs are waxing eloquent against such a trend, which they believe is eroding civil liberties under the banner of fighting against terrorism momentum.

Some proposals, which were put forth by the British government recently, raised the hackles of both the right and the left, as also the Human Rights Groups who categorized these measures as undemocratic.

All this scare-mongering and suspicion reinforces the idea that libertarian arguments are being dismissed as absolete. Consequently, the fear is that no aspect of citizen's life will remain his private domain.

In this scenario there are more and more indications that the present state is no longer benign and such as intrusive state Nozik vigorously maintained, "violates moral side constraints on how individuals may be treated."

Today when we see more and more re-balancing of powers towards the state and when more and more people are trying to shove libertarian arguments into the background trying to label them as belonging to a different political reality, Nozik's libertarian arguments become all the more relevant.

Robert Nozick (1939-2002)

Before starting with an introduction of the political theory of Robert Nozick, it would be appropriate to give an introduction of the man himself.

Variously hailed as an 'Eclectic intellectual', 'A creative force' having 'one of the most versatile, piercing and agile minds', this intellectual giant burst into the public consciousness in 1974 with his path-breaking book 'Anarchy

State and Utopia'. This book was followed by five other works : 'Philosophical Explanations' (1981)–which is a book on the nature of knowledge, the self, free will and ethics, and which won the Ralph Waldo Emerson Award of the Phi Beta Kappa; 'The examined life' (1989) is a book of reflections on such themes as love, happiness, creativity, evil and the holocaust, 'The nature of rationality'–(1995) studies and develops formal models of rational action and rational belief; and in 1997, the "Socratic Puzzles" was published which is a collection of his articles, reviews and works of fiction.

In 2001, 'Invariances' was published, which was his last published work.

Besides these books, his Ph.D. dissertation, 'The normative theory of individual choice' was reprinted in 1990.

Though it was his first book, 'Anarchy, State and Utopia (1974)'–(which won a 'National Book Award' and was listed by 'The Times Literary Supplement' as one of 'The Hundred most influential books since the war'–it was even translated into eleven languages)—which propelled him into the public eye, he was already well-known at Harvard, where he came from an assistant professorship at Princeton University in 1965. He served as an assistant professor here for two years and went to Rockfeller University in 1967 as an associate professor. He returned to Harvard at the age of 30–as a full professor of philosophy in 1969, and served as Chair of the philosophy department from 1981 to 1984.

'Philosophical Meditations' was published in 1989 and in this book, he describes how his interest in philosophy was stimulated. He came to philosophy via a paperback edition of 'Plato's Republic', which he found intellectually thrilling. To quote him :

"When I was 15 years old, or 16, I carried around on the streets of Brooklyn a paperback copy of 'Plato's Republic' front cover facing outward. I had read only some of it and I was excited by it and knew it was something wonderful."

Hungry for more, he took an introductory philosophy course when he arrived at Columbia College, later he took a non-philosophy course in contemporary civilisation, which was taught by a Philosophy Professor, Sidney Morgenbesser, who greatly inspired and influenced him by his sharp reasoning and intellect. Later, he was to quip, that he, had 'majored in Morgenbesser'.

Nozick, who had been fighting a battle with stomach cancer since 1994, died on January 23, 2002, at the age of 63.

He was a man who was always rethinking his own views, always probing, always learning new subjects.

This heavy-weight among philosophers took up a battery of core metaphysical questions–like, the nature of truth, objectivity, necessity, ethics and consciousness–in his last published book, before his death, 'Invariances : The structure of the objective world' (October 2001, Harvard University Press), which was hailed as 'Intriguing' 'Engaging', interesting 'Useful and Enlightening' and 'Highly readable'.

Not only has this brilliant and provocative scholar had an important influence on contemporary philosophy but his work crosses the boundaries of different disciplines. In the U.S.A. he has been hailed as one of the nation's most influential philosophers.

Born in Brooklyn, New York, in 1939 he attended public school there and later attended Columbia College. From Columbia, Nozick entered graduate school at Princeton, where he received an MA in 1961 and a Ph.D. in 1963–writing his dissertation on theories of rational decision.

He had been the recipient of many awards and honours. The Presidential Citation from the American Psychological Association in 1998 described him as 'One of the most brilliant and original living philosophers.'

In the following pages, I shall try to summarise his two most influential works 'Anarchy, State and Utopia', and

'Philosophical Questions'–the former written in 1974 and the latter in the year 1981–'Anarchy State and Utopia' was a path-breaking book which gave the libertarian movement large scale academic attention. Through this book, he revived the Lockean State of Nature, and defended the libertarian doctrine that the 'minimal state' performing the narrow function of protecting against force, theft fraud and enforcement of contracts is the most powerful state morally justifiable. It is inspiring as well as right.

In 'Philosophical Explanations', he dealt with philosophical questions like Metaphysics, epistemology, value, knowledge, scepticism, evidence and the concept of free-will.

Anarchy, State and Utopia

'Anarchy, State and Utopia' has three parts and ten chapters spread over 365 pages. Part I has 6 chapters 1-6, Part II has 3 Chapters–7-9, and Part III and concluding part comprise the final chapter 'UTOPIA'.

Part I deals with the 'State of Nature theory or how to Back into a state without really trying'. In the Chapter I, 'Why State of Nature Theory' he revives the Lockean state of nature, and asks, 'whether there should be any state at all. Why not anarchy ...... 'which anarchic situation should we investigate to answer the question of why not anarchy.'[14]

In other words he tries, to state that neither the 'minimax' criterion, nor the 'maximax' criterion–the former represented by the Hobbesian state of nature–and the latter by the Godwinian assumption of how things would work out–is feasible because one is too pessimistic and the other too optimistic. But the Lockean state of nature is neither too pessimistic, nor too optimistic–hence the best choice. To quote him–

"This state-of-nature situation is the best anarchic situation one reasonably could hope for. Hence investigating its nature and defects is of crucial importance to deciding whether there should be a state rather than anarchy."[15]

He further states that a rationale for the state's existence would be provided, if :-

(a) One could show that the state would be superior even to this most favoured situation of anarchy

(b) Or would arise by a process involving no morally impermissible steps or would be an improvement if it arose.

Moreover, the state-of-nature theory, according to Nozick has a twofold purpose :

(a) Its importance for political philosophy.

(b) Explanatory purposes.

Nozick states that there are three possible ways of understanding the political realm. In his words :

1. "to fully explain it in terms of the non-political;
2. to view it as emerging from the non-political ...
3. to view it as a completely autonomous realm."[16]

Nozick further states the first alternative appears to be the most desirable theoretical alternative–and he calls it the 'Fundamental Explanation' of the realm, because he finds it the most desirable and complete kind of explanation. In his words 'the more fundamental the starting point (the more it picks out basic, important and inescapable features of the human situation) and the less close it is or seems to its result (the less political or statelike it looks), the better."[17]

Hence, it follows that we should pursue this alternative of showing how a political situation would arise out of a non-political one–The state of nature, being non-political–and well-known within political philosophy, Nozick believes, it would be prudent to begin a fundamental explanatory account' with something with which one is familiar–hence the revival of Lockean state of nature. In Nozick's words, "State of nature explanations of the political realm are fundamentally potential explanations of this realm and pack explanatory punch and illumination, even if incorrect. We learn much by seeing how the state could have arisen, even if it didn't arise that way."[18]

Nozick begins the second chapter, entitled 'The state of nature' by quoting extensively from Locke's 'two treatises of government'. He says that the individuals in Locke's state of nature are in "a state of perfect freedom to order their possessions and persons as they think fit, within the bounds of the laws of nature, without asking leave or dependency' upon the will of any other man."[19]

The bounds of the laws of nature require that "no one ought to harm another in his life, health, liberty or possessions (sect 6) some persons transgress these bounds, invading others rights and ..... "doing hurt to one another." "everyone has a right to punish the transgressors of that law to such a degree as may hinder its violation." (section 7)

Despite the fact that 'individuals are in a state of perfect freedom' in the Lockean state of nature there are 'inconveniences of the state of nature', for which, Locke says "I easily grant that Civil government is the proper remedy". (section 13)[20].

In the Lockean state of nature since the natural law may not provide for every contingency, feelings of being mutually wronged will be all pervasive, because the wronged individuals 'will overestimate the amount of harm or damage they have suffered and passions will lead them to attempt to punish other more than proportionately and to exact excessive compensation (sections 13, 124, 125). Thus private and personal enforcement of one's rights leads to feuds, to an endless series of acts of retaliation .... and moreover there is no firm way of settling or ending disputes. Furthermore, in certain cases, an individual may lack the power to enforce his rights, he may not be in a position to exact punishment from a stronger adversary.

"How might one deal with these troubles within a state of nature" Nozick asks–He can do it individually or collectively–Individually he "may himself enforce his rights, defend himself, exact compensation and punish (or atleast try his best to do so)."[21]

The second way of dealing with these troubles is through mutual-protection associations–To quote Nozick :

"Groups of individuals may form mutual–protection associations : all will answer the call of any member for defense or for the enforcement of his rights. In union there is strength."[22]

But Nozick also asserts that there might arise certain inconveniences in these MPAs–some members might want to misuse the MPA–As Nozick says :

"Protective associations will not want to be at the beck and call of their cantankerous and paranoid members not to mention those of their members who might attempt, under the guise of self-defense to use the association to violate the rights of others."[23]

Because of the mutual bickerings, mutual conflicts among MPAs, a dominant Protective Association will come into effect. While referring to its origin, Nozick talks of an 'invisible hand explanation'–which means "Every individual intends only his own gain, and he is in this, as in so many other cases, led by an invisible hand to promote an end which was no part of his intention." In order to give the reader a clearer account of what he has in mind when he talks of an IHE, he cites 16 examples of IHE.

He further states that this DPA, although superior to all the other MPAs, is not a state because of two reasons:

"1. It appears to allow some people to enforce their own rights. and

2. It appears not to protect all individuals within its domain."[24]

Nozick admits that "formulating sufficient conditions for the existence of state thus turns out to be a difficult and messy task"[25], because some writers in the tradition of Max Weber, hold that a monopoly on the use of force in a geographical area is crucial to the existence of a state, while others like Marshal Cohen point out that a state may exist without actually monopolising the use of force, and even within the state there may exist such groups as the Mafia, the KKK etc.–who also use force.

Nonetheless, the state, according to Nozick 'claims a monopoly on deciding who may use force'

"Thus it appears that the dominant protective agency in a territory not only lacks the requisite monopoly over the use of force, but also fails to provide protection for all in its territory, and so the dominant protective agency falls short of being a state."[26]

Chapter III is entitled–'Moral Constraints and the State', and here he talks of 'the minimal state and the ultra minimal state' and imagines a social arrangement which falls between 'the night-watchman state of classical liberal theory' and the scheme of private protective associations–and he calls this arrangement the 'Ultra Minimal State' : Defining the ultra minimal state, he says,

"An ultra minimal state maintains a monopoly over all use of force except that necessary in immediate self-defense, and so excludes private (or agency) retaliation for wrong and exaction of compensation, but it provides protection and enforcement services only to those who purchase its protection and enforcement policies."[27]

Nozick states that "an individual and his rights are inviolable and instead of incorporating rights into the end state to be achieved, one might place them as side constraints upon the actions to be done: don't violate constraints C. The rights of others determine the constraints upon your action."[28]

Nozick believes that "side constraints upon action reflect the underlying Kantian principle that individuals are ends and not merely means. They may not be sacrificed or used for the achieving of others' ends without their consent."[29] Individuals can not be sacrificed for the greater overall good– using or rather misusing people in this way–"does not sufficiently respect and take account of the fact that he is a separate person."[30]

No one can force him to make sacrifices for some overall social good, because that way the sacrosanct nature of the rights-bearing individuals will be sacrificed. To quote Nozick :

"He does not get some overbalancing good from his sacrifice and no one is entitled to force this upon him–least of all a state or government that claims his allegiance."[31]

Thus we see, that these moral side constraints are based on the root idea that there are separate individuals with separate lives and none of them can be sacrificed to benefit the others. The logical corollary of these moral side constraints are the Libertarian Constraints on aggression against another, and this aggression involves (a) Aggression Against Individuals (b) Aggression Against Nations.

In the words of Nozick, "libertarian prohibitions are usually formulated so as to forbid using violence on innocent persons."[32]

Nozick states that the individualist anarchists complaint against the state is that it monopolises the use of force, and– "When the state monopolises the use of force in a territory and punishes others who violate its monopoly, and when the state provides protection for everyone by forcing some to purchase protection for others, it violates moral side constraints on how individuals may be treated. Hence, he concludes the state itself is intrinsically immoral."[33]

He further adds that "to get to something recognisable as a state we must show 1. how an ultra minimal state arises out of the system of private protective associations; and 2. how ultra minimal state is transformed into the minimal state, how it gives rise to, that 'redistribution' for the general provision of protective services that constitutes it as a minimal state. To show that the minimal state is morally legitimate, to show it is not immoral itself, we must show also that these transitions in 1. and 2. each are morally legitimate."[34]

This is exactly what he proceeds to do in the remaining chapters of Part I. In trying to show how each of these transitions occurs and is morally permissible, he argues 'that the first transition, from a system of private protective agencies to an ultra minimal state will occur by an invisible hand process in a morally permissible way, that violates no one's rights', secondly, he argues that the transition from an ultra minimal state to a minimal state morally must occur. He says:

"It would be morally impermissible for persons to maintain the monopoly in the ultra minimal state without providing protective services for all, even if this requires specific 'redistribution'. The operators of the ultra minimal state are morally obligated to produce the minimal state."[35]

He concludes the last chapter of Part I by saying

"Having gotten from anarchy to the minimal state, our next major task is to establish that we should proceed no further."[36]

Chapter IV is entitled prohibition, compensation and risk–and also tackles the problem of independents, who do not deal with any protective agency, and enforce their own rights against one and all–In Nozick's words :

"Let us suppose that interspersed among a large group of persons who deal with one protective agency lives some miniscule group who do not. These few independents (perhaps even only one) jointly or individually enforce their own rights against one and all, including clients of the agency."[37]

This chapter answers the questions as to how a dominant protective agency may act towards independents.

It investigates the moral status within a state of nature of procedural rights and of prohibitions upon risky activities.

It also tries to find out as to what knowledge is presumed by principles about the exercise of rights, including especially rights to enforce others' rights.

Referring to the independents, he mentions Locke, saying,

"Locke held that no one may be forced to enter civil society, some may abstain and stay in the liberty of the state of nature even if most choose to enter (595)."[38]

Unravelling the question of prohibition occupies much of this chapter. The moot question is why is prohibition essential. He says :

"A line (or hyper-plane) circumscribes an area in moral space around an individual Locke holds that this line is determined by an individual's natural rights, which limit the actions of others. Non-Lockeans view other considerations as settling the contours of the line. In any case the following question arises : Are others forbidden to perform actions that transgress the boundary or encroach upon the circumscribed area, or are they permitted to perform such actions provided that they compensate the person whose boundary has been crossed."[39]

He states that those who are prohibited from indulging in risky activities should be adequately compensated for–To quote him :

"We need only claim the correctness of some principles such as the principle of compensation, requiring those imposing a prohibition on risky activities to compensate those disadvantaged through having these risky activities prohibited to them."[40]

He, however, admits that he does not feel quite comfortable in presenting a principle which has 'not been worked out fully', but claims that as a beginning it is all right to leave a principle in a somewhat fuzzy state.

Chapter V entitled 'The State', has a few subtitles :

(a) Prohibiting Private Enforcement of Justice

(b) The Principle of Fairness

(c) Procedural Rights

(d) How May The Dominant Protective Agency Act :

(e) The Defacto Monopoly

(f) The State

(g) The Invisible Hand Explanation of the State.

In this chapter he provides an invisible hand explanation of the state and concludes the chapter by saying:

"If the state is an institution 1. that has the right to enforce rights, prohibit dangerous private enforcement of justice, ... and 2. that effectively is the sole wielder within a geographical territory of the rights 1, then by offering an invisible hand explanation of 2, though not of 1, we have partially explained in invisible hand fashion the existence of the state .... The dominant protective association with the monopoly element is morally required to compensate for the disadvantages it imposes upon those it prohibits from self-help activities against its clients. Those operating an ultra minimal state are morally required to transform it into a minimal state."[41]

Following Herbert Hart and John Rawls he talks of a 'Principle of Fairness', but calls it objectionable and unacceptable. "This principle holds that when a number of persons engage in a just, mutually, advantageous cooperative venture according to rules and thus restrain their liberty in ways necessary to yield advantages for all, those who have submitted to these restrictions have a right to similar acquiescence on the part of those who have benefited from their submission."[42]

Talking about procedural rights, Nozick says that in the state of nature theory, there is no clarity regarding these rights. To quote him :

"The notions of procedural rights, public demonstration of guilt, and the like, have a very unclear status within the state of nature theory."[43]

Yet, this does not imply that there are no procedural rights and that one may not defend oneself against unfair procedures, but the DPA, according to Nozick, believes that its own procedures are both reliable and fair, therefore it will not allow anyone to defend against them–it will punish anyone who does so. By virtue of its unique position it can enforce prohibitions on others' procedures of justice.

Thus we see that, although the DPA has no monopoly,– it emerges 'as the most powerful applier of principles which it grants everyone the right to apply correctly, it enforces its will which from the inside it thinks is correct."[44]

Because of its strength, it is the ultimate enforcer and the ultimate judge to its own clients–and as such, although it has no dejure monopoly–it can claim to have the de facto monopoly, and thus is in a position to say : 'only those procedures we deem appropriate will be used on our customers."[45]

He quotes an anthropologist Lawrence Krader, who says that 'the concentration of all physical force in the hands of central authority is the primary function of the state' and since the DPA appears to have this quality–Nozick asks, can the DPA be characterised as a state. He says :

"It is plausible to conclude that the dominant protective association in a territory is its state, only for a territory of some size containing more than a few people."[46]

Moreover, Nozick states, that it is wholly desirable and appropriate to call a DPA a state because it has the de facto monopoly to make judgements over the permissibility of violence–But, instead of calling it a state, he prefers to call it a state like entity.

Chapter VI is entitled 'Further considerations on the argument for the state', and in this chapter he considers various arguments and objections to the argument detailing how a minimal state arises. He makes some further comments and connects it with some other issues, thus ending Part I of the book, which had established how the minimal state arises from Anarchy through an invisible hand process. Now starts Part II, which is called 'Beyond The Minimal State' and has 3 chapters.

Chapter VII 'Distributive Justice' is a significant chapter which deals at length with his Entitlement Theory of Justice. He begins it by asserting that "the minimal state is the most extensive state that can be justified. Any state more extensive violates peoples rights."[47] Despite this Nozickean claim, many persons have tried to justify a more extensive state. Herein, he focusses upon 'the most weighty and influential' reason given in favour of a more extensive state. In section I, he outlines his Entitlement Theory–the gist of which is 'From each as they choose to each as they are chosen.'

He tries to reinforce his conclusions by referring to Amartya Sen's arguments, he talks of redistribution and property rights, refers to Locke's theory of acquisition (pp. 174-182).

In the II section of the chapter, he refers to Rawls' Theory of Distributive Justice, and calls his book 'A Theory of Justice' as a 'Powerful deep, subtle, wide-ranging systematic work in political and moral philosophy'[48] and goes on to refute his theory.

Chapter VIII is entitled 'equality, envy, exploitation etc' He begins it by stating :

"The legitimacy of altering social institutions to achieve greater equality of material conditions, is though often assumed rarely argued for."[49]

He states that changes can definitely be brought about provided people's entitlements are not violated, but—"The entitlement conception of justice in holdings makes no presumption in favour of equality or any other over-all end state or patterning. It cannot merely be assumed that equality must be built into any Theory of Justice."[50]

He refers to Bernard Williams' influential essay 'The idea of equality', and says that when the layers of Williams' argument are pealed away we arrive at the conclusion that society should make provision for the important needs of all its members, but despite appearing to do so, Williams presents no argument in favour of it.

Similarly, Nozick also opines that 'the major objection to speaking of everyone as having a right to various things such as equality of opportunity, like and so on and enforcing this right, is that these rights require a substructure of things and materials and actions and other people must have rights and entitlements over these. No one has a right to something whose realisation requires certain uses of things and activities that other people have rights and entitlements over."[51]

Similarly, he talks of self-esteem 'and envy, and asks whether 'it is plausible to connect equality with self-esteem'. He is "sceptical of the chances of equalising self-esteem and reducing envy by equalising positions along that particular dimension upon which self-esteem is importantly based."[52]

The ninth chapter is entitled 'Demoktesis', and in this chapter, he makes a modest effort in the direction of illuminating 'essential aspects of the more extensive states people, every where now live under', and tries to lay bare their nature.

The tenth and final chapter is entitled 'A Framework For Utopia,' wherein he claims that the 'minimal state, no doubt, has many virtues, but it is 'no utopia, and utopian theorists might find it pale and feeble when compared to their hopes and dreams'.

Such an investigation would serve a two fold purpose :

(a) It would highlight the defects and shortcomings of the minimal state as the end of political philosophy.

(b) Moreover it would also prove to be 'intrinsically interesting.'

Nozick states that all utopian authors have been very confident of the virtues of their own visions, and have differed among themselves "No utopian author has everyone in his society leading exactly the same life, allocating exactly the same amount of time to exactly the same activities."[53]

So he concludes that there will not be one kind of community existing and one kind of life led in utopia, on the contrary 'utopia will consist of utopias, of many different and divergent communities in which people lead different kinds of lives under different institutions. Utopia is a framework for utopias, a place where people are at liberty to join together voluntarily to pursue and attempt to realise their own vision of the good life but where no one can impose his own utopian vision upon others."[54]

In his concluding remarks under 'Utopia and The Minimal State' he says :

"The framework for utopia that we have described is equivalent to the minimal state .... we argued in Part I that the minimal state is morally legitimate; in Part II we argued that no more extensive state could be morally justified ..... This morally favoured state, the only morally legitimate state, the only morally tolerable one, we now see is the one that best realises the utopian aspirations of untold dreamers and visionaries....... Is not the minimal state, the framework for utopia, an inspiring vision."[55]

He further states that the minimal state treats us as inviolate individuals having sacrosanct rights. "Treating us with respect by respecting our rights, it allows us individually, or with whomsoever we choose our life and to realise our ends and our conception of ourselves in so far as we can, aided by the voluntary cooperation of other individuals possessing the same dignity. How dare any state or group of individuals do more or less."[56]

Thus ends this magnum opus, packed between the pages of which is his path-breaking political philosophy which will later be critically evaluated.

Philosophical Explanations

When his other book 'Philosophical Explanations' was published in the year 1981, it received rave reviews. It was hailed as a 'remarkable book', 'an important book', which displays a 'striking and imaginative originality.' Which proposes a new way of doing philosophy.

In the introduction of 'Philosophical Explanations' he says, that all philosophical questions 'stem from one : how are we valuable and precious.'[57]

In trying to answer this question he wants to avoid 'Coercive Philosophy' which seeks to prove things by providing a Knock-Down argument.

So, in place of a Knock Down Philosophical Argument, he offers a 'Philosophical Explanation, which renders things 'coherent' and better understood."[58]

He believes that there are various philosophical views, and they cannot be rejected outright–so a philosophical explanation should be the sum–total of these views–after they have been modified and shaved.

We find that the conception of Philosophical Explanations is intertwined with another goal which is more radical. He believes that exploring hypotheses may lead to "radically new and surprising truths and insights."[59]

Nozick has no qualms about accepting alternative hypotheses, or, what he prefers to call 'Philosophical Pluralism', which is not synonymous with relativism. He admits that philosophy is definitely not a science yet "the philosopher's existential hypothesis may suggest detailed investigation to the scientist."[60]

In the end of the book he maintains that philosophy is an art form, which presents a shaped view or vision.

Subscribing to 'Philosophical Pluralism', he is very tolerant towards other philosophical views, and about his own philosophical explanations, he states that they have been put forth in a very tentative manner though that does not necessarily imply that they are not illuminating.

Following the introduction the book is divided into three parts :

1. Metaphysics
2. Epistemology
3. Value

'Metaphysics' is further divided into two main chapters:

(a) The identity of the self

(b) Why is there something rather than nothing

The Identity of the Self–is again divided into two parts: the first deals with the problem of Identity through time. The second deals with the notion of reflexivity. Both these parts are intimately related, and reflexivity emerges as one of the dominant themes of the book.

What are the important features of the entity which is called 'self'? In Nozick's words, the "Capacity for reflexive self-reference is essential to being a self."

Referring to Fichte's notion of self-positing, Nozick maintains that the self is created by a primordial act of self-reference which is also a decision about what to be. To quote him :

"The self which is reflexively referred to is synthesised in that very act of reflexive self-reference."

In other words, the primordial act is self-reflexive (seen from the inside) and at the same time, it refers to itself. The Act of Reflexive Self–Reference has also been described as a 'Reflexive Act of Craftsmanship' The conception of the self is instrumental in satisfying the original impulse to engage in philosophy.

"Self-subsumption is a way a principle turns back on itself, yields itself, applies to itself, and refers to itself."

Chapter II of Metaphysics is entitled:

"Why is there something rather than nothing?" For Nozick this is a question loaded with meaning, and it is also an issue about the nature of explanation. Philosophy attempts to explain everything but if we push explanation to its outer limits, we find ourselves on the horns of a dilemma, and this dilemma is explained by Nozick in the following words :

"Explanatory self-subsumption I admit appears quite weird–a feat of legerdemain. When we reach the ultimate and most fundamental explanatory laws however there are few possibilities. Either there is an infinite chain of different laws and theories, each explaining the next, or there is a finite chain. If a finite chain ..... the endmost laws are unexplainable facts or necessary truths or the only laws there can be if there are laws of a certain sort at all ..."

Nozick claims that self-subsumption is the only way out, because of the traditional and apparently 'stubborn problem of justifying first principles within a deductive explanation'. In the words of Capaldi.

"What we need, according to Nozick, is a fundamental explanation of the totality of reality which loops back onto itself without circularity and without an unexplained residue of brute fact".

Nozick discusses many such explanations, however, he does not recommend any of them.

Out of the several explanations offered by Nozick, Capaldi selects two as the most representative and indicative of the direction of Nozick's thinking. In the words of Capaldi:

"First, Nozick speculates on going beyond existence and nonexistence to a nothingness force that 'nothed' itself and let in reality. This hypothesis would seem to give non-being a power of its own. Second, Nozick considers the possibility of a self-subsuming principle of organic unity. "one that best fits in with the other facts" and which "would be explained by its mesh with other facts" (p. 149). This hypothesis would seem to reinstate particulars within the universal concept."

The second section of the book is entitled epistemology, and is further subdivided into:

(a) Knowledge (b) Scepticism (c) Evidence

Nozick tries to show that in spite of scepticism, knowledge can be possible, and this section of the book is mainly devoted to answering the question–'How is knowledge possible?"

He defines knowledge as having "a belief that tracks the truth" and tracking is a "real factual connection to the world". Tracking is the case where, "to know that is to be someone who would believe it if it were true, and who wouldn't believe it, if it were false."[61]

Ultimately, what Nozick is offering us is a speculative hypothesis about knowledge as tracking which is compatible with evolution. In other words, Nozick believes that the evolutionary process is capable of giving organisms the capacity to vary beliefs with the truth of what is to be believed.

The third and final chapter is entitled value, and it constitutes the largest section of the book.

It is further subdivided into three chapters : (a) Free Will (b) Foundations of Ethics (c) The Meaning of Life.

The Concept of Free Will

Nozick is seriously concerned with formulating a coherent account of the concept of Free Will, because like Locke, Nozick's rights are also grounded in a conception of free action, in Philosophical Explanations he remarks that he has "spent more time thinking about the problem of free will ...... than about any other philosophical topic except perhaps the foundations of ethics".[62]

Nozick intends that his discussions of Free Will and the foundations of ethics should provide the moral foundations of his political theory, though he admits that there might be some difficulties in trying to do so.

His central concern is with rescuing the idea of individual freedom from its 'enemies', who want to deny the existence of free will and "think it important to deny for instance, that we have free will that we can do something because it is right, that we know reality, that we are anything other than a congery of physiochemical processes and properties."[63]

Action : Defining an action he says it is "an intentional doing arising out of a process of choice among alternatives."[64]

He repeats the central question about freedom of action many times–and that is, how can a person freely perform an action, "if his doing it was causally determined eventually by factors originating before his birth, and hence outside his control"? He tries to answer this oft repeated question by asserting that true causal explanations of the genesis does not necessarily imply that we cannot make genuinely free choices–To quote his exact words:

"The question is not whether there will be evolutionary explanations of how consciousness, language and self-consciousness arise and are selected for. The question is whether once these do arise by a blind process, they then operate and lead to some things unblindly. That there is an invisible hand explanation of our having our cognitive capacities does not mean there is an invisible hand explanation of my writing the contents of this book."[65]

Nozick does not argue that man's will is free, on the contrary, he attempts to frame a theory of free action that, in his words: "Is compatible with determinism and sufficient for our value purposes."[66]

Foundations of Ethics : Through his ethical theory, Nozick tries to show how the world can be moulded into an embodiment of human purpose. He admits that his views on morality cannot be linked with views expressed in his earlier book 'Anarchy, State and Utopia', because in the latter, he was merely presenting a political philosophy without presenting any moral foundations. In his words :

"In Anarchy, State and Utopia' I presented a political philosophy ..... but did not ..... present any moral foundations for that view".[67]

Although Nozick does not present moral foundations of his political philosophy in 'Anarchy State and Utopia', in 'Philosophical Explanations', he does, and tries to define the task of ethical theory in accordance with the dialectical relation between right and morality, or, to put it in Nozickean terms, the "moral pull and the moral push."

Nozick admits that in the realm of values 'the highest organic unity is not possible' so there is the possibility and "room for new and even radically different organic unities."

Nozick says that value is an 'organic unity', and it exists, because we have chosen that values be there, but their character is not dependent on us. Nozick puts it better in these words :

"We choose that there be values, that they exist, but their character is independent of us."[68]

The Meaning of Life

The final conclusion that Nozick reaches is that philosophy is a part of the humanities, as it aims not only at explanation, but at the explanation of value and meaning.

Life gets its meaning also from the choice that there be value, and it is meaningful in the sense that, it is, to quote Nozick "a choice to connect and accord with something external, a choice to transcend one's own limits."[69]

Nozick believes that Philosophy is an art form and it is the duty of the philosopher to be 'true enough to the world'– In other words he should strike a balance between the real and the ideal :

'Philosophical Explanations' when published in 1981 was heralded as a bold new step into the future–it was no doubt, also criticised on many counts–but there is no denying the fact that it introduces new concepts, daring hypotheses, rigorous reasoning, playful exploration, which one finds–and as Nozick had hoped, 'illuminating and 'worth considering.'

Conclusion

The preceding pages gave a brief account of the political theory of Robert Nozick, whose path-breaking book 'Anarchy, State and Utopia' (1974), besides being a rejoinder to the liberal egalitarianism of John Rawls as enunciated in 'A Theory of Justice' (1971), was also responsible for giving the libertarian movement large scale academic attention.

In accordance with the doctrine of libertarianism, which believed in inviolable rights of the individual, and disbelieved in social justice and the welfare state, Nozick upheld and revived the classical liberal–individualistic theory of the state, believing that individual rights can be safeguarded only when a society has strong private property rights, a free market and minimal government.

Although libertarianism has its roots in the classical liberalism of the past, which emphasised negative liberty, or the absence of restraints, it took a new meaning in the 1960s and 1970s, challenging the reigning assumptions.

In the post-communism scenario, there had been many socio-economic changes, and more and more nations had been adopting the capitalist mode of development, the welfare model was being dismantled in a number of developed as well as developing countries, it is against this backdrop that Nozick's views become extremely important.

With his emphasis on minimal government, individual rights, specially property rights, his theoretical lineage can be traced to the classical liberalism of Locke, which reemerged after the 1970s under a new name–Libertarianism–and which was given vigorous support by Nozick in his book, 'Anarchy, State and Utopia'.

The following pages will deal at length with his political theory, followed by a critical evaluation of his views.

Notes and References

1. Held, David (1984) 'Liberalism, Marxism and public policy' in 'Political theory and the modern state : essays on state, power and democracy', Polity Press.
2. Spragens, Thomas (1999) 'Civic liberalism : reflections on our democratic ideals : New York, Rowman and Little Field Publishers Inc.
3. The Dictionary of important ideas and thinkers (2002) arrow books–The Random House Group Ltd. pp. 335-36.
4. Rawls, John (1993) 'Political Liberalism'–introduction Columbia : Columbia University Press, p. xix.
5. Bellamy, Richard, Liberalism and Modern society : An Historical Argument, Cambridge, Polity Press, 1992.
6. Nozick, Robert (1974) 'Anarchy State and Utopia' New York : Basic Books, Inc, Publishers, p. ix.
7. *Ibid.*

8. Harper Collins Dictionary of Thought (1988) New York : Harper and Row Publishers.
9. Rothbard, Murray, 'The Blackwell Encyclopedia of Political Thought' Oxford : Basic Blackwell.
10. Lafolette, Hugh (1979) 'Why Libertarianism Is Mistaken' In John Arthur and William Shaw (Eds.) 'Justice and Economic Distribution'.
11. Miller, David (1987) 'Libertarianism' In the Blackwell Encyclopaedia of Political Thought', Oxford : Basil Blackwell.
12. Hagopian, Mark N., (1985) 'Ideals and Ideologies of Modern Politics', London, Longman, p. 92.
13. Spragens, Thomas Ajr (1999) *op. cit.*
14. Nozick, Robert (1974) 'Anarchy, State and Utopia', p. 5.
15. *Ibid.*, p. 5.
16. *Ibid.*, p. 6.
17. *Ibid.*, p. 7.
18. *Ibid.*, p. 9.
19. *Ibid.*
20. Locke, John. 'Two Treatises of Government Section–4. Quoted In 'Asu–Nozick, p. 10.
21. Nozick, Robert (1974), *op. cit.*, p. 12.
22. *Ibid.*, p. 12.
23. *Ibid.*, p. 13.
24. *Ibid.*, p. 23.
25. *Ibid.*, p. 23.
26. *Ibid.*, p. 25.
27. *Ibid.*, p. 26.
28. *Ibid.*, p. 27.

29. *Ibid.*, pp. 30-31.
30. *Ibid.*, p. 33.
31. *Ibid.*, p. 33.
32. *Ibid.*, pp. 34-35.
33. *Ibid.*, p. 51.
34. *Ibid.*, p. 52.
35. *Ibid.*, p. 52.
36. *Ibid.*, p. 146.
37. *Ibid.*, p. 54.
38. *Ibid.*, p. 54.
39. *Ibid.*, p. 57.
40. *Ibid.*, p. 87.
41. *Ibid.*, p. 119.
42. *Ibid.*, p. 90.
43. *Ibid.*, p. 96.
44. *Ibid.*, p. 109.
45. *Ibid.*, p. 109.
46. *Ibid.*, p. 117.
47. *Ibid.*, p. 149.
48. *Ibid.*, p. 183.
49. *Ibid.*, p. 222.
50. *Ibid.*, p. 233.
51. *Ibid.*, p. 238.
52. *Ibid.*, p. 244.
53. *Ibid.*, p. 311.
54. *Ibid.*, p. 312.

55. *Ibid.*, p. 333.

56. *Ibid.*, p. 334.

57. Nozick, R. (1981) 'Philosophical Explanations' Cambridge, Mass, Harvard University Press, p. 1.

58. *Ibid.*, p. 8.

59. *Ibid.*, p. 12.

60. *Ibid.*, p. 13.

61. *Ibid.*, p. 278.

62. *Ibid.*, p. 293.

63. *Ibid.*, p. 444.

64. *Ibid.*, p. 304.

65. *Ibid.*, p. 347.

66. *Ibid.*, p. 292.

67. *Ibid.*, pp. 498-99.

68. *Ibid.*, p. 555.

69. *Ibid.*, p. 618.

2

The Liberal Milieu Locke to Nozick

Liberalism—a very flexible and at the same time resilient ideology has so many diverse strands—that it is indeed a Herculean task to disentangle these inter-related strands from each other, as they shoot out in all spheres–the social, political, moral and economic.

Right from the natural rights Liberalism of Locke, to the libertarianism of Nozick, it has undergone many changes but true to it resilient spirit, there has been one strand which has surfaced as the common strand among all the types of liberal strands and that strand has been the principle of liberty. Without any fear of criticism, it can be stated that liberalism has been the only ideology, which has proved tenacious enough to array its forces against any attack on the liberty of an individual. It is an ideology, which wants a world where free and equal individuals can flourish.

So many people have spoken the liberal language in varying degrees and diverse ways, a host of eminent philosophers, statesmen, politicians and social theorists have jumped into the bandwagon of liberalism and in the ensuing Babelesque confusion that has followed, it has indeed become a formidable task to make some sense of the bewildering variety of definitions. "Its popularity is obvious: from the ancient Greeks to the present day politicians, religious leaders and philosophers have vied with each other to yoke liberty firmly to their particular banner, creed or cause."[1]

Similarly, Mills and King say: 'It is perfectly understandable that many of the political and economic changes since the early 1980's–particularly in Europe and North America should go by the label of 'liberal'.[2]

Hence, the two believe that liberalism "is a rather problematic and inconsistent phenomenon."[3]

In this context, another writer writes:

"Emerging in Great Britain in the middle and late seventeenth century, liberalism spread to Europe and America where strong movements flourished, and often came to power in the course of the nineteenth century. While the eruption of communism and fascism in the middle of the twentieth century threatened liberalism's very survival, it came through World War II with renewed vigour specially in the United States and Western Europe."[4]

Mansfield in the preface of his book 'The spirit of liberalism' states:

"Liberalism was born in revolt against the tradition of Plato and Aristotle, rejecting its high-mindedness as giving opportunity to tyranny but accepting its public-spirited character against the temptation of high and low-minded hedonism. In the early version of Hobbies and Locke, liberalism represents an attempt to be public-spirited without being high-minded. The later fate of this attempt, degenerating, to today's cool cucumber liberalism, which is neither public-spirited nor high-minded but very broad minded suggests that liberals might do better to borrow from the classical tradition...."[5]

He maintains that liberalism has changed its tone, tenor and complexion right from the days of Locke to the present.

We find that there are so many definitions of the term 'liberal' that it is quite easy for a political party to select a convenient definition that fits in snugly with its particular profile. Tim Gray wonders whether this way the notion of freedom is not being stretched too far, whether liberties are being taken with the concept of liberty.[6]

Needless to say, liberties are really being taken with the concept of liberty and liberalism, because it has been moulded and manipulated in such a way, that it assumes a variety of postures and assumes a number of positions. In the words of a writer:

"It is a movement within a movement and thus has been forced to react to a number of changing circumstances."[7]

So, it is universally acknowledged that it is indeed a daunting task to arrive at a comprehensive definition of liberalism because it is not unambiguous and straightforward in meaning. The term liberal is quite slippery and hence there has been a lot of wrangling over what liberalism 'really' is, or involves. Numerous difficulties are involved in understanding, characterizing, and defining it, because the definitions are diverse and conflictual.

While Gayle McKeen wonders whether it can be characterised as a coherent whole, Mansfield succinctly maintains that 'It is evident that liberalism, if it is a whole, is a whole that is afraid to be a whole...."[8] implying that it has many different strands, resulting in ambiguity and hence, it does not lend itself to a universally accepted definition. Moreover, there are so many different writers bracketed as liberals that it is indeed difficult to define liberalism as a coherent whole.

In the words of a writer:

"I believe that the term liberalism was in fact infrequently used in the English-speaking countries until the last half of the nineteenth century. Even then it usually referred to the programme of specific political parties–the liberal party in England or the Liberal Republican faction in the United States–much more than to any distinct broader tradition in the history of the political thought."[9]

The above view-point is indicative of a narrow view of liberalism. It limits it to the programme of specific political parties–thus excluding the broader view-point which emphasises the humanitarian outlook–the concept of human worth, of human dignity and of man as the end.

The Harper Collins Dictionary of Thought says : "Although protean in nature and not easily reducible to a set of general propositions liberalism springs from a vision of society as crucially composed of individuals (rather than, for instance classes) and of their liberty as the primary social good."[10]

It was in the early 1950s that the educated classes began to define the liberal tradition in the ways we usually do today—"As running in its infinite diversity from roots to John Calvin to John Locke, to John Marshall to John Stuart Mill to John Dewey and in our day to John Rawls."[11]

The Real life dictionary of American politics: what they are saying. and what it really means, defines liberalism as:

"A political concept and attitude whose definition has changed over the centuries and has different meanings depending on one's position in the political spectrum".[12]

Dewey dated the use of the term to the first decade of the nineteenth century, but traces it ideas further back to Locke.[13]

Hobhouse states that liberty is the hall-mark of liberalism–and it is not merely a right of an individual but a necessity of society.

To Jean Hampton, the term liberalism is 'really a kind of umbrella that can include a variety of particular liberal philosophies.'[14]

She emphasises five liberal commitments that are shared by all liberals:

1. A commitment to the idea that people in a political society must be free. This can be understood either in individualistic or collectivist terms.
2. A commitment to equality of the people in a political society.
3. A commitment to the idea that state's role must be defined so that it enhances freedom and equality– some talking of a minimal role (Nozick) and the others talking of an extensive role (Rawls).
4. Any political society must be justified to the individuals who live within it, if that society is to be legitimate.
5. Reason is the tool by which the liberal state governs.

Liberalism can be categorised into :

1. Classical Liberalism
2. Revisionist Liberalism
3. Modern Liberalism
4. Contemporary Liberalism

In classical liberalism, the representative thinkers included are John Locke and Adam Smith.

In revisionist liberalism, the revisionist liberals included are Jeremy Bentham and J.S. Mill.

The representative liberals included in modern liberalism are John Dewey, Milton Friedman, Friedrich Hayek, Isiah Berlin and C.B. MacPherson.

In contemporary liberalism, Ronald Dworkin, Brian Barry, Nozick and Rawls have been included, who lent a new complexion to liberalism after the 1970's.

Besides this, from the 1980s there has been an ongoing debate between communitarians and libertarians. Some of the important communitarians included in this chapter are Alisdair MacIntyre, Michael Sandel, Michael Walzer and Charles Taylor. With their emphasis on community, common good, they questioned the entire liberal family of theories, and their ire was also directed against libertarianism and its emphasis on individual liberty.

Classic Liberalism : This was the first stage of liberalism and it stressed laissez faire–being, passionately committed to the doctrine of individualism. Extolling the virtues of the individual, it pledged to uphold liberty–As a writer says :

"....this freedom was understood negatively, namely, as freedom from arbitrary coercion. One of the areas where freedom was most in demand was in the economy. A free economy was most conducive to the satisfaction of human beings."[15]

John Locke and Adam Smith have been included under classic liberalism–John Locke and his natural rights liberalism, proved quite influential in his time, and even in contemporary liberalism, we find libertarians like Nozick toeing his line, and Adam Smith, who has been called the father of classical economics was a liberal in the field of economics, and has a lasting impact.

CLASSICAL LIBERALISM

John Locke (1632-1704)

John Locke—Classic liberalism had several major forms, which reflected specific rational traditions as well as divergent philosophical backgrounds. In Locke, the basic themes of classic liberalism are evident. His defense of property, individualism, representative and limited government and separation of church and state set the stage for the evolution of liberal thought in the eighteenth and nineteenth centuries.

The natural rights liberalism epitomised–some say founded–by John Locke in the late seventeenth century England, believed in certain rights that people do not derive from, or depend upon their membership in specific human societies. As Locke saw it, man has been endowed with reason and the ability to know the basic principles of morality or natural law, and natural law dictated that each rational person possesses three fundamental natural rights–the right to life, liberty and property (or 'estate' in Lockean language).

In the words of a writer :

"I believe Locke's theory shaped the economically and socially conservative nature of liberalism as a political ideology in important and lasting ways."[16]

Louis Hartz also believes that 'Lockean Liberalism early became the dominant current in the mainstream of the American political tradition"[17] and the American Declaration of Independence was animated by natural-rights liberalism. Its author, Thomas Jefferson wrote of the "in alienable rights" with which the creator endowed all men, who were thereby 'created equal', His only departure was to encompass "life, liberty and the pursuit of happiness" in those rights, whereas Locke said, "life, liberty and estate."[18]

Since the individual has inalienable natural rights, that government is the best which governs the least.

In the words of a writer :

"Since government is instituted to protect the God-given rights of men its functions are inherently limited. Jefferson's dictum that government is best which governs the least is Lockean in Spirit ......"[19]

Locke's political teachings may be stated briefly thus :

'All government is limited in its powers and exists only by the consent of the governed. and the ground Locke builds on is this : All men are born free.[20] The theme of human freedom pervades all his writings. In 'A letter concerning toleration' (1689) he wrote of religious freedom; in 'Two treatises of government' (1690), of political freedom and in 'Some considerations of the consequences of the lowering of interest and raising the value of money' (1691), of economic freedom. But this theme receives its fullest treatment in the two treatises.

State of Nature

He draws a rosy picture of the state of nature which is one of 'peace, goodwill, mutual assistance and preservation'– and this halcyon state of nature provides "a complete equipment of human rights and duties. The defect of the state of nature lies merely in the fact that it has no organisation, such as magistrates, written laws, and fixed penalties, to give effect to the rules of right."[21] Thus we find that Locke interpreted natural law as a claim to innate rights inherent in each individual–and as such, the government and society exist for the preservation of these individual rights.

Natural Rights

As Andrew Vincent says :

"The place of natural rights in liberal thought is often traced back to thinkers like John Locke. Behind the original natural rights ideas was the panoply of natural law ideas and an optimistic deism which saw the world as ruled by Laws of God implanted in our reasoning. Such, rights were seen to be asocial, universal, inalienable claims premised on human nature. The possession and respect of such rights was the precondition to human flourishing."[22]

To put it in simpler terms, natural rights theorists like Locke, believed man possessed certain rights 'by nature' irrespective of any particular social, legal or political institutions and that these inherent rights are demonstrated by reason. Just as God endows man with arms, legs, eyes and ears, he also endows him with these rights so that he may realise himself to his fullest potential.

In a nutshell, these rights of 'life, liberty and estate' are inherent in the personality of man. They are non-transferable, inalienable immutable, and they belong to man independent of society and state. They are prior even to the primitive society which he described as the state of nature.

In Contemporary Liberalism, we find followers of Locke, in libertarians like Robert Nozick.

Adam Smith (1723-1790)

Adam Smith has been aptly named the father of the school that later came to be known as 'Classical Economics', and he has often been credited with being the father of Scientific Economics. As Gerald O'driscoll says:

"Smith is at the beginning of a tradition developed and carried on *inter alia* by Thomas Robert Malthus, James Mill, David Ricardo, James Ramsay, Mc Culloch Nassau, William Senior and John Stuart Mill."[23]

He was a liberal in the field of economics and advocated the doctrine of minimum possible state activity to ensure maximum possible individual liberty.

In 1759, Smith published his first work, 'The Theory of Moral Sentiments'–which lays the psychological foundation on which 'The Wealth of Nations' was later to be built. According to the Encyclopaedia Brittanica "Despite its renown as the first great work in political economy, 'The Wealth of Nations' is in fact a continuation of the philosophical theme begun in 'The Theory of Moral Sentiments.'"[24]

'An inquiry into the nature and causes of the wealth of nations' was published in the year 1776, and it was indeed a revolutionary event. As Thomas Sowell so aptly put it :

"Adam Smith's 'The Wealth of Nations', was a revolutionary event in 1776–an intellectual shot heard round the world. It attacked an economic system prevalent throughout European civilisation, both in Europe itself and the Western Hemisphere Colonies."[25]

Smith was a staunch defender of a liberal market economy, and in 'The wealth of nations', he put forward an economic programme which was embodied in whiggery. Being greatly influenced by the eighteenth century liberalism which "Was synonymous with a defense of private property rights and the political autonomy of the individual and with an opposition to state power or control over the lives of citizens, whether economic or political."[26]

Adam Smith's classic, spreading over 900 pages is a scathing attack of the status quo :

Heaping a virtual torrent of abuse upon the businessman, he alluded to 'the sneaking arts of underling tradesmen ...... The mean rapacity, the monopolising spirits of merchants and manufacturers .... The impertinent jealousy of merchants and manufacturers (p. 406).'

Smith was passionately and vigorously opposed to mercantilism, not merely because merchants were rapacious and self-seeking, but because "mercantilism was a collection of government measures that made it possible for businessmen to achieve their own selfish goals without at the same time advancing the public interest. Mercantilism represented a successful assault of the business community upon a helpless public."[27]

It was by advocating laissez faire that Smith hoped to bring about an elimination of special privileges which had helped the merchant in enriching himself without enriching the nation.

Restricting the sphere of State Activity was the means by which the public welfare could be advanced. As Rosenberg says :

"If only the state would leave the economic arena and give each individual an equal chance to 'better his condition', the public would benefit immensely."[28]

Smith believed that the naturally predatory acts of the businessman can be effectively curbed by a genuinely competitive order, where all mercantilist restrictions and privileges are eliminated, and an individual is given complete freedom in his economic pursuits.

'Civil government' he wrote, 'so far as it is instituted for the security of property is, in reality instituted for the defence of the rich against the poor, or of those who have some property against those who have none at all......'

According to Smith, society moves from simple to complex, and all the stages bring requisite alterations in the super structure of laws and civil institutions–and the final stage is the one which Smith characterizes as 'a system of perfect liberty' which is characterised by new institutions', such as market-determined rather than guild-determined wages and free rather than government–constrained enterprise–this later came to be known as laissez faire Capitalism–In all this, the primal moving agency is human nature, 'driven by the desire for self-betterment and guided (or misguided) by the faculties of reason.'

The Invisible Hand : 'This is the focus of Books I and II of 'The wealth of nations,' and through this, he tries to explain 'how a system of perfect liberty, operating under the drives and constraints of human nature and intelligently designed institutions will give rise to an orderly society–He refers to an institutional mechanism that acts to reconcile the disruptive possibilities inherent in a blind obedience to the passions alone. This protective mechanism is competition, an arrangement by which the passionate desire for bettering one's condition–'a desire that comes with us from the womb, and never leaves us until we go into the graves'–is turned into a socially beneficial agency by pitting one person's drive for self-betterment against another.

It is in the unintended outcome of this competitive struggle for self-betterment that the invisible hand regulating the economy shows itself."[29]

Smith believed that the wealth of nations would grow only if there were no inhibitions 'only if individuals, through their governments, did not inhibit this growth by catering to the pleas for special privilege that would prevent the competitive system from exercising its benign effect."[30]–hence much of 'The wealth of nations', particularly Book IV, is an onslaught on the restrictive measures of the 'mercantile system' that favoured monopolies at home and abroad.

Although Smith preached laissez faire, his argument was directed as much against, monopoly as government.

Heaping praise on his classic, N. Rosenberg says :

'Many of his arguments continue to be illuminating, relevant and full of insight even though we may have cogent reasons today for rejecting a policy of laissez faire."[31]

He further says that Smith was a 'complete realist', who realised that government intervention was likely to benefit a small privileged group rather than the entire nation. "His plea for laissez faire was not based on the assumption .... that government should stand idly by regardless of the abuses or anti-social behaviour of merchants and manufacturers. He saw clearly that the powers of government had in the past been used to dispense monopolies and special favours to a small privileged group.

In arguing for non-intervention, Smith was pleading for the elimination of all special treatment and privilege. He believed very deeply that laissez faire would lead not only to greater production but to greater equality as well."[32]

He strongly believed that economic welfare is maximised when each individual is allowed to pursue his own interests, without the intervention of kings and ministers. As he puts it so sardonically :

"It is the highest impertinence and presumption in kings and ministers, to pretend to watch over the economy of private people .... Let them look well after their own expence, and they may safely trust private people with theirs. If their own extravagance does not ruin the state that of their subjects never will."[33]

Revisionist Liberalism : Bentham and J.S. Mill

The second stage of Liberalism can be labelled as revisionist liberalism, and the representative thinkers included are Jeremy Bentham and J.S. Mill, who tried to revise liberalism in the context of utility, understood in terms of the greatest good of the greatest number.

The nineteenth century produced a group of writers called Philosophical radicals–Bentham and J.S. Mill–their doctrine, utilitarianism dominated English political thought for more than half a century, and it "provided a new theoretical foundation to liberalism."[34]

The following pages will try to throw light on the ideas of Bentham and J.S. Mill and how their novel ideas revised liberalism in the context of utility.

Philosophical radicalism had immense practical importance in nineteenth century politics.

As a writer says :

"Here was a doctrine to rock the foundations of all accredited political theory. With ruthless logic, Bentham..... had put it down that divine right, feudal right, historical right, natural right, contractual right and constitutional right equally and alike were rubbish and nonsense...."[35]

The philosophical radicals were able to disseminate novel ideas, without attaining the status of a political party, and in the light of these ideas, 'a vast amount of antiquated political lumber was swept away, and legislation, administration, and judicial process were made both, more efficient and more democratic."[36]

As Wayper says :

"They were as trenchant and vigorous and fearless in their attack on aristrocratic privilege as any new industrialist could desire, but were bitterly critical of the theory of natural rights....."[37]

But the consequences of the application of Benthamism to political life, led to a rethinking of the relationship between individual and society. In the words of Sabine :

"A thoroughgoing revision of liberal theory, therefore required a re-examination of the nature and functions of the state, the nature of liberty..... the relationship between individual human nature and its social milieu. To deal with this last question the old ready explanations, in terms of self-interest, pleasure and utility proved steadily less convincing."[38]

Although Bentham was an individualist, as he regarded the individual as the ultimate unit and reality, he tended to exalt the powers of the legislator far too high.

In its efforts to promote the greatest good of the greatest number, the British government had started interfering with the freedom of the individual, hence Bentham's successor J.S. Mill reached the conclusion that popular majorities could also be tyrannical and despotic, and it was against this tyrannical majority, that an individual needed to be guarded–hence he proclaimed in vociferous tones in his path-breaking, essay, 'On Liberty' (1859) which Sabine calls the 'most characteristic and.... most lasting contribution to political thought' :

"Over himself, over his own body and mind, the individual is sovereign."

As Ivor Brown says :

"It was Mill who saw through the facile optimism of his predecessors in democratic theory and determined to make of liberty, the liberty of men and women, not of groups and abstractions, a political concept of primary importance."[39]

Jeremy Bentham (1748-1832)

In England, the industrial revolution created a new manufacturing class, and their 'social and economic status rendered them intolerant of the old regime, urged them to a demand for freedom of trade and contract, infuriated them with the clumsy cruelties and procrastinations of the positive law which Black stone had lauded to the Skies, and made of them the most fruitful nursery for planting a new liberalism."[40]

The economic tenets of this new manufacturing class were the expression of its economic necessities.

"The old fetters, which encumbered every form of human activity, had to be broken in order to liberate the tremendous forces that were surging up within the community.... and the political passion for liberty was the obvious reflex of the commercial doctrine of laissez faire .... Weary of the old stagnation, they believed that any flowing current would carry them to happiness."[41]

Jeremy Bentham, was the intellectual fountain from whom the waters flowed and in his hand, "Social contract and Natural Law vanish from the social theory of the day and their place is taken by the impressive and solid figure of the greatest good of the greatest number."[42]

Thundering against the statists who believed in kneeling down and offering up 'incense to a deified Leviathan', he said that the state's interference must be jealously watched, and that its claim to infallibility is the rankest insolence.

In 1776 when he was but twenty-seven years old, Bentham published 'Fragment on Government' in which he waxed eloquent against the sentimental optimism of people like Blackstone who had lauded the British Constitituon and the positive law to the Skies. Regarding this work Dunning says : "Though he lived to be eighty-four and wrote to the very end, it was never superseded.."[43]

In 1789, he wrote 'Introduction to the principles of morals and legislation' which contains the essence of Bentham's social theory.

Bentham claimed to have found the key both to describing actual human behaviour and prescribing the 'Principles of morality and legislation.' The starting point being a psychological one' and this starting point, as he writes in 'Introduction to the principles of morals and legislation' is, "nature has placed mankind under the governance of two sovereign masters, pain and pleasure. It is for them alone to point out what we ought to do as well as to determine what we shall do."

In short, he emphasized that only those laws are useful which do not conform to the vague and abstract natural law, but which promote the greatest good of the greatest number, and this test of utility was for Bentham a complete and final guide for all those who might be interested in morals and legislation, and he had a deep and unwavering loyalty to this conviction which found expression in the many pleas that he made for practical reform.

As Dunning says, 'his services to ethical and juristic science ...... were of utmost value ...... he formulated codes of international law, of constitutional law, of criminal law, which ...... embodied ..... principles and suggestions that have not failed to fruitfulness in later generations."[44]

John Stuart Mill (1806-1873)

A manifest shift in Liberalism from a negative side to a positive one can be seen in the thought of J.S. Mill, who was in the direct line of utilitarian succession. His task, 'was to set the coping stone on the great edifice of thought planned by Bentham, elaborated by James Mill, his father ..... He softened away the crudities of Benthamite ethics and in so doing he made utilitarianism at once more human and less consistent : he admitted superior quality in one form of happiness as opposed to another .... He made innovations in the ruthless economics of laissez faire, and was not unsympathetic to socialism. But throughout his life he was guided by the idea of liberty:"[45]

Although Mill began his intellectual career as a disciple of Jeremy Bentham–he disagreed with the Benthamite perspective that all pleasures were equal in value. He stated his disagreement in the eloquent words, "It is better to be a human being dissatisfied than a pig satisfied; better to be Socrates dissatisfied than a fool satisfied".

In other words, he tried to emphasise the inherent nobility and sublimity of certain pleasures as compared to others, and with that qualitative modification in the 'greatest happiness' principle, he made it the essence of 'social utility', stating that public policy should be guided by social utility.

Despite his father's efforts of bringing J.S. Mill up in the utilitarian gospel of Bentham, Mill was able to bring about some changes in the utilitarian creed of Bentham–firstly, he emphasised the qualitative basis of utility as reflected in his famous words, mentioned earlier, and secondly, he elevated liberty over utility.

Although Mill started with a negative function of state, implying that liberty means the absence of restraint, in the final stage of his philosophy, a tilt towards the positive conception of liberty and a positive function of the state can be discerned.

Dividing individual actions into two groups 1. Self-Regarding and 2. Other Regarding, he says... that regarding the former, man's liberty involves the absence of restraints, but in the latter an individual's liberty can be checked in order to guarantee the similar liberty of others.

Regarding his views, a writer says :

"The liberal political philosophy of John Stuart Mill represents a type of liberalism that gives up much of the Lockean baggage of natural law, state of nature, and social contract",[46] yet shares the basic egalitarianism of Locke.

Mill believed that his father's generation had desired liberal government not for the sake of liberty but because they believed that it would be efficient government .... But for him "freedom of thought and investigation, freedom of discussion and the freedom of self-contained moral judgment and action were goods in their own right."[47]

Mill had reached the conclusion that the individualism of early liberal theory was inadequate, hence he feared an oppressive and intolerant public opinion.

Sabine, says that Mill's contribution to liberal philosophy can be summed up under four heads :

1. Mill's utilitarianism rescued Bentham's version from that form of ethics which was calculated merely on the basis of pleasures and pains.

   "Mill's ethics was utilitarian" chiefly in the sense that he thought of the value of personality not as a metaphysical dogma but as something to be realised in the actual condition of a free society."[48]

2. Freedom is the proper condition of a responsible human being, hence, Mill's liberalism accepted political and social freedom as itself a good, not because it contributed to an ulterior end but because ..... To live one's own life, developing one's own native traits and capacities is not a means to happiness; it literally is a substantive part of happiness. A good society must, therefore, be one which both permits freedom and opens up the opportunity for free and satisfying ways of life.

3. Liberty is not only an individual good, but also a social good ..... Individual right and public utility are closely connected.

4. "The function of a liberal state in free society is not negative but positive. It cannot make its citizens free merely by refraining from legislation or assume that the conditions of freedom exist merely because legal disabilities have been removed."[49]

The function of a Liberal State, in Mill's perspective was to, 'Make life more humane and less coercive'

Despite varied criticisms of utilitarianism the idea that the individual is the best judge of his own interest remained very strong in western countries, although it took a different form under modern liberalism.

Modern Liberalism

The third stage of liberalism is modern liberalism and the main thinkers included here are Milton Friedman, F.A. Hayek, I. Berlin, C.B. MacPherson, all of whom lent a new tenor and complexion to liberalism.

Despite the enormous reputation of Jeremy Bentham and J.S. Mill as the founding figures of liberalism, some modern liberals criticised and doubted their liberal credentials, emphasising that their greatest happiness principle could never be the basis for sound liberal legislation. Hayek doubted the rationalist premise built into utilitarianism, namely, that anyone could calculate the general happiness of society. He argued that the utilitarian committed the philosophical mistake of not identifying the limits to reason. Similarly, Friedman argued that freedom is the right of individuals to choose their own course of action.

John Dewey with his emphasis on 'Specific Reform Programmes', also tried to bring liberalism up-to-date, although, unlike, Hayek and 'Friedman he did not espouse the atomistic view of the individual.

In the post-Second World War period, liberalism donned the mantle of a saviour–a good Samaritan–trying to save mankind from the tyranny of a totalitarian system. The all-pervasive welfare state had slowly but surely degraded into a totalitarian state where civil liberties had been woefully undermined. In the words of a writer : "By letting the state fox into the market chicken coop, those developed societies entering into the project of creating a regulatory planned economy and a redistributive welfare state were putting themselves on a slippery slope that inevitably ended in Nazi or Soviet style despotisms."[50]

In the immediate aftermath of the Second World War, a lot of intellectual churning started taking place and this churning was most apparent in the United States, where the works of liberals like Hayek and Friedman had astonishing success. Both criticised the excessive government that had been developing ever since the New Deal Programmes and the War on Poverty, and the interventionist social engineering, which interfered with the market and produced a bloated and corrupt political class. "Welfare was also perverse in its effects, futile in its ambitions and jeopardised the very accomplishments on which it depended."[51]

There was an attack from all–the Marxists left and the neo-liberal right–on the arrogance of government over reach, and they all agreed unanimously that the belief in a social state which guaranteed steady and incremental progress must be rejected.

The post-Second World War period was indeed a gloomy scenario, where "much of the optimistic perfectibilism of the nineteenth and early twentieth century liberals was dashed on the fields of the Somme, Ypres and by the later knowledge of Dachau and Buchenwald."[52] and now liberalism became redefined in contradistinction to the supposed totalitarianism of communist and fascist regimes–the hall-marks of this modern variant of liberalism being scepticism, individual self-cultivation and self-examination.

John Dewey (1859-1952)

John Dewey wrote various books in a life spanning, a well-lived ninety three years. 'Liberalism and social action', 'the 'public and its problems', 'problems of men', 'reconstruction in philosophy' being some of the books in which he expressed his views.

Criticising classical liberalism for its lack of 'historical relativity', and its 'atomistic' view of society, he tried to bring liberalism up-to-date. He believed that it was the short-sightedness of the 'early liberals' that 'condemned the principles of classic liberalism eventually to become outworn cliches.

In the words of Dewey, the unhistorical method, "blinded the eyes of the liberals to the fact that their own special interpretations of liberty, individuality, the intelligence were themselves historically conditioned and were relevant only to their own time."[53]

He believed that the classic liberals did not view individuality as a moving thing.

To the classic liberal, "individuality was something readymade, already possessed, and needing only the removal of certain legal restrictions to come into full play. It was not conceived as a moving thing, something that is attained only by continuous growth."[54]

Unlike the classical liberals, Dewey did not view the society as atomistic, which viewed individuals as social atoms with only a limited involvement in the social whole. "Dewey's rendition of 'positive' freedom includes a strong social dimension. Liberty thus becomes "that secure release and fulfillment of personal potentialities which takes place only in wide and manifest association with others."[55]

In the words of S.E. Frost :

"He conceives of a world which is in the making, and man is doing some of the creating...... Human wants, desires, willings are determiners of the universe".

For Dewey, the pivot of progress is the intelligent human being freely foreseeing the possible consequences of events and throwing himself into the stream in order to, in a degree at least, change the course of the stream so that it conforms more fully to his ideals."[56]

In a similar vein, another writer says :

"Appeals to nature and the rest struck Dewey as an abdication of human responsibility for human destiny. By assigning such responsibility to mystical cosmic forces, they condemned society to drifting and back-sliding. True progress is not a gift of the cosmos; rather, it is an achievement that man must earn."[57]

Being a pragmatist, he mistrusted absolutes, believing that important truths are not fixed once and for all. For the pragmatist, the world is dynamic and evolving, and truth is not a static relation between ideas–it is related to the multifarious processes which make up the world.

He believed that change is the law of life, and ideas live only so long as they are relevant. In the words of a writer :

"Ideas therefore are condemned to obsolescence. Change is the law of life and no constellation of ideas or attitudes can hope to live beyond its time of relevance."[58] He saw his belief confirmed by the changing history of liberalism.

In Dewey's opinion 'social action' should be the watchword of any philosophy. He pleads for thorough-going changes in the entire social system. A 'do-nothing' view of progress does not conform to Dewey's pragmatic philosophy. "Progress itself requires 'social action' which may well mean using government in ways alien to classic liberalism and its contemporary defenders. Accordingly, Dewey argues that modern liberalism must take on a 'radical' cast."[59]

Radicalism, according to Dewey involves the necessity of thorough-going changes in the set-up of institutions and corresponding activity to bring the changes to pass.[60]

Rejecting both the extremes of pure capitalism and pure socialism, the pragmatist in him emphasises specific reform programmes, without which the society can only drift and back-slide.

For him, liberty and democracy were compatible. In fact, he believed that democracy captured the very essence of liberalism.

"Quite naturally, Dewey dispelled any classic liberal doubts about the compatibility of democracy with liberty. Like Green, he considered the modern democratic idea simply an extension of truly liberal notion of individuality. A true belief in individuality involves a sense of human equality that rejects the old-fashioned ideas of superiority and inferiority. Individuals, morally speaking, are unique–not identical, not superior, and not inferior to each other."[61]

In the words of Dewey :

"No matter how great the quantitative differences of ability, strength, position, wealth, such differences are negligible in comparison with something else–the fact of individuality...."[62]

Thus democracy, for Dewey was compatible with individuality. It was within the democratic set-up that an individual's full worth could be realised.

In a nutshell, Dewey's views can be summarised thus :

1. Ideas are not 'immutable truths', good at all times and places. Change is the law of life.
2. Individuality was not something readymade, but it was something created by an individual. His wants and desires shape his individuality, hence individuality is a moving thing–it's in a state of continuous growth.
3. An individual is deeply rooted in the social firmament, and he can realise his potentialities only in association with others.

4. His view of society is not atomistic, like the classic liberals.
5. True progress is not a gift of the cosmos, it is achieved by the intelligent human being through thinking, planning, inquiring and deciding.
6. Individuality and democracy go hand in hand. Democracy is a way of life, rather than a rigid structure of government.

Friedrich Hayek (1899-1992)

Hayek was born in 1899 into a family of civil servants and academics in Vienna, the capital of the Austro-Hungarian empire. In 1931, he accepted a chair at the London School of Economics and Political Science, where he was to remain for two decades.

He was a free-market oriented economist, who strongly opposed extensive government intervention in economic life. In the 1930s, he became a stout opponent of the British economist John Maynard Keynes, criticising him for his interventionist conception of government role in the capitalist economy. In 1974 he was awarded the Nobel Prize for Economics.

'The road to serfdom', published in 1944, fetched him popular fame in Britain and in America, and this book was an attack on socialism, government ownership of the means of production, and economic planning. He emphasised that Britain's enemy German National Socialism, was the result of socialist roots, and the very processes which led to the rise of Nazism in Germany were gaining strength in England and America. The thrust of his argument was, that socialism, even when it was pursued with democratic intentions, tended toward governmental control over evermore spheres of life leading toward totalitarianism.

Although Hayek spent the bulk of his remaining years until his death in 1992, in Austria and Germany, it was in the English-speaking world that his influence could be seen.

'The Constitution of Liberty' was published in 1960, and in this he critically examined 'The Welfare State', objecting to what he regarded as the abuse of the welfare state in pursuing the traditional socialist goal of equality of income. He was suspicious of government monopolisation of the provision of social, medical or educational services. He tried to show how social security could be provided in a manner that did little damage to individual freedom.

This inquiry continued in the trilogy, 'Law, Legislation, and Liberty' published from 1973 to 1979.

Hayek argued that the 20th century concept of social justice (implying a redistribution of society's resources by the state) is manifestly unjust, believing that it results in an authoritarian political order.

"For Hayek, the concept of social justice has no role or meaning in economic order based on the market, nor is it possible within a market order to redistribute society's resources according to some assessment of individual performance within it. Should this happen, the logical outcome is steady progression toward an authoritarian political order."[63] The pursuit of social justice, Hayek believes, can be realised justly in a directed economy where actions are guided by specific directions and not by rules of just individual conduct. Governments which supposedly try to establish social justice refuse 'to recognise the autonomous spheres of individuals, hence are unjust.'

Social justice is indeed a mirage for Hayek because it undermines the stability of the market order. Apart from riding roughshod over individual freedom, this mirage, prolongs the dependency culture of the needy and it also gives rise to vested interests. This tarnishes the spontaneity of the market, thus circumventing the free liberal order– hence, 'Economic Planning', which runs against the diversity and complexity of society is an imposition, hence, it is unjust.

Constraints Upon the State

In order to prevent the state from interfering with the market order, Hayek proposed a range of constraints aimed specifically at insulating the economic sphere from the political sphere.

In this context, Hayek emphasises the Rule of Law, and 'the rule of law' for Hayek is not simply a rule of law but 'a rule concerning what the law, ought to be, a meta legal doctrine or political ideal' (Hayek, 1960 : 206). Hayek's 'basic principles' (Hayek 1982 : 111) are based upon universal rules upholding an abstract order. These rules .... would require limits upon what government may do and would go beyond the traditional contents of a Bill of Rights. In short, the state may only use its powers of coercion–which he concedes exists irrespective of politico–economic organisation–if it can be shown to uphold the universal rules of a just order, i.e., based upon the principle of individual liberty."[64]

To this end, Hayek talks of dual representative bodies–one which is charged with legislation, and the other with fundamental law–making to prevent laws that would inhibit individuals liberty.

Although the Hayekean brand of liberalism has been criticised a lot, his views are important as they have lent a new tenor to liberalism.

Milton Friedman (1912– ....)

A great believer in the power of the free-market, he won the Nobel Prize for Economics in 1976 and his work influenced the Tory Government of Margaret Thatcher to adopt his policies in 1979 when it was elected. Friedman, believing in a limited government, felt that the major function of government was 'to protect our freedom from the enemies outside our gates.'

The political views he espoused are clearly rooted in the concept of early liberalism found in the late eighteenth and early nineteenth centuries–which considered individual freedom a natural right. Friedman believed that political power would eventually corrupt even the best intentioned person, hence instead of trusting a few to wield the political reins, he emphasised separation of powers among the three different branches of government.

His brand of liberalism was a traditional laissez faire liberalism–a hands–off approach to government interference in the private market.

A proud student of the eighteenth century economist Adam Smith, he founded the Mont Pelerin society in the post-Second World War period, the aim of which was to "promote a classical, liberal philosophy, that is, a free economy, a free society socially, civilly and in human rights. 'Capitalism and Freedom' (1962) was an extension of his liberal economic views.

His views stand in stark contrast to the welfare statists who believed that social and economic problems could be solved by the direct intervention of the state in the economic affairs of the individuals. In 'Capitalism and Freedom' he writes that the United States has no doubt, progressed by leaps and bounds, but all this progress 'has been the product of the initiative and drive of individuals cooperating through the free market. Government measures have hampered not helped this development.... The invisible hand has been more potent for progress than the visible hand for retrogression."[65]

With his emphasis on limited government, Friedman would appear to be a libertarian, but he refuted such a label, although he had followed the libertarian movement closely. Instead, he considered himself a republican, and believed the libertarians to be 'cultist in their theories, trying to invent something new when–the old ways are best.'

Sir Isaiah Berlin (1909–1997)

This most important liberal philosopher of our time was witness to a century, he was in Washington during World

War II, in Moscow at the dawn of the cold war and dining with President John F. Kennedy on the eve of the Cuban Missile crisis.

Born in Riga in the twilight of the Czarist Empire, he lived long enough to see the Soviet state collapse. This son of a Jewish timber merchant, defended the liberal idea of freedom against Soviet Tyranny, and when he died in 1997, he was hailed as the most important liberal philosopher of his time.

He gave a new impetus to the liberal individualist tradition and sharpened it by "his insistence that liberty amounts to the permitted range of individual potential choices, by his separation of the negative liberty from all varieties of 'positive' liberty."[66]

Moreover, he also warns against positive liberty, because it is liable to become an 'Engine of oppression.'

In the words of a writer :

"Berlin was not the first (or the last) to distinguish between a negative and a positive concept of liberty. Indeed, that distinction in one form or another has been implicit, if not always explicit, in political thought since the ancient Greeks. Berlin's contribution was to elaborate the distinction to such an extent that it has now become part of the staple fare of every analysis of freedom."[67]

Berlin's 'Two Concepts of Liberty' was first published in 1958, being hailed as a landmark in the history of attempts to elucidate the meaning of freedom, while one writer calls it a 'minor classic of modern political theory'[68] another hails it as 'a rare intellectual treat',[69] which emphasises that the negative view of liberty is' a truer and more humane ideal' than positive liberty. About the latter, he maintains, that it is inimical to the spirit of liberalism, because it lends a dangerous theoretical sanction to every type of authoritarianism.

The distinction between positive and negative liberty was elaborated by Berlin in such a way that it has now 'become part of the staple fare of every analysis of freedom.'

He believes that there should be a certain minimum area of personal freedom, which must on no account be violated. To quote Berlin :

"If it is overstepped, the individual will find himself in an area too narrow for even that minimum development of his natural faculties which alone make it possible to pursue and even to conceive, the various ends which men hold good or right or sacred."[70]

So what follows is, that a frontier must be drawn between the area or private life and that of public authority–but where it should be drawn is indeed a matter of argument.

Regarding the notion of 'negative' freedom, Berlin says:

"I am normally said to be free to the degree to which no man or body of men interferes with my activity. Political liberty in this sense is simply the area within which a man can act unobstructed by others."[71]

Positive Freedom

Four basic assumptions can be traced in Berlin's concept of positive liberty :

1. All men have one true purpose and one only, that of rational self-direction',
2. That the end of all rational beings must of necessity fit into a single universal, harmonious pattern which some men may be able to discern more clearly than others.
3. All conflict and consequently all tragedy, is due solely to the clash of reason with the irrational or the insufficiently rational–the immature and undeveloped element in life–and such clashes are

avoidable–(Rationality, Berlin claims can be acquired by education).

4. When all men have been made rational, they will obey the rational laws of their own natures, which are one and the same in them all, and thus they will become wholly law-abiding and wholly free."

Berlin believes that positive liberty has lead, and can also lead to 'monstrous denials of liberty'.

Despite his claim that the two aspects of liberty cannot be distinguished in practical terms, we find him, in the ultimate analysis defending the negative view of liberty. He emphatically affirms :

"Emphasis on negative liberty, as a rule leaves more paths for individuals or groups to pursue. Positive liberty, as a rule opens fewer paths...."[72]

A brief analysis of his views on negative and positive liberty reveals, that like Michael Oakeshott, Berlin believes that 'rights are liberties and therefore arise not from law but from the silence of law.'

Although the concept of negative liberty was replaced by positive libety in the twentieth century, people like Isaiah Berlin have revived it in the twentieth century, and it appears that the influence of John Locke is obvious on him, and, like this seventeenth century English philosopher, he also believes that liberty "is the power a man has to do or forbear doing any particular action according .... as he himself wills it" ("Essay concerning human understanding," Book II, Chapter xxi, Section 15) and as Locke says in the second treatise of civil government, (Sec. 57) that the 'end of law is not to abolish or restrain but to preserve and enlarge freedom."

Contemporary Liberalism

There was one final manifestation of liberalism after the seventies, which represented diverse and contradictory impulses of the liberal ideology–This vigorous efflorescence which had a great impact, specially in the USA, saw writers like Michael Walzer, Ronald Dworkin, John Rawls, Brian Barry, Robert Nozick, C.B. MacPherson and others enunciating their views on major political issues from diverse angles of liberal thought. Rawls, as we know, was the spokesman of liberal–egalitarianism, Nozick upheld the ideology of libertarianism, Dworkin emphasised the liberal virtue of equal concern and respect to individuals, C.B. MacPherson maintained that liberal-democracy should consider man as a doer, and not as utility maximiser or a power maximiser and communitarians like Michael Sandel, Charles Taylor, Alasdair MacIntyre and others, emphasised the community as opposed to the individual, thus giving rise to the libertarian communitarian debate.

John Rawls

It was John Rawls' 'A Theory of Justice' (1971) which gave him a prominent place in contemporary liberalism and also credited him with the revival of political theory. With his emphasis on the welfare state, redistribution and social justice, he provided an egalitarian tenor to liberalism and tried to replace utilitarianism, the eminent ideology of the time by his alternative Theory of Justice, which tried to improve the lot of 'The Least Advantaged Person'. In the words of a writer, 'Not only did Rawls set the stage for a large scale reconsideration of the nature of distributive justice by philosophers critical of utilitarianism but he also gave new life to the discipline of political philosophy, which was largely moribund in the Anglo-American world in the first half of the twentieth century."[73]

I have dealt with the political theory of John Rawls in chapter V, and hence, here. I would just like to emphasise the point that his Theory of Justice explicitly mandates equalising each citizen's opportunities and liberties and also securing the grounds for self-respect for every citizen, and by so doing he tries to lay the foundations of a just state which is deeply egalitarian in spirit, which has excited and influenced many, and provoked some like Robert Nozick into writing a, rejoinder to 'A Theory of Justice', in the form of 'Anarchy, State and Utopia' (1974).

Robert Nozick

Robert Nozick, as already mentioned, restated the classical liberal case in his path-breaking book 'Anarchy, State and Utopia' (1974). Greatly influenced by John Locke, he supported the minimal state, which is limited to the narrow functions of protection against force, theft, fraud, enforcement of contracts, etc.

While Rawls supported an extensive state, which is involved in social engineering, through the adjustment of entitlements which benefits the least advantaged, Nozick refutes such a view-point, on the grounds of inalienable rights of individuals which cannot be interfered with, on the same grounds, he opposes redistribution taxation and welfare programmes. For Nozick, justice is not a matter of attempting to reorganise society and its institutions to achieve some distributive pattern but is one of respecting the inalienable rights of individuals.

By his emphasis on liberty and the inalienable rights of individuals, Nozick revived libertarianism, and the following pages will deal it length with his libertarian ideology, which encompasses his theory of the minimal state and the entitlement Theory of Justice.

C.B. MacPherson

In the 1970s, normative theorising, which emphasised participatory democracy, started flowering, wherein many theorists articulated their views regarding the active and not passive participation of citizens in the democratic process. One such theorist was C.B. MacPherson and the two important books which spell out his political theory are 'Democratic Theory' (1973) and 'The life and times of liberal democracy' (1978).

He criticised the passivity and utility of the dominant conceptions of liberal democracy, and tried to give an alternative and more active conception of democracy. Regarding his analysis, an analyst says, 'MacPherson's analysis of political theories according to whether they assume the nature of human beings as primarily acquisitive consumers of goods or primarily as developers and exercisers of capacities remains a useful way to orient democratic political theory."[74] He redefined the human good as the development and exercising of capacities giving a different turn to democratic theory. He emphasised that distributive justice is only a means to the wider good of positive freedom, which is itself a social good, because it is realised in cooperation with others. For MacPherson, freedom is the opportunity to develop and exercise one's capacities, an actively engaged citizen democracy is both a condition and expression of such freedom, and liberal democracy should base itself on the concept of man as essentially an actor, a doer, and the developer of human attributes.

MacPherson's interest in capacities was motivated by a conviction that the meaning of freedom should be deepened in political theory and practice.

He emphasises the fact that the image of man as an infinite consumer and infinite appropriator, as a being whose rational purpose in life is to devote himself to an endless attempt to overcome scarcity, needs to be demolished as it is 'unnecessary and deleterious, and if this is not done, then the liberal-democratic heritage of western society has a poor chance of survival.

Thus, MacPherson, tried to recast liberal-democratic theory by dropping from it the market assumptions about the nature of man and society.

Ronald Dworkin

Brian Barry and John Rawls can be labeled as liberal democratic theorists. Another important contemporary thinker is Ronald Dworkin–who, along with them can also be labeled as a liberal democratic theorist.

The two important works of Ronald Dworkin are 'Taking rights seriously' (1978) and 'A matter of principle' (1985) 'Taking rights seriously' is a collection of essays regarding 'rights', and the upshot of these essays is that rights do not have any metaphysical character, but that they are 'Political trumps held by individuals', and all political rights derive from the abstract right to concern and respect.

In the introduction of 'Taking Rights Seriously' Dworkin writes :

"The book nevertheless suggests one favoured form of argument for political rights, which is the derivation of particular rights from the abstract right to concern and respect taken to be fundamental and axiomatic."[75]

'Taking Rights Seriously' is, sharply critical of two theories, namely (a) The theory of legal positivism' (b) The theory of utilitarianism–which holds that law and its institutions should serve the general welfare and nothing else.

Legal positivism holds that individuals have legal rights only in so far as these have been created by explicit political decisions or explicit social practices.

In his essay on 'Liberalism', Dworkin succinctly sums up the neutralist case when he says that the constitutive morality of liberalism consists of a theory of equality.

"Since the citizens of a society differ in their conceptions, the government does not treat them as equals if it prefers one conception to another."[76]

Dworkin, emphasises the point that all laws in some way diminish Liberty, for example, Laws can restrict a citizen 'from driving his car uptown on Lexington Avenue', and hence he announces, 'it seems to me absurd to suppose that men and women have any general right to liberty at all....."[77]

As a writer puts it :

"For Dworkin, drawing deeply upon Rawls' 'Theory of Justice', it is equality, or more precisely equal concern and respect that must fill the empty concept of liberty."[78]

In fact, it is the defining duty of the liberal state to provide equal concern and respect to individuals without imposing any sacrifice or constraint on them which would make him abandon their 'sense of equal worth.'

In two important articles 'What is Equality Part I' : 'Equality of Welfare' and 'What is Equality? Part II' : 'Equality of Resources', Dworkin spells out his views regarding equality.

Resource Egalitarianism

Espousing resource egalitarianism, he maintains, that the state should equalise resources and not welfare, which implies a way of distributing resources, which while not resulting in everyone having exactly the same amount, however, leaves each person satisfied. He bases his solution on a hypothetical auction in which participants bargain with an equal number of worthless counters (clam Shells) for the resources of an imagined island–which is meant to replicate an idealised market.

He believes that although the liberal institutions of the market economy and representative democracy can help in the realisation of the liberal idyll, there are two aspects of the real world which might prevent this realisation. First, people do not begin on an advantage. Second, people are not equal in their 'Raw' skill, intelligence or other capacities–and hence he concentrates on producing an equal distribution of resources against which individuals choose their plan of life, but they must do so on the basis of their own abilities and those of like-minded fellow citizens.

Although there are many practical difficulties that bedevil Dworkin's account of rights, his assertion that government must show concern for its citizens as 'beings who are capable must show concern for its citizens as 'beings who are capable of forming and acting on intelligent conceptions of how their lives should be lived' is an appeal to the liberal model of the self-developing rational, chooser of ends, which is characteristic of the rationalist tradition of Kant and Mill, and it is this conception which makes him rank the 'rights of the individual' above everything else, and in order to uphold the moral fabric of liberal society he imagines a judge of Herculean powers–thus we see him holding a liberal ethical view-point which supports equality of individuals.

Brian Barry

Brian Barry, R. Dworkin and J. Rawls form a triumvirate of political theorists, who held a plea for social justice, and can be labeled as liberal–democrats.

Some of his important books are 'Political Argument' (1965); 'The liberal Theory of Justice, (1973) 'Democracy, power and justice : Essays in political theory' (1989), 'Liberty and justice : Essays in political theory 2' (1991) 'Justice as impartiality' (1995), 'Culture and Equality : An egalitarian critique of Multiculturalism' (2001).

Expatiating on liberalism, Brian Barry says that, 'the basic idea of liberalism is to create a set of rights under which people are treated equally in certain respects, and then to leave them to deploy these rights (alone or in association with others) in the pursuit of their own ends."[79]

He states that although, in the past two hundred years, there have been widespread changes in accordance with the precept of equal treatment, for example, slavery has been abolished in the West, India and Latin America, as well as in the U.S.A., but the liberal agenda is by no means complete _ 'Anti–discrimination provisions can be strengthened .... The principle of 'equal pay for equal work' can be pressed much further ...... equal opportunity in education is still far from achievement. Above all, the kind of economic security that is necessary to give value to other rights is conspicuously lacking."[80]

He tries to drive home the point that some theorists in modern times have argued for the abandonment of the liberal idea of equal treatment, under common laws, because they believe that liberalism pretends to the tolerant to diverse, beliefs and ways of life while actually it is highly restrictive.

Refuting such an allegation, Barry maintains, that people who try to make additional claims, in the name of liberal values, are not being fair ....

Communitarianism

Since the 1980s there have been political theorists who have criticised not just particular liberal values, but the entire liberal family of theories, claiming that 'they are too focused on the importance of individual liberty, and insufficiently appreciative of the way in which human beings require a place in a well-functioning community in order to flourish.' This has resulted in a liberal vs communitarian debate, and the following pages will throw some light on communitarianism and the views of some important communitarian writers like, Alasdair MacIntyre, Charles Taylor, Michael Walzer and Michael Sandel.

Communitarianism is a reaction against individualism, subjectivism, atomism, alienation and the contract-based and market-oriented character of liberalism. It was also a reaction to the resurgence of libertarianism.

All Communitarians appeal to the idea of community as an inescapable ideal–Unlike the libertarians who uphold the individual and his individual rights, their emphasis is on the existence of community–on the common good, rather than on individual good.

For them, society is less an aggregate of individuals, and more a system of shared values and commonly subscribed practices and institutions–Their emphasis is on values, practices and institutions which form an integral part of the society.

They view individuals in the context of society and believe that common good, springs from the individuals, but only when they see themselves as part of a larger whole–the society. Individual freedom becomes meaningful only in its societal context.

For the libertarians, for example, for Nozick, individuals have rights, and there are things no person or group may do to them,' and these rights are 'so strong and far-reaching', that they put constraints on others, while the communitarians believe that an individual and his rights can be understood only in the wider context of community. For them rights emerge in their true character as secondary rather than primary principles. So, their emphasis, unlike Hayek and Nozick is on their belief that community instead of diminishing rights helps enlarge them.

They believe that no abstract philosophical reasoning can help us in developing cogent views regarding the good–for, according to them, the idea of the good is not the product of individual preferences, on the contrary, they believe that it is embodied in the ways of life of particular communities.

For the communitarians, it is the community which is the basis of practical reason, and political judgment, and the individual is important only so far as it is influenced by the values of the community–

In a nutshell :

1. Community, and not the individual is the source of all values.
2. Common good lies within the ambit of the community itself.
3. Community is more than the aggregate of individuals. It is the sum-total of values combined together.

5. The individual is the constitutive organ of the community-born, nurtured and developed in it.

Although the writers who have been labelled as communitarians may have expressed some disquiet about being so labelled, there can be discerned a distinctive anti-individualism in much of their work.

In a very illuminating work Frazer outlines three theses of Communitarianism namely:

1. It is not the case that all there is in the world is individuals–They have to be viewed in the context of collectives, institutions, etc.
2. Ethically, we need to look to the social individual or collective and the significance of trust, solidarity, etc.
3. Methodologically, it is necessary to interpret and refine values that are immanent in the ways of life of really living groups–societies, communities, etc.

Providing a very helpful overview, Frazer draws three important inferences from these three theses :

1. Communitarians take issue with the idea that the individual stands and should stand in direct unmediated relationship with the state and with society.
2. Unlike the libertarians, the communitarians dispute the place of a free unregulated market as the key social institution, and the idea that free market exchanges are a particular right and even natural pattern of human relationships.
3. Communitarians promote a distinctive set of values: They hold the community in high esteem, and value tradition. They believe that there cannot be a universal list of significant values–for what is

> a universal list of significant values–for what is important will depend on the traditions and ways of life in that community.[83]

Some of the communitarian rhetoric has found its way into political discourse in the UK and USA (specially through the language of the new labour in the former).

If we compare the communitarian perspective with the liberal perspective, we find that right from the classical liberals–Locke, to the revisionist liberals Bentham Mill–to the modern and then to the contemporary liberals–there has hardly been any substantial change in their conception of the common good–Their commitments to the ideals of liberty and the autonomous individual was never questioned. For them, common good has meaning only within the framework of the individual good–when the individual good is fulfilled, it will ultimately result in the fulfilment of the whole society, while for the communitarians, it is the other way round. For them, all moral and political relations are based on social relations, which cannot be wished away–As Roger Eatwell and Anthony Wright say :

"To remove this social foundation is to deny those formative experiences which make us moral and political agents."[84]

For the liberals, the values of freedom and equality are of paramount importance, and for the communitarians, the values of community life are most important.

They are particularly vehement in 'rejecting the idea that in order to ensure human liberty the state must refrain from articulating a conception of the good to which all people must conform ..... instead they believe that in order to ensure that its citizens flourish, the ideal state must use its power and authority to encourage the continuation and health of the cultural traditions."[85]

Michael Sandel

With 'liberalism and the limits of justice' (1982) Michael Sandel launched the current contemporary political theory : Communitarianism. He argued that 'Rawls' Theory of Justice wrongly presupposes a moral self prior to social relationships guided by principles of justice, a self 'unencumbered' by particular culture and commitments into which he or she is thrown."[86] Such principles, Sandel argues, which are generated from an abstract notion of self, can only regulate public relations among strangers. His suggestion for a robust political theory of social union is that justice must be supplemented by recognition of particular community bonds, without which the view of a person is woefully impoverished, as he says that we cannot regard ourselves as independent of the loyalties and convictions which help us in understanding ourselves "as the particular persons.... We are–as members of this family or community or nation or people as bearers of this history, as sons and daughters of that revolution, as citizens of this republic ..... those more or less enduring attachments which taken together define the person that I am."[87]

So, the upshot of his argument is that liberal theories fail to come to grips with the nature of one's "embeddedness". He believes that a 'deeper commonality' can be created, not when we try to understand human beings independently of all activities, desires, ideas, roles and pursuits (as Rawls' people in the original position), but "by thinking about how people with attachments that partially constitute their identities can come to know and relate to one another as friends."[88]

Michael Walzer

Michael Walzer believes that if the liberal values of equality and pluralism are to be endorsed, then we must accept the different strands communities adopt when evaluating the justice of their social arrangements.

He says that goods cannot be conceived abstractly as something we may or may not want on the basis of our personal preference. In his words :

"Rather, goods with their meanings because of their meanings–are the crucial medium of social relations; they come into people's minds before they come into their hands; distributions are patterned in accordance with shared conceptions of what the goods are and what they are for."[89]

Walzer is of the opinion that different communities have different conceptions of the good life, and these must be respected by us, and we must also show respect towards the diverse natures of the goods which people follow.

In order to judge the justice, both of the range of goods available in a given society and of the chosen patterns of distribution, he provides us with two criteria.

1. He maintains that the set-up must have the uncoerced allegiance of all the members of the society. Citing an example from the caste system, he says that it cannot be legitimately condemned as long as those affected by it, endorse it–and if members of a particular community challenge the system of beliefs on which it is based, then it is no longer just.

2. He tries to argue that each good gives rise to a set of relevant reasons for its distribution and he substantiates his argument by many examples. He says that medical care should be distributed to a person who really needs it, and not to a person who is wealthy–similarly, he argues that places in education should be distributed to those who are really meritorious and not to those who lack intellectual capabilities.

His theory is based on two powerful intuitions :

1. A background sense of the worth of a particular pattern for the life of our community influences us when we think about justice.

2. We should respect the various goods as valuable for different sorts of reasons–not allowing the pursuit of some goods by people having a different set of tastes and capacities to hinder individuals with different capacities to follow different paths successfully.

Eatwell and Wright believe that "These are important concerns which no viable form of liberalism can ignore"[90] and they also maintain that "the communitarian liberals can be praised for atleast being aware of how autonomy presupposes certain societal conditions."[91]

Alasdair MacIntyre

MacIntyre is one of the most profound and most controversial moralists and social thinkers of our time. His works have sparked controversy among political theorists, social critics as well as professional philosophers. Conferences have been convened to discuss his ideas, critical studies of his works have been compiled and many of his articles and books have been translated into foreign languages.

In political theory, there has been a steady stream of writings in which liberalism has been defended against MacIntyre's criticisms. He ridicules the liberals' autonomous moral agent who operates disconnected from any social context–He believes that individuals can flourish only within the context of 'practices', which are "any coherent and complex form of socially established cooperative human activity."[92]

So, communitarians like MacIntyre believe that the state's role is to develop and protect practices that encourage the development of human excellence. Social disintegration and moral disaster would result, if the state would let the individuals loose to realise their autonomy, as liberals seem to desire, treating them as socially disintegrated beings, who are solely concerned with their rights. They go on to argue that such a disintegration has already started in liberal states–where crime and violence have begun to reign supreme.

In the words of a writer, "in this modern world-view moral agents are released onto the landscape as disconnected, commodified and often cynical atoms. The malaise can best be treated by looking for living communities of shared values and virtues that can serve as contemporary analogues of medieval guild communities."[93]

Charles Taylor

Born on November 5, 1931 this Canadian philosopher, known for his viewpoints on morality and modern western identity of individuals and groups has also been classified as a communitarian.

The important books written by him are Hegel (1975); Hegel and Modern Society (1979), Sources of the self : The making of modern identity (1989), The Ethics of Authenticity (1992).

Like the communitarians mentioned earlier, Taylor also rejects wholesale the notion of individual rights, and also the notion that justice is the primary standard by which political arrangements are to be judged.

Toeing the communitarian thinking, Taylor also believed in the key communitarian notion that the 'person' in the sense of a modern self, is a secondary notion, and that since selves emerge only in the context of communities, these communities are where all the moral weight lies.

In an article, Charles Taylor, commenting on I. Berlin's, twin concepts of liberty, and his preference for the negative concept, says that in accordance with the negative concept, if a person is left totally unfettered to pursue his fundamental purpose, he might go downhill, because of a "very distorted sense of his fundamental purposes marred by confusion and error and hence, at best he is liberated into a very impoverished freedom."[94]

The upshot of his argument is that an individual cannot always be the sole judge of his fundamental purpose, because of 'confusion, illusion and distorted purpose' and hence it is the positive view of freedom–which is more important. The negative view implies that an individual is independent from others, hence free to decide about himself, but the positive freedom believes that an individual cannot be the final authority on his own freedom–He cannot be free outside a society, he can be free only in a society–where he is governed collectively.

Taylor, echoes the criticisms of MacIntyre, attacking the plausibility of the liberals 'atomistic' conception of human beings as autonomous choosers, which ignores the complexities of the human personality and the fact that in order to develop, a personality has to be embedded in society.

The communitarians have led to classical and welfare liberals making common cause to defend liberalism as a whole against this new onslaught. Welfare liberals believe in norms of individual choice, and those social freedoms which they falsely believe can be divorced from economic freedoms, and as we have seen, their arguments are still couched in terms of individual rights, as represented by Robert Nozick.

This debate between communitarians and liberals as we have seen 'dominated the 1980s, specially in the United States, with Europeans as interested but somewhat puzzled observers',[95] raising important questions about the nature of the self, the relation between the society and self, culture and politics the nature and grounds of morality etc., but critics say that "communitarianism could not formulate fundamental questions adequately, and moreover, despite stressing the moral importance of community, hardly any of them could develop a systematic theory of community some communitarians, equating the community with the nation-state 'unwittingly endorsed an insidious form' of nationalism and collectivism."[96]

Moreover, with liberalism having once again become the dominant voice today, it has more or less become the absolute standard of moral and political evaluation, with the surprising result that 'everyone is anxious to appear as a liberal and legitimises even his radical departures from liberalism in liberal terms.'[97]

By the mid 1980s, the liberalism–communitarianism debate had started flooding the pages of books and journals in political theory, but it was believed that the debate was too abstract and based on a false dichotomy. Marion Young believes that 'despite the fact that the aim of communitarians was to situate moral and political norms in the particular social contexts of full blooded agents, they rarely discussed any particular communities."[98]

Moreover, despite their critique of liberalism, there are hardly any communitarians who reject liberal values of equal respect, freedom of action, speech and association of tolerance, for example Charles Taylor insists "Quebec's concern to preserve its distinct way of life with its consequent curtailment of some individual rights is a perfectly legitimate attempt to set up one type of good society... it represents a different kind of liberalism."[99]

Conclusion

The preceding pages amply reveal the chameleon-like nature of liberalism. With a mind-boggling dexterity, it has changed colours. Spreading over a period of more than four centuries, it has proved to be a highly flexible and fluid philosophy which has invited bouquets as well as brick-bats from its advocates and opponents. The leading thinkers of the day have denounced, revised rejected and defended this bafflingly flexible ideology, which has taken into its all-encompassing arms the natural-rights liberalism of John Locke, the utilitarian liberalism of Bentham and its revision at the hands of J.S. Mill, the pragmatic liberalism of John Dewey the economic individualism of Hayek and Friedman, egalitarian liberalism of John Rawls, the libertarianism of Nozick, and the communitarian ideology of Micheal Sandel, Charles Taylor, Alasdair MacIntyre and Michael Walzer–which has been called a post-liberal view and has been developing great currency in political and ethical thought after the 1980s.

No person who studies political theory "would reasonably deny the name of liberal to any of the men represented in this connection. Yet each of them held views widely different in some respect from those of others. and these differences are differences not only of policies and programmes–those are more easily explained–but also of principles, for example of the role of the state, the vexed question of laissez faire."[100]

It is a mark of its tenacity and resilience that despite its changing colours and complexion, it continues to permeate much of our thought, taking different forms and labels. In Nozick, it tried to return Western societies to a somewhat mythical and utopian vision of the classical Lockean individualistic liberalism, under a new name–libertarianism– The following pages will deal at length with the libertarian ideology of Robert Nozick.

Notes and References

1. Gray, Tim (1991) 'Freedom : Issues in Political Theory'– New York; MacMillan, p. 1.
2. Mike Mills and Fraser King (eds) (1995) 'The Promise of Liberalism : A Comparative Analysis of Consensus Politics', USA; Dartmouth Publishing Co., p. 215.
3. *Ibid.*
4. Hagopian, Mark (1985) 'Ideals and Ideologies of Modern Politics', New York, London : Longman, p. 181.
5. Mansfield, Harvey, C. Jr. (1978) 'The Spirit of Liberalism', Harvard, Harvard University Press. Preface, pp. X–XI.
6. Gray, Tim, *op. cit.*, p. 1.
7. Wiser, James L (1978) 'The Structured Soul and The Open Self' in McGrath (ed) 'Liberalism and The Modern Polity : Essays in Contemporary Political Theory', New York, Margel Drekker, p. 11.

8. Mansfield, Harvey, *op. cit.*, p. 16.

9. Smith, M. Rogers (1999), 'Liberalism and Racism : The Problems of Analysing Traditions' in 'The Liberal Tradition in American Politics : Reassessing the Legacy of American Liberalism' Ericson and Bertchgreen (eds), New York, London : Routledge.

10. The Harper Collins Dictionary of Thought; (1988) New York, Harper and Row.

11. Smith, M. Rogers, *op. cit.*

12. Thompson, Kathleen Hill and Gerald (eds) (1994), Los Angeles : General Publishing Group.

13. Dewey, John (1963) 'Liberalism and Social Action'–New York, Capricorn Books.

14. Hampton, Jean (1998) 'Political Philosophy', Delhi, O.U.P.

15. Vincent Andrew (1992) 'Modern Political Ideologies' : Blackwell Publishers, p. 42.

16. Shapiro Ian (1986), 'The Evolution of Rights in Liberal Theory' Cambridge, Cambridge University Press, p. 80.

17. Hartz, Louis (1955) 'The Liberal Tradition in America', New York : Harcourt, Brace and World.

18. Hagopian, Mark, *op. cit.*, p. 171.

19. *Ibid.*, p. 171.

20. Goldwin, Robert (1963) 'John Locke' in Strauss, Leo and Cropsey Joseph (ed) 'History of Political Philosophy'–Rand Chicago : McNally and Company, p. 433.

21. Sabine, G. H. (1973) 'A History of Political Theory', Oxford, Oxford and IBH Publishing Co., p. 485.

22. Vincent, Andrew (1992) *op. cit.*, p. 42.

23. O' Driscoll, Gerald (1979) 'Introduction in O' Driscoll (ed) 'Adam Smith and Modern Political Economy', IOWA, USA, IOWA State University Press, p. ix.

24. Encyclopaedia Brittanica : Macropaedia : 27. pp. 308–311, 15th edition.

25. Sowell, Thomas (1979) 'Adam Smith in Theory and Practice in O' Driscoll ed. 'Adam Smith and Modern Political Economy'–IOWA, USA, The IOWA State University, p. 3.
26. O'Driscoll (1979) 'Introduction', *op. cit.*, p. ix.
27. Rosenberg, N (1979) 'Laissez faire Revisited' in O'Driscoll, Gerald (ed) 'Adam Smith and Political Economy', Iowa, USA, Iowa State University Press, p. 23.
28. *Ibid.*, p. 24.
29. Encyclopaedia Brittanica : Macropaedia, Vol. 27, pp. 308–11.
30. *Ibid.*
31. Rosen Berg, N., *op. cit.*, p. 20.
32. *Ibid.*, p. 26.
33. Smith, Adam (1776) 'An Inquiry into Wealth of Nations', quoted in *Ibid.*
34. Thakurdas, Frank (1982) 'Essays in Political Theory', N. Delhi, Gitanjali Publishing House, p. 186.
35. Maxey, 'Political Philosophies', p. 409.
36. Sabine, *op. cit.*, p. 632.
37. Wayper (1963) 'Political Thought'–London : Hutchinson–pp. 101-02.
38. Sabine, *op. cit.*, p. 637.
39. Brown, Ivor (1929) 'English Political Theory' London, Methuen and Co. Ltd., p. 121.
40. *Ibid.*, p. 94.
41. *Ibid.*, p. 95.
42. *Ibid.*, p. 96.
43. Dunning (1920) 'A History of Political Theories from Rousseau to Spencer', New York, MacMillan Co., p. 214.
44. *Ibid.*, p. 224.

45. Brown, Ivor, *op. cit.*, p. 119.
46. Hagopian, Mark, *op. cit.*, c. 171.
47. Sabine, *op. cit.*, V. 641.
48. *Ibid.*, p. 646.
49. *Ibid.*, p. 646.
50. Spragens, Thomas, A (1999) 'The Appeal and Limits of Libertarianism' in 'Civic Liberalism : Reflections on our Democratic Ideals' New York, Rowman and Little Field Publishers Inc. p. 19.
51. Rose, Nikolas (1999) 'Powers of Freedom : Refraining Political Thought', Cambridge, O.U.P. pp. 140-41.
52. Vincent, Andrew, *op. cit.*, p. 53.
53. Dewey, John (1963) 'Liberalism and Social Action', New York, Capricorn Books, p. 32.
54. *Ibid.*, p. 39.
55. Dewey, John (1954) 'The Public and Its Problems', Denver : Allen Swallow, p. 150.
56. Frost, S.E. (1948) 'The Basic Teachings of the Great Philosophers', New York : Halcyon House, Garden City. p. 169.
57. Hagopian Mark, *op. cit.*, p. 180.
58. *Ibid.*, p. 179.
59. Hagopian, *op. cit.*, p. 180.
60. Dewey, John (1963) *op. cit.*, p. 62.
61. Hagopian, *op. cit.*, p. 180.
62. Dewey, John (1970) 'Characters and Events', Vol. II. New York, Octagon Books, p. 854.
63. King, Fraser (1995) 'The Promise of Liberalism "Comparative Analysis of Consensual Politics" Mike Mills and Fraser King (ed.)–USA; Dartmouth Publishing Co., p. 21.
64. *Ibid.*, p. 22.

65. Friedman, Milton (1962) 'Capitalism and Freedom', Chicago, University of Chicago Press.
66. MacPherson, C. B. (1973) 'Democratic Theory : Essays in Retrieval' Oxford, Clarendon Press, p. 95.
67. Gray, Tim, *op. cit.*, p. 17.
68. MacFarlane, L. J. (1996) 'On Two Concepts of Liberty' in Political Studies, Vol. 14.
69. Thakurdas, Frank (1982), *op. cit.*
70. Berlin, I. (1991) 'Two Concepts of Liberty' in David Miller (ed.) Liberty, Oxford, OUP.
71. *Ibid.*, p. 34.
72. *Ibid.*, pp. xvi–xiix.
73. Hampton, Jean (1998) *op. cit.*, p. 133.
74. Young, Iris, Marion (1996), 'Political Theory : An Overview' in Robert E. Kringeman Goodin (eds.), 'A New Handbook of Political Science–Oxford OUP, p. 484
75. Dworkin, Ronald (1977) 'Taking Rights Seriously' Harvard, Harvard University Press, pp. xiv–xv.
76. Dworkin, R. (1978) 'Liberalism', in S. Hampshire 'Public and Private Morality'; Cambridge CUP, pp. 113-43.
77. *Ibid.*, p. 267.
78. Brubaker, Stanley, C. (1988) 'Can Liberals Punish" in American Political Science Review, Vol. 82, No. 3, September.
79. Barry Brian (1996) 'Political Theory, Old and New' in Goodwin, Klingemann (eds), A New Handbook of Political Science Oxford, OUP, p. 538.
80. *Ibid.*, p. 539.
81. Brian Barry, 1996, *op. cit.*, pp. 539-40.
82. Hampton, Jean, *op. cit.*, p. 182.
83. Frazer, E (1999) 'The problem of communitarian politics: Unity and conflict' Oxford, OUP.

84. Eatwell, Roger Wright, Anthony Contemporary political ideologies–London, Printer Publishers, p. 7.

85. Hampton, Jean, *op. cit.*, p. 185.

86. Young, Marion, Iris, *op. cit.*, p. 495.

87. Sandel, Michael (1982) 'Liberalism and The Limits of Justice,' Cambridge, CUP, p. 1981.

88. *Ibid.*

89. Walzer, M (1983) 'Spheres of Justice', Oxford, Oxford University Press, p. 7.

90. Eatwell, Roger and Wright Anthony, *op. cit.*, p. 244.

91. *Ibid.*, p. 250.

92. MacIntyre, Alasdair (1981) 'After Virtue' Notre Dame; University of Notre Dame, Press, p. 187.

93. Young, Marion (1966), *op. cit.*

94. Taylor, Charles M (1979) 'What's Wrong with Negative Liberty', in 'The Idea of Freedom' (ed.) Ryan, A, Oxford, OUP, pp. 175-93.

95. Parekh, Bhikhu (1995) 'Political Theory : Traditions in Political Philosophy' in King and Mill (ed) 'The Promise of Liberalism', p. 511

96. *Ibid.*, p. 511.

97. *Ibid.*, p. 511.

98. Young, IRIS M, *op. cit.*, p. 479.

99. Parekh, Bhikhu (1996), *op. cit.*, p. 512.

100. Allan Bullock and Maurice Shock ed. (1956) 'The Liberal Traditions From Fox to Keynes' London; A and C Black, p. xix.

3

Entitlement Theory of Justice

The notion of justice, is an ancient notion, having its roots in the past changing its nature, its shades of meaning and its various connotations. It has various dimensions, various meanings. For some, it is a unifying force, for others, it is the adjustment of persons and principles, some identify it with the rule of reason, others believe it is synonymous with law. For Plato, it meant performing one's duties–with all abilities and capacities towards the social whole, and for Aristotle it meant equal share to the equals and unequal, to the unequals distributing power and position proportionately according to the worth of an individual. For the Romans, justice referred to a body of laws emanating from legislative declarations, customs and judicial pronouncements.

In the medieval age, justice became synonymous with the idea of morality and righteousness, and this was due to the predominance of the Church and Christianity. During this age, justice came to be associated with a body of ethical rules emanating from the scriptures, from man's sense of morality, and man-made rules which were in conformity with the principles of eternal, divine and natural law.

In the early modern period, the natural right theorists identified justice with the rule of reason–thus creating a bridge between the medieval religious notion of justice and the ethical concept of justice as developed by a modern rationalist being. This was the concept of justice, that Locke and his followers subscribe to.

With the advent of democracy and democratic institutions, justice came to be identified with equal participation in all social and political spheres.

For the liberals, justice is legal and political equality– and it includes rule of law, equality before law, equal protection of laws etc.

With the advent of industrialization, it was the economic aspect which was asserted by socialists, syndicalists and anarchists–for them, justice implied the establishment of a just social order, which was characterised by the absence of economic exploitation and political enslavement. For the Marxists, justice meant the end of exploitation and the creation of a communist society based on the principle of 'to each according to his need, from each according to his capacity'.

This chapter will deal with :

(a) The meaning, etymology of justice.

(b) The various sources of justice.

(c) The kinds of justice.

(d) The libertarian perspective : Hayek and Robert Nozick's entitlement Theory of Justice, and its comparison with the different theories of justice– past and present.

Meaning and Etymology of Justice

The word 'Justice' has been derived from the latin word 'Jus' and also includes 'Justis' and 'Justitia', and is connected with another latin word 'Jungere'. Prof. Ernest Barker says that justice is:

'Primarily a joining or fitting, a bond or a tie".

"The joining or fitting implied in this root idea is that between man and man is an organised system of human relations. But we may also conceive of the 'just' and 'justice' as connected with, and expressed in a joining or fitting between value and value."[1]

Earnest Barker further states that in any organised system of human relations, there are a number of different values which are essential–these values are liberty, equality–fraternity or which can be better called co-operation:

"All these values are present in any system of law, but they are present in different degrees, at different periods of time, and there is a constant process of adjustment and readjustment between their claim. The claims of liberty have to be adjusted to those of equality; and the claims of both have also to be adjusted to those of co-operation. From this point of view the function of justice may be, said to be that of adjusting, joining, or fitting the different political values."[2]

Sources of Justice

Further elaborating on the notion of justice, Prof Barker asks, "What is the source of its justifying grace and obliging power?" and says, that four different answers may be given to that question–and these four answers are :

(a) Religion (b) Nature

(c) Economics (d) Ethics

(a) Religion

"The medieval church held, and the Roman Catholic church still holds today that it is God who gives through His church the notion of justice ... This is plainly expressed in the theory of St. Thomas Aquinas."[3]

(b) Nature

Another source of justice is nature–In the words of Barker :

"When 'nature' is adduced to the origin of justice the suggestion is that law has value or may be made to have value, by being in accordance, or by being brought into accordance with ...... the natural order of things."[4]

The idea of nature as a source of justice is as old as the stoics and goes as far back as the end of the fourth century B.C. or even farther.

To the stoics nature provided a two-fold view–

1. A view of the order of things in the material world.

2. A view of the spiritual order of the human world.

"There was a single premise on which stoicism was based and that was–that men in their essential nature were rational beings and from this basic premise three conclusions could be drawn :

'The first conclusion drawn from this premise was that men, being rational in their nature should all be regarded as free and self-governing in their actions. This was the conclusion of liberty–The second conclusion was that men being all in their nature rational, should all be regarded as equal in status. This was the conclusion of equality. The third conclusion was that men being united to one another by the common factor of reason, should all be linked together in the solidarity of a world society–a single city of Zeus—this was the conclusion of Fraternity."[5]

This stoic premise from which the above three conclusions are drawn, formed a current of thought which Barker believes–has flowed "through ancient times and the Middle ages through the Age of Enlightenment and the French Revolution, and is still flowing in our own age. This current of thought carries in its course an idea of justice, professing and claiming to be drawn from nature, which is a synthesis of the three values of liberty, equality and fraternity."[6]

Economics

The third source of justice according to Barker was economics. In the nineteenth century, economics was put forth as an important source of justice. As Barker so aptly puts it:

"With the development of modern industry which began on the continent in the nineteenth century, the theory began to be advanced first by French and German thinkers and then, from Bakunin onwards by Russian thinkers and revolutionaries that the origin of the idea of justice could and should be discovered in the area of economics."[7]

In this context, he refers to the theories of Marx, Proudhon and Duguit

Marxian theory is a theory of the dominance of matter, and the material conditions of man's economic activity. For Marx, all history is a history of class–struggle, and in this struggle, it is always the economically stronger class that dominates and exploits the weaker one. The state, for him is the "executive committee of the exploiting class"–In the capitalist society, the bourgeois class, being economically stronger, dominates and exploits the workers. Justice, for Marx is removal of economic inequality through communism, and communism in its highest and purest form will be a society, which "will be non–political and non–legal; and being without law it will be informed by a disembodied spirit of justice."[8]

Proudhon also drew the notion of justice from an economic source–'mutualite'–upon which French syndicalism was based, which thought, not in terms of 'warring and colliding classes, but of occupational groups complementary to one another and knit together by mutual need and the bond of mutual service."[9]

Such a notion of justice is not based on the interest of a class of society but of the entire society and all its complementary groups. Duguit believed that a national society must mainly be regarded as an economic society, and the 'basic fact of such a society is the existence of different occupational groups, producing different things, but bound to one another by mutual need of one another's products and by a consequent system of mutual exchange. The essential principle is therefore Solidarity."[10] (and none can do anything contrary to the principle of solidarity and all should try to cooperate as far as possible in the realisation of that principle.)

Ethics

Thc forth source on which justice is presumably based is Ethics–in other words, justice is related to the 'Moral Conscience', and if law is to have value it must satisfy, in the last resort, the demands of the general moral conscience. "The moral standard of the community, precipitated in and enforced by the general moral conscience, will be the source of a notion of justice, containing a system or synthesis of values...."[11]

In order to solve the baffling predicament of several–bottomed justice, Arnold Brecht divides it into two broad categories which he calls the :

(a) Traditional Justice.

(b) Trans-traditional Justice.

(a) **Traditional Justice :** This category of justice accepts the basic institutions which constitute the basis of our daily life–The traditional justice is positivistic, in the sense that it has faith in these institutions which have been established by the positive law, written constitution, legislation, judicial precedents.

(b) **Trans-traditional Justice :** This category of justice has no faith in the existing institutions and criticises them in accordance with the ideas of a party of revolutionary junta, or merely in deference to the opinion of a strong personality.

Apart from these two distinct levels in the idea of justice there may also be a third level wherein 'he discovers, what he "really thinks and where he may be critical also of the trans–traditional ideas of his friends. Within a single day he may move through all three levels in his business hours living and feeling with the traditional sense of justice, in the evening joining with his friends in their criticism, and at night isolating himself from his friends."[12]

The traditional and trans-traditional aspects of justice are simply other names for objective and subjective justice– The subjective justice deals with the variety of conditions of state of affairs which people "regard as standard goals in their idea of justice either for the distant future or for the present moment".[13]

Brecht identifies a few ideal types of subjective justice thus :

1. **The Equalitarian :** For the equalitarian, equality is of utmost importance, and it has the highest place in matters of justice.
2. **The Libertarian :** He measures everything by the yardstick of liberty, and any steps violating liberty are condemned as unjust by the libertarian.
3. **The Revelationist :** For him, God's will and its execution is of utmost importance.
4. **The Conservative :** He wants no change in the traditional institutions and disrespect to them constitutes injustice.
5. **The Authoritarian :** For him, leadership is the principle of highest value. To follow leadership is just, but to counteract it, is unjust.
6. **The Majority Worshipper :** He is of the opinion that whatever the majority decides, is the highest value to be accepted by everyone. Justice lies in

following the majority will, and opposition to it, involves an injustice.

7. **The Hedonist :** He looks for individual happiness for the greatest good of the greatest number.

8. **The Group Worshipper :** He believes in the subordination of the desires of an individual to the interest of the group.

9. **The Harmoniser :** For him, harmony is the ultimate value. Justice resides where there is peace, harmony–and no disturbance.

10. **The Pyramid-Builder :** He associates justice with the spiritual part of his country's culture or civilisation or some specific achievements of his race.

11. **The Man of Duty :** He believes that a man should be given as much freedom as he needs to fulfil his moral duties–because for him life is a chain of duties rather than of rights.

12. **The Peace and Order Fanatic :** For him, peace and order is of utmost importance and he wishes that reforms should be there, but should be brought about in an orderly way.

All that has been said about justice, in the preceding pages leaves the strong impression that justice is a multi-dimensional concept, and a flexible term which can be stretched to fit any idea of good. Justice can be called a synthesiser which synthesises other political values like rights, liberty, equality and property.

In the words of Earnest Barker, Justice "is the reconciler and synthesiser of political values : it is their union in an adjusted and integrated whole : it is in Aristotle's words 'what answers to the whole of goodness.... being the exercise of goodness as a whole .... towards one's neighbours."[14]

Robert C. Solomon, waxing eloquent about the importance of justice in everyday life says :

"I think that .... Justice simply stated is an ever increasing sense of the importance and dignity of the individual."[15]

Brecht calls it a "barrel with several bottoms".

Ever since the time of Plato, all of us have been asking, the question, 'What is Justice', and the answers to this question differ from person to person, but there can be no difference of opinion regarding the universal significance of justice, because in one form or the other, it has been governing the world.

To quote Proudhon :

"Justice under various names, governs the world–nature and humanity, science and conscience, logic and morals, political economy, politics, history, literature and art Justice is that which is most primitive in the human soul, most fundamental in society, most sacred among ideas and what the masses demand today with most ardour."

In the similar vein, Robert C. Solomon, says that 'it was perhaps, the first great philosophical question, and it is still the most important and unavoidable philosophical question, embracing, as it does, not only those essential questions about what we desire in life and .... all of those basic questions about the good life ...... what it is, how to find it, how to live it :[16]

Even in the realm of political theory, the concept of justice has a great significance, because the aim of both state and government has been identified as the preservation of justice. In this context, it would be worthwhile to quote James Bryce and Arnold Brecht, both of whom believe that the efficiency of state and government depends on its capability of preserving justice. To quote Bryce:

"There is no better test of excellence of government than the efficiency of its judicial system, for nothing more nearly touches the welfare and security of the average citizen than his sense that he can rely on the certain and prompt administration of justice."[17]

In the words of Brecht "Two axioms have been generally accepted without question : First, that governments' own actions ought to be just, second, that governmental institutions, such as law courts ought to ensure the preservation of justice."[18]

It is indeed a Herculean task to define justice in precise terms, because what a person considers just, varies from person to person. Moreover, different societies have different conceptions of justice, different ideas about what is fair, and what is unfair, varying interpretations are given of this baffling and dynamic term–there is the Roman concept of justice the secular concept of justice, the utilitarian view of justice, the contractarian Theory of Justice–the Rawlsian view of justice, wherein he describes justice as the first virtue of social institutions–the entitlement Theory of Justice advocated by libertarian writer, Robert Nozick–the Marxist Theory of Justice–the democratic socialist concept of justice, which aims at removing the prevalent inequalities through peaceful democratic means–the Anarchist view of justice–which wants to do away with property and state.

Confronted with so many dimensions of justice, it is indeed very difficult to give an exact and unambiguous definition of justice-What we call justice would not have been recognised as such in Homeric Greece, or in the Athens of Plato and Aristotle four hundred years later. It is very different from the sense of justice that one would find in feudal France, in the Florentine renaissance, or in the bourgeois London society. It is very different, indeed from the sense of justice one finds in contemporary Japan or Iran and it may well differ from New York city to Dallas, Texas."[19]

While tackling the problem of justice, we cannot gloss over the paramount fact that "our ideas and feelings of justice may be twofold or threefold, or even more fold, in accordance with different systems of values to which we respond positively at different times, or even simultaneously. Justice, in the light of personal ideas is, ... a barrel with several bottoms."[20]

This 'barrel with several bottoms' indeed provides a baffling array of definitions and viewpoints.[21]

According to Gould and Kolb, justice can be used in two senses :

1. To give man his due.
2. Rectifying a wrong either by compensation or punishment.

In the first sense, justice is concerned with deciding the principles of allocation of rights and duties, material goods, dignity, security and opportunities in the society. In this context, it is worth noting, that the historical circumstances of a particular society determine the distribution of goods and services, hence the principles of justice are never absolute and keep on changing with the change in circumstances.

The second sense of justice pertains to the legal aspect of justice–If what is due to man, is because he is a human being–then what is implied is natural justice. If what is due to him, is in consonance with certain customary rules–then it is conventional justice, that we are talking of. If the due is in virtue of a rule, the violation of which makes the violator answerable for his action to the public power, then the justice is legal.

For another writer justice is dual–faced or Janus–like–one is its legal face and the other is the moral face.[22] It is conservative–because it looks to the past, and also reformative–because it looks to the future.

George Gurvitch opines that the term justice is used in two senses :

1. It is the faithful realisation of the existing laws against any arbitrary violation.
2. The second sense is a broader sense and involves the entire sphere of morality–it represents the ideal element in law—the idea which the law tends to subserve.[23]

The preceding pages have thrown ample light on the meaning, definitions and sources of justice. Now, in the following pages, I will try to give a synoptic view of some important theories of justice, and also Nozick's entitlement theory–and then try to compare the Nozickean theory with the important theories of justice mentioned.

KINDS OF JUSTICE

Platonic Justice

Plato–423-347 B.C.

In 'The Republic', Plato propounds his Theory of Justice which is not a juristic definition, but a metaphysical-ethical one–

"For it lacks the notion, connoted by the Latin word 'Jus' and the English word 'right' of powers of voluntary action in the exercise of which a man will be protected by law and supported by the authority of the state."[24]

His entire philosophy revolves round justice. His famous doctrine of ideas tries to solve the problem of justice. Ideas, for him, are absolute values which should be, but never can be, realised entirely in this world–and it is the idea of eternal good which is the main idea, all other ideas being subordinate to it. The idea of absolute good–of righteousness, implies justice.

Justice, for Plato is harmony. He believed that the state is the individual writ large, and justice is the virtue both of the individual and the state.

"The theory of the state culminates in the conception of justice. Justice is the bond which holds a society together, a harmonious union of individuals, each of whom has found his life work in accordance with his natural fulness and his training. It is both a public and private virtue because the highest good both of the state and of its members is thereby conserved. There is nothing better for a man than to have his work and to be fitted to do it; there is nothing better for other men and for the whole society than that each should thus be filling the station to which he is entitled."[25]

In a nutshell, Plato's justice is 'giving every man his due' :

"For what is due to him is that he should be treated as what he is in the light of his capacity and his training, while what is due from him is the honest performance of those tasks which the place accorded him requires."[26]

For Plato, justice is one of the four virtues, the other three being wisdom, temperance and courage. He believes that everything in the universe has its own station and tasks, and it is virtue which enables each man to do his own task best. The structure of the state and the government should be such that every man is entrusted with a job, to which his nature is best suited. Thus, Platonic justice serves a two-fold purpose :

(a) The rational division of work.

(b) Specialisation of functions, as a result of this, there is an all-pervasive harmony, because an individual is doing the task, towards which he is by nature inclined, and moreover, there is also the greatest utilisation of the resources of the state in the form of human labour.

In the words of Barker:

"Social justice thus may be defined as the principle of a society, consisting of different types of men ... who have combined under the impulse of their need for one another, and by their combination in one society and their concentration on their separate functions have made a whole which is perfect because it is the product and the image of the whole of the human mind."[27]

In precise terms, we can say, that Platonic justice is the harmonious blending of different men and different functions in a perfect whole.

Socialist Theories of Justice

In the nineteenth century, the socialist movement that emerged out of the criticism of capitalist society, came forth with its own ideas of liberty, equality, democracy and justice. The anarchists, the Marxists and the democratic socialists, all can be justifiably clubbed together as socialists–because they were unanimous in their criticism of capitalism. The anarchists condemned capitalism as a charter of economic exploitation, the Marxists severely criticised the capitalist mode of production, and for the democratic socialists, capitalism is the symbol of the worst form of moral degradation.

Thus, though they can be bracketed together as socialists of varying degrees, they differ in the strategies and objectives.

For the anarchist, the abolition of state comes first, followed by the abolition of capitalism, a Marxist, on the other hand, would abolish capitalism first and state later, a democratic socialist would neither abolish the state nor capitalism, and as far as the means to be adopted for the realisation of those objectives are concerned, the anarchists would not mind using violence (at least the revolutionary anarchists would) the Marxists would adopt peaceful methods if possible, and violent if necessary, and the democratic socialists would try to bring socialism through peaceful democratic methods, and of course with the help of the state.

All these Socialists start with the premise, that justice exists where there is no injustice. The socialist idea of justice emerges from the injustice that pervades society.

The anarchist believes that the presence of the law and the state, throttles the liberty of the individual, hence for the anarchist, such a situation is a symbol of injustice and justice exists where there is freedom for the individual–where there is no state, no property and no religion–but freedom.

The democratic socialists, being both socialists and democratic believe that justice exists in a democratic order–where there is liberty and equality, and no exploitation.

The Marxist Perspective of Justice

The Marxist perspective of justice integrates the idea of justice with the doctrine of class war. The Marxists are vocal about uneven distribution of income as an example of injustice. They believe that the state is the executive committee of the exploiting classes, which makes laws to exploit the poor.

The theory of Class War, being an integral part of his theory, Marx believed that history bears eloquent testimony to the fact, that society has always been divided into two classes–the 'haves' and the 'have nots'; and since their interests always clash with each other–the one exploiting the other–the class struggle continues.

In capitalism, there is a struggle between the capitalist and the labcur class, and the capitalist identifies the social good with his own preservation, and even "education, justice, religious teaching are tempered to serve their interests... But the class excluded from the privileges of possession naturally also deserves a share in them. Hence arises in every society, a struggle between classes for its control."[28]

So, Marx believed that in such a class-ridden society, where economic inequality and class-war, hold sway, to talk of social justice is futile.

Thus, for Marx, justice could be established only when there were no classes and consequently, no class-struggle. His view of justice stemmed from his invincible faith in the final triumph of the proletariat and the liquidation of the capitalist order–the establishment of his state-less, class-less society under communism, where economic equality would reign supreme and there would be no exploitation.

He believed that the proletariat would unite together because they had nothing to lose but their chains, and unitedly they would wage a war against the exploitative capitalists, and snatching power from their hands, would establish their dictatorship. This transition period would later lead to the stage where the state would wither away–there would be no classes–and communism would be established, where the principle 'from each according to his ability, to each according to his needs' would reign supreme. In the communist society, justice would be synonymous with equality for all, there being no discrimination, exploitation and oppression–a justice without coercion, without the repressive state machinery.

The Anarchist Theory of Justice

For the anarchists, justice resides where there is no property, no state and no religion. State for them is an unnecessary evil, a symbol of political coercion. Property is theft–a negation of social justice–and religion is a falsehood which debases and corrupts the people.

There are different shades of anarchists, but all of them wax eloquent against exploitation and oppression, and political authority, they believe is a symbol of evil, hence unnecessary and undesirable. They have many desirable aims–like the creation of a just society–which is a 'Natural Society' i.e., a self-regulated society of individuals and freely formed groups where personal freedom is at a maximum. But there are major differences of opinion regarding how these desirable aims could be achieved.

Some of the prominent anarchists are William Godwin (1756-1836) (An enquiry concerning political justice and its influence on general welfare and happiness). Pierre Joseph Proudhon (1809-1865) (What Is Property?), Bakunin (1814-

1876), Kroptokin (1842-1921), Tolstoy (1828-1910) and Mahatma Gandhi and Bertrand Russell.

Godwin believed that neither laws nor law courts can ensure any justice, for they are the products of the jealousies, passions, ambition of people over the ages.

The myriad writings of the aristocratic Russian revolutionaries Michael Bakunin and Kroptokin also cover the keynotes of classic anarchist doctrine :

1. The negation of the state.
2. The abolition of private property.
3. The attack on religion.
4. Revolution.
5. The new cooperative order.

Bakunin denies that the state is "a natural human society which supports and reinforces the life of everyone by the life of all–quite the contrary, it is the immolation of every individual as well as of local institutions.... It is the limitation, or rather the complete negation of the life and the rights of all the parts of the whole society."[29]

Bakunin believed even a democratic state is a 'cruel hoax' on the people because democratic paraphernalia like 'majority rule' and the 'will of the people' cannot, disguise the minoritarian character of the state. Although, he believed in pure socialism, he was convinced that even that would not be able to moralise and humanise the state, because it too would involve a government.

"It will be the reign of scientific intelligence, the most aristocratic, despotic, arrogant and elitist of all regimes."[30]

Both Bakunin and Kroptokin believed that private property inevitably produces classes–and justice for them would follow only if the state and private property were abolished–and the individuals were free–and this individual freedom can be real only if "the state accompanies private property into the museum of historical antiquities."[31]

Kroptokin was of the belief that if people are left to themselves to work out a way of life they would develop a number of voluntary associations to make social life possible, and they would maintain peace, practise mutual aid and create justness.

Similarly Bakunin said, "There is no fixed and constant authority, but a continual exchange of mutual, temporary, and above all, voluntary authority and subordination."[32]

Kroptokin also pointed out :

"Self jurisdiction was the essential part, and self-jurisdiction meant self-administration."[33]

So, according to both, justice would exist where leadership is voluntary, provisional and without special privileges or prestige. There would be no chance for it to solidify into a rigid hierarchy. Justice, for them finds expression not in bondage, but in freedom. It is a sense of liberty, not of slavery, of emancipation, and not of exploitation, and above all, of acting not in accordance with some coercive external force, but in accordance with the free will.

Mahatma Gandhi was a spiritual and moral anarchist, for whom the stateless non-violent society in which there will be no police and military, no law courts, doctors, heavy transport and centralised production is an inspiring ideal."[34]

This was an ideal, and Mahatma Gandhi admitted, 'but the ideal is never fully realised in life', yet it could be achieved if people grow accustomed spontaneously to observe their social obligations without the operation of the state.

This justice for him would exist in a society, where there is the 'rule of unadulterated non-violence',[35] where there is no oppression, no exploitation, no discrimination, no coercion, where an individual is able to defend his liberty against the whole world, where there is no corruption and hypocrisy, where there is 'freedom for the meanest of our countrymen."[36]

The Democratic Socialist Theory of Justice

Democratic Socialism defined justice in the context of prevailing inequalities and unfairness of distribution of goods and resources, and it aimed at rectifying these wrongs through peaceful democratic methods.

Refuting the Marxian contention, that the state was the symbol of oppression and exploitation, and that socialism could be achieved only through revolutionary transformation, the democratic socialists, believed that socialism should be achieved through 'ballots rather than bullets'.

A just society for them was one, which was based on democracy, appropriation of the means of production by the workers through political power and trade union pressure.

In the words of a writer :

"Democracy is both a means to an end (a socialist economy) and an end in itself (a just political order)."[37]

In its Fabian form, many writers tried to bring a synthesis between liberalism, democracy and socialism. It aimed at a reorganisation of society by abolishing private property and tried to free land and industrial capital from individual and class ownership and invest them in the community for general benefit–and all this it planned to do through positive state intervention.[38]

David Miller says that democratic socialism combined justice with traditional concerns of mixed economy and redistribution of wealth for greater equality and industrial decentralisation.

We can understand the democratic socialist view of justice at three levels:

(a) **Political Level :** At the political level, justice means equal dispensation of political rights, democratization, decentralisation, and a general consensus among the people regarding the fundamental issues.

(b) **Social Level :** At the social level, justice results, where there are equal opportunities for development, and non-discrimination, when the uneven distribution of natural talents is rectified, and when there is social security, old age pension, unemployment allowance etc.

(c) **Economic Level :** It believes in correcting the imbalance of property through drastic economic reforms. It wants a central authority to distribute property according to its own criterion of merit–It believes that justice can be achieved through social and economic institutions.

Sidney Webb, an eminent Fabian, emphasised the fact that all important organic changes should be : 1. Democratic 2. Gradual 3. Not Demoralising 4. Constitutional and Peaceful.[39]

According to Harry Laidler, a just society is where capitalism has been abolished, and where there is full employment, high education, rising standard of living, social security, fair distribution of property and income, equality of opportunity, nationalisation of existing industries, where economic power has been decentralised and an individual is rewarded according to his efforts.[40]

The democratic socialists, hold that justice exists where law exists, but the kind of law that is an embodiment of 'Social Service' and not of awful majesty and they believe that the function of the courts is to dispense justice but they should not be puppets in the hands of the politically powerful people.

They believe in the rule of law, and justice for them is a frame, a system, a goal to be set and attained by laws. For the courts, they provide a heavy agenda of diffusion, decentralisation and federalisation of political and economic power.

They believe that justice and a democratic order are synonymous; an undemocratic system, according to them can never be just, because it is characterised by its lack of equality and liberty, whereas in a democratic set up there is people's participation, hence liberty and equality are the hallmarks of democracy–and democracy and justice go together.

Libertarian Perspective

Friedrich Hayek (1899-1992)

This Austrian born British economist is a philosopher of freedom, who, in his various works has called social justice 'empty and meaningless'. Some of his important works are :

1. The Constitution of Liberty–1960
2. The Road to Serfdom–1944
3. Law, Legislation and Liberty : The Mirage of Social Justice, 1976.

He considers social justice a mirage, and voices his views very eloquently in the following words :

"For, in such a system in which each is allowed to use his knowledge for his own purposes, the concept of social justice is empty and meaningless ..... because in it, nobody's will can determine the relative incomes of the different people or prevent that they be partly dependent on accident."[41]

For Hayek, justice should attain individual good, rather than what is called social good. His contention is that social justice does not secure liberties for the individual through which he or she can pursue his or her own good. The Hayekian justice is synonymous with unfettered freedom of the individual through which he can obtain his or her good, and when there is interference in individual freedom–the result is injustice.

Condemning social justice, he opines that it stands for a particular purpose (of distribution of goods/or/and services to be given to the individuals in society). It is concerned more with the procedure rather than with the result–patterning the norms of distribution in such a way that people share goods/services equitably, ignoring as to what an individual should get in return. So, for Hayek justice seeks a spontaneous order that helps develop rules of conduct.

He believes that legislation is based on coercion, because it attempts to alter 'the material position of particular people or enforce distributive or 'social justice.'[42]

In the words of David Held :

"Hayek .... Is unequivocal about this : a free liberal order is incompatible with the enactment of rules which specify how people should use the means at their disposal. Governments become coercive if they interfere with people's own capacity to determine their objectives.[43]

Criticising social justice, he cites two adverse consequences of the idea of distributive social justice :

1. It will be based on a preferential treatment. In order to achieve a particular pattern of justice, one set of values related to human purpose will be given a preference over others in a society and this is utterly incompatible with a liberal and free society in which diversities of ends is recognised.

2. Moreover, there will be a lot of ambiguity about these values, and hence attempting to distribute goods, income and services, in accordance with any one of these criteria, will involve the concentration of power in the hands of the officials–which will naturally lead to coercion, arbitrariness, and this will open the gates of an unjust era, where the government and state will become increasingly

> powerful, coercive and arbitrary and will ultimately yield to the interest groups which stand for private and not for public interest–and this would result in a Civil War among various interest groups and the government would itself become a party to it, and thus it would be responsible for changing a free society into a totalitarian one, as Hayek says.

"The worst danger entailing from the whole case of social justice is that its obstinate pursuance eventuates in totalitarianism since it requires an ever–increasing use of coercion at the hands of the state in social and economic life of the people."[44]

Hayek states that social justice 'is not only unjust but also highly unsocial in the true sense of the word; it amounts simply to the protection of entrenched interests."[45]

Striking at the very root of socialism, Hayek asserts that the very idea is atrocious, because socialism believes that political power ought to determine the material position of the different individuals and groups which is wrong.

'The Road to Serfdom' published in 1944 was an attack on the ever–increasingly activist state, which had become the order of the day–where political leaders undermined civil liberties and abandoned democracy for dictatorships. In the words of Thomas A Spragens :

"The pump-priming, regulating redistributive welfare state became well-established and institutionalised during Franklin Delano Roosevelt's NewDeal; it was essentially accepted as part of normal policy even by Republicans during the Eisenhower years, and it expanded its purchase and its ambitions under the aegis of Lyndon Johnson's Great society in the 1960s......"[46]

It was against such an ever-increasingly-powerful welfare state that Hayek's arguments were directed–and the solution that he comes forth with is :

(a) A state that acts neutrally between the competing interests of numerous groups.

(b) A set of abstract laws that will be able to secure the maximum amount of individual freedom through minimum coercion.

(c) A free-market unfettered by the distributive principles of social justice.

Hayek argued that there was no third way between capitalism and socialism–it was essentially an either/or proposition.

In the words of Spragens :

"The choice between a free-market system and a socialist command economy was essentially an either/or proposition."[47]

The free-market is a sensitive mechanism–it is dynamic, innovative and responsive.

Thus, it was free-market, a neutral state, rule of law that Hayek believed could ensure justice in a society–The neutral state as opposed to the all powerful state, would provide essential conditions for the preservation of an overall order. The rule of law would secure the maximum freedom for an individual with the minimum of state coercion, and a dynamic, responsive and innovative free-market unconstrained by the distributive principles of social justice, would determine collective choice on an individual basis. In the words of Zenon Bankowski :

"The market is presented as the saviour of society. The remarketisation of society is supposed to bring both efficiency and morality back to peoples' lives. It gives them freedom",[48] as opposed to command economics which undermines civil liberties and attacks individual freedom–and hence is unjust.

Although the free-market has its shortcomings, yet for Hayek, by keeping the 'State Action' to a minimum, it ensures justice for the individuals. In the words of David Held :

"The free-market does not always operate perfectly; but Hayek insists, its benefits radically outweigh its disadvantages."[49]

For people like Hayek, the free-market is the saviour of society, and it appears to be the magic wand, the waving of which will solve all existing problems of society. As he argues:

"There can be no freedom of the press if the instruments of printing are under the control of government, no freedom of assembly if the needed rooms are so controlled, no freedom of movement if the means of transport are a government monopoly."[50]

Nozick's Entitlement Theory of Justice

Part II Chapter VII of 'Anarchy, State and Utopia' entitled 'Beyond the Minimal State', deals with his Entitlement Theory in Section I.

The salient features of Nozick's theory of entitlement can be stated as follows:

(a) Nozick's argument begins with individual rights. As he states in the preface :

"Individuals have rights, and there are things no person or group may do to them."[51]

(b) These rights are 'so strong and far reaching' that they put constraints upon others' actions.

(c) The paramount fact that there are separate individuals with separate lives implies that none can be sacrificed for the other.

(d) This theory is historical, as compared to other conceptions of distributive justice. It is historical in the sense that it emerged in the course of time, and not through any set formula or pattern. To quote Nozick :

"In contrast to end-result principles of justice, historical principles of justice hold that past circumstance or actions of people can create differential entitlements."[52]

(e) It is the task of justice to protect individual rights, to which they are entitled. As Nozick puts it, "Things come into the world already attached to people having entitlements over them."[53]

(f) Any type of interference in the rights or entitlements of an individual is unjust and illegitimate. Nozick justifies the right to property on the ground that it is an entitlement of an individual, hence cannot be violated.

(g) Following in the Lockean footsteps, he believes in the inviolability of individual rights–including the right to property', and no one has the right to question the property right to which an individual is entitled.

(h) The slogan of the Entitlement Theory of Justice is "from each as they choose, to each as they are chosen."

The Entitlement Theory of Justice as sketched by Nozick in 'Anarchy, State and Utopia' has three parts :

1. A principle of justice in original acquisition of holdings.
2. The second principle concerns the transfer of holdings from one person to another.
3. The third deals with the rectification of unjust holdings.

"The first principle sets the conditions for creation of property; the second for passage of property from one owner to another; and the third, for remedies, should one of the other two principles be violated."[54]

Referring to the first principle of original acquisition, Nozick tells us that on the basis of this principle we come to know :

"How unheld things may come to be held, the process or processes, by which unheld things may come to be held the things that may come to be held by these processes, and so on."[55]

Elaborating the second principle he says :

"The second topic concerns the transfer of holdings from one person to another. By what processes may a person transfer holdings to another? How may a person acquire a holding from another who holds it."[56]

Under this topic are included :

(a) General descriptions of voluntary exchange (b) Gift (c) Fraud (d) Reference to particular conventional details fixed upon in a given society. It goes without saying that it also includes "principles governing how a person may divest himself of a holding, passing it into an unheld state."[57]

An exhaustive definition of justice in holdings, would, in the words of Nozick be :

1. A person who acquires a holding in accordance with the principle of justice in acquisition is entitled to that holding.

2. A person who acquires a holding in accordance with the principle of justice in transfer, from someone else entitled to the holding, is entitled to the holding.

3. No one is entitled to a holding except by (repeated) applications of 1 and 2.[58]

Thus, 'the complete principle of distributive justice would say simply that a distribution is just if everyone is entitled to the holdings they possess under the distribution."[59]

Thus the three principles of Nozick's Entitlement Theory can be further explained by an example:

If someone owns a plot of land, Nozick's first principle will tell us how this piece of land was initially acquired, 'the second principle will tell us that, since this piece of land, is justly acquired, it can be justly and legitimately transferred, the third principle will tell us, that if 'past, injustice has shaped present holding' how this past injustice regarding this piece of land can be rectified.

Referring to the third principle, Nozick says :

"Not all actual situations are generated in accordance with the two principles of justice in holdings : the principle of justice in acquisition and the principle of justice in transfer, some people steal from others, or defraud them or enslave them, seizing their product and preventing them from living as they choose, or forcibly exclude others from competing in exchanges."[60]

Since none of these means is considered a permissible mode of transition from one situation to another–the question arises how to rectify past injustices. To quote Nozick :

'If past injustice has shaped present holdings in various ways, some identifiable and some not, what now, if anything, ought to be done to rectify these injustices? What obligations do the performers of injustice have toward those whose position is worse than it would have been had the injustice not been done? Or, than it would have been had compensation been paid promptly?"[61]

Nozick believes that there are many types of injustices involved, and many types of questions regarding past injustices that come to mind–questions like :

(a) How do things change if those who have benefitted, and those who have been made worse off, are not the direct perpetrators of injustice, but their descendants.

(b) Is an injustice done to someone whose holding was itself based upon an unrectified injustice.

(c) How far back must one go in wiping clean the historical state of injustices?

(d) What may victims of injustices do in order to rectify the injustices meted out to them, including the many injustices done by persons acting through their government?

Nozick admits that he is not aware of a 'thorough or theoretically, sophisticated treatment of such issues', but hopes that theoretical investigation will produce a principle of rectification.

"This principle uses historical information about previous situations and injustices done in them ...... and information about the actual course of events that flowed from these injustices, until the present, and it yields a description (or descriptions) of holdings in the society. The principle of rectification presumably will make use of its best estimate of subjunctive information about what would have occurred if the injustice had not taken place. If the actual descriptions of holdings turns out not to be one of the descriptions yielded by the principle, then one of the descriptions yielded must be realised."[62]

In short, Nozick maintains that "The general outline, of the Theory of Justice in holdings are that the holdings of a person are just, if he is entitled to them by the principles of justice in acquisition and transfer, or by the principle of rectification of injustice."[63]

A Comparative Analysis of Nozick's Theory of Justice and other Popular Theories of Justice

Platonic Justice/Entitlement Theory

In 'The Republic', Plato defines justice in meta-physical and ethical terms, emphasising the fact that justice is synonymous with harmony. For him, the state is the individual writ large, and justice is the virtue both of the individual and the state. It is both a public and a private virtue–by which individual fills the station to which he is entitled, and honestly performs his task.

For Plato, justice is one of the four virtues, namely :

1. Wisdom
2. Temperance
3. Courage
4. Justice

His justice was related more to morality, rather than to legality. In Nozick's entitlement theory, morality does not figure.

Platonic justice was based on social justice, because it was reflected in the three-dimensional society, in the form of division of labour and specialisation of functions.

This meta-physical–ethical Platonic justice cannot be accepted in the modern times.

Nozick's justice, on the other hand, is an argument against social justice, because he does not want the state to be an interventionist state, which interferes in people's lives–because, as he maintains, individuals have rights and there are things no person or group may do to them.

Nozick's justice is more a theory of rights, unlike the Platonic justice, it has nothing to do with division of labour and specialisation of functions, it is concerned with the protection of the rights of the individuals, because, he believes that 'things come into the world already attached, to people having entitlements over them,' and justice demands that there should be no tampering in these entitlements either by the people or by the state through redistribution.

Nozick's Theory of Justice is more a justification of property rights. He believes, in the tradition of Locke that an individual has unquestionable property rights in unowned things, and any Theory of Justice should respect these property rights.

Anarchist Justice/Entitlement Theory

The anarchist justice has a two-fold thrust–a negative and a positive thrust.

The State

The negative thrust is directed against the state, which it believes, is an abomination–an unnecessary evil, which redistributes awards making the rich richer and the poor poorer.

All anarchists are unanimous in their condemnation of the State, which they believe is neither necessary nor sufficient to resolve the gigantic problems confronting the common man.

Historically speaking, the emergence of the state has not been based on choice, on the contrary, it is a blatant imposition resulting from conquest and colonisation, hence their firm conviction is that justice can be established only when the state is abolished and replaced by a completely "free organisation of society."

On the other hand, in the Nozickean justice, the 'state is not altogether abolished, but it arises from anarchy (Locke's state of nature), and through different stages of voluntary progression, assumes the role of a minimal state, which performs "the limited functions of protection against force, theft, fraud and enforcement of contracts, hence, it follows that it is merely a protective agency which, however, maintains a monopoly of force for protecting the rights of the people.

Hence, for Nozick, justice can result only by the least intrusive form of political power, commensurate with the defence of individual liberty.

Property

While in the anarchist conception of justice, property is equated with theft, Nozick, we have seen, is not convinced with any argument given against property–therefore, he does not want any governmental interference with existing property rights. In fact, he favours existing inequalities in terms of property, and justifies property if it is not stolen, or fraudulently acquired. He emphasises, that the existing inequalities in terms of property are the result of a long historical process and therefore justified.

Its positive thrust is directed towards the creation of a just society, which is a 'natural society'–a self-regulated society of individuals and freely-formed groups, where individual freedom is at its maximum, in which there is a fair distribution of material goods, and the common tasks are carried out by voluntary agreement.

During the last two hundred years, many varieties of anarchism have appeared but despite this rich variety, there is a common strand holding them together and that is:

(i) All anarchists want to put an end to the coercive and authoritarian power of the state.

(ii) All emphasise and rely on self-regulatory methods of organisation, where intervention is not involved–and oppose those highly-regulatory procedures, which are based on paternalism and centralism.

(iii) The imposed methods are to be replaced by voluntary methods.

(iv) Emphasis on decentralisation and deconcentration, in place of centralisation and concentrated structures.

(v) Empowerment to be a replaced by depowerment.

Although, all shades of anarchists believe in the above-mentioned common features of the just society, they differ in detail–mostly about the economic arrangements that should characterise a stateless society.

Marxian Justice/Entitlement Theory

If we compare the Marxian Theory of Justice with Nozick's entitlement theory, we see that Marx talks of justice in the context of class-war and believes that in capitalism, the capitalists exploit the labourers, the state is the executive committee of the exploiting class, and that capitalism carries within itself the seeds of its own decay. He believes that under Communism, a state-less and class-less society will emerge–which will be based on equality.

Nozick's theory, on the other hand, is a strong supporter of the market–a passionate believer in the inalienable rights of the individual–holding that 'Each individual is his own master' and he cannot be obliged to help others–because taxation, in Nozick's terms, is extortion.

Views on Property

For Marx, economic equality is the true basis of social justice–and the entire Marxian theory is geared towards establishing it.

Marxian justice does not want equalisation of property, but it wants the abolition of private property–on the other hand, Nozick, under Lockean influence, passionately believes in the rights of an individual, which cannot be violated. For him, the right to property is the most important right, and his entitlement theory, is in fact, a theory, which tries to protect the entitlements of an individual. It emphasies the fact that the holdings of a person are just if he is entitled to them by the principle of acquisition and transfer or by rectification.

In other words, the entitlement Theory of Justice favours inequalities in terms of property, because the existing inequalities in terms of property are the result of a long historical process and hence justified. Hence, Nozick emphatically states : "we are not in the position of children who have been given portions of a pie by some one who now makes last minute adjustments to rectify careless cutting."

For the Marxists, private property is a hindrance to the real development of society–because all history, according to Marx has been the history of class struggle, where one class has dominated the other on the basis of private property and this has given rise to exploitation. The haves not only control the apparatus of the state, but they also control ethics, religion etc. on the basis of their ideology.

In a nutshell, in the Marxian concept of Justice, private property has no role. "The Communist Manifesto" had declared in strong terms that the theory of Communism may be summed up in only one sentence : The abolition of private property.

The State

In the Marxian view of justice, justice will result only when there is a state-less class-less society. Property, the Marxists believed, was also responsible for the creation of state because the state had not existed from eternity, there had been societies where there was no state–the state was the inevitable result of the division of society into classes and it became the 'executive committee of the exploiting class'– exploiting the have-nots. Thus, the highest purpose of the state was the protection of private property–as Engels said, 'the state is "the state of slave-owning citizens, in the middle ages, the feudal lords; in our own, the Bourgeoise"—

In other words, from times immemorial, the state, according to the Marxists has always indulged in exploitation–hence, justice can result only when property, state, and classes have been totally abolished–and a communist society based on equality is established–and in this communist society, all the vestiges of capitalism are destroyed–and so the state which was a weapon in the hands of the capitalist class withers away, because without the classes, it has no existence.

The Entitlement Theory of Justice, on the other hand, does not want the abolition of the state altogether but, as we have seen, it upholds the minimal state, which protects an individual against the use of force, theft, fraud and enforcement of contracts, because any more extensive state is unjust, uninspiring, immoral and illegitimate.

Thus, instead of the abolition of the state, Nozick's Entitlement Theory of Justice emphasises the fact that what is needed is the least intrusive form of political power commensurate with the defence of individual liberty–the less the state interferes in the lives of the individuals–the better it is for this individuals.

Equality

In the Marxist view of justice, equality is very important–Marxism arose as a reaction against liberalism–which in spite of advocating liberty, freedom, human Rights–etc. ended up in inequality, exploitation and alienation. Hence, Marxism emerged as a corrective that advocates equality unlike the Entitlement Theory of Justice which strongly believes that 'if the state attempts, to promote equality, it steps beyond its legitimate boundaries.'

Briefly summing up Nozick's Theory of Justice and Marxist Theory of Justice, we can conclude by saying that Nozick argues that the state has to perform only the minimum of functions, unlike the Marxist, who believes in a total abolition of the State, which is a:

1. A Class Institution
2. A Man Made Institution
3. It Belongs to the Economically Dominant Class
4. The State is a Means of Exploitation

5. It is a Coercive Insitution

6. The State is a Temporary Institution

In Nozick's Theory of Justice, if the state does something against the individual to which he is entitled, it is a case of injustice. Passionately believing in individual rights, he emphasises, that if the state tries to take away these rights, it is performing an injustice.

Thus, justice for Nozick implies–no disruption of individual entitlements–and any policy or law that tries to disrupt them through any patterned device is illegitimate and unjust.

The Marxist principle : 'from each according to his ability to each according to his need', Nozick believes, is a patterned device. Against this, Nozick's principle is "from each as they choose, to each as they are chosen : unlike the patterned devices, which Nozick believes, would involve appropriating the actions of other persons."

In the final analysis, Nozick's justice is a matter of protection of one's entitlements–property being the most important entitlement of an individual–which is 'so strong and far-reaching' that it puts constraints on the others.

Such a type of justice, Nozick believes is compatible with a minimal and not with an extensive state.

Democratic–Socialist Theory of Justice and Nozick's Theory of Entitlement

As mentioned earlier, the democratic–socialist Theory of Justice, does not want to throw out capitalism, or the state, on the contrary, it wants to find justice through the state, while in the Nozickean justice, the state is limited–it is a minimal state, entrusted with the task of protection against force, theft, fraud and enforcement of contracts.

For the Democratic socialists, justice is not merely a matter of liberty–liberty which is not licence to do anything, but an atmosphere in which one grows without impeding the liberty of others–but also a matter of equality, but, in the Nozickean justice, we find, that while he extols liberty, emphasising the fact that individual liberty has to be defended at all costs, against all sorts of encroachments, he also emphatically maintains that if a state tries to promote equality it tries to step beyond its legitimate boundaries.

The Democratic Socialist view of justice can be understood at the three following levels :

1. **At the Political Level :** Justice involves equal dispensation of political rights, decentralisation and democratisation.

2. **At the Social Level :** It is associated with equal opportunities for development, and also wants to correct the arbitrary and uneven distribution of talents and natural abilities, which is vehemently opposed by Nozick, who believes that no state can intervene in an individual's right of self-ownership.

3. **At the Economic Level :** It calls for drastic economic reforms in order to correct the imbalance of property, and defends a central authority which will distribute property proportionality, in accordance with its own criteria of merit–which is again strongly opposed by Nozick, who does not want any interference in the property rights of individuals, in order to rectify the economic imbalances of society.

In a nutshell, we can say that the anarchist justice would want to abolish state first and capitalism later, the Democratic socialist justice would never want to abolish the state, on the contrary, they would want the state machinery to be used in a positive manner, in order to bring about social justice. The Marxist justice would result only when the state had withered away, and in Nozick's justice, the state would perform a non-interventionist role, not entrusted with the task of establishing social justice.

The Marxist view of justice can be stated thus : "share the burden according to your capacity; and benefits, according to your needs." The Democratic socialist view of justice is : 'take in proportion to what you give' and the Nozickean justice is : from each as they choose, to each as they are chosen.'

Conclusion

The preceding pages gave a synoptic view of how justice, which has been an ancient notion has changed its nature–right from Platonic justice to the Nozickean justice. For Plato, justice was synonymous with the performance of one's duties–in the medieval age, it becamc synonymous with morality and righteousness, in the early modern period, the natural right theorists identified it with the rule of reason, with the advent of democracy, justice meant equal participation in all social and political spheres.

The liberals emphasized legal and political equality as the hall-mark of justice–which included rule of law, equality before law and equal protection of laws.

With the advent of industrialization, the economic aspect was asserted by Socialists, Syndicalists and Anarchists, for whom a just social order was characterized by the absence of economic exploitation.

For the Marxists, justice meant the end of class-war, the withering away of the state, and the establishment of a communist society, which was state-less and class-less.

Nozickean justice is a passionate believer in the inviolable rights of an individual, and these rights are so 'strong and far-reaching', that Nozick maintains, that justice lies in protecting these rights–and the most important right being–the right to property.

Thus, we see that Nozick's Entitlement Theory of Justice, makes a passionate plea for the protection of individual entitlements–any infringement of those entitlements results in injustice.

Notes and References

1. Barker Ernest : 'Principles of Social and Political Theory'–Oxford, Oxford Paperbacks, OUP, p. 102.
2. *Ibid.*, p. 102.
3. *Ibid.*, p. 103.
4. *Ibid.*, p. 106.
5. *Ibid.*, p. 108.
6. *Ibid.*, p. 108.
7. *Ibid.*, 110.
8. *Ibid.*, 111.
9. *Ibid.*, 112.
10. *Ibid.*, p. 112.
11. *Ibid.*, p. 117.
12. Brecht, *op. cit*
13. *Ibid.*, p. 151.
14. Barker, Ernest (1967) : Principles of Social and Political Theory, London : Oxford Univ. Press, p. 102.
15. Solomon Robert C. 'A Passion For Justice : Emotions and The Origins of The Social Contract'–Addison–Wesley Publishing Co. Inc. California, p. 8.
16. *Ibid.*, p. 5.
17. Bryce James : 'Modern Democracies' (London : Macmillan 1921, Vol. II, p. 421.
18. Brecht Arnold : 'Political Theory : Foundations of Twentieth Century Political Thought' Princeton : Princeton University Press, 1965, p. 136.
19. Solomon Robert C. *op. cit.*, p. 5.
20. Brecht : *op. cit.*, pp. 147-48.

21. J Gould and W. I Kolb, 'A Dictionary of Social Sciences'– Free Press, New York, 1965, p. 363.

22. Raphael. D (1977) 'Problems of Political Philosophy', Macmillan (India) N. Delhi, p. 165.

23. Gurvitch George, 'Justice' In Encyclopaedia of Social Science' Vol. VII, p. 509.

24. Sabine GH. (1973) 'A History of Political Theory'–Oxford + Ibm Publishing Co., N. Delhi, p. 65.

25. Sabine, *Ibid.*, p. 64.

26. *Ibid.,* p. 65.

27. Barker Earnest (1925). 'Greek Political Theory, Plato and His Predecessors', p. 176-F.

28. Laski : 'Communism', p. 63.

29. Michael Bakunin, 'The Political Philosophy of Bakunin Et. G.P. Maximoff', NY–The Free Press, 1964, p. 206.

30. Michael Bakunin, 'On Anarchy' Ed. S. Dolgoff, N.Y. Vintage Books, 1972, p. 319.

31. Hagopian, *op. cit.*, p. 110.

32. Bakunin, (1970) 'God and The State', NY–Dover Publications, 1970, p. 25.

33. Peter Kroptokin, 'The Essential Kroptokin' Ed. E. Capouya and Tomkins, N.Y. Livereghi 1975, p. 184.

34. Gopinath Dhawan : 'The Political Philosophy of Mahatma Gandhi' Navjivan Publishing House, Ahmadabad, 1946, p. 326.

35. Harijan, October 13, 1940, p. 320.

36. Young India, II, p. 602.

37. Hagopian, *op. cit.*, p. 144.

38. David Miller Blackwell Encyclopaedia of Political Thought, pp. 484-85.

39. Sidney Webb : In "Fabian Essays In Socialism–G.B. Shaw (Ed.) Garden City, N.Y., Dolphin Books, p. 51.

40. Harry Laidler, (1968) 'History of Socialism', Routledge and Kegan Pal, pp. 863-64.

41. Hayek, F. (1976) 'Law, Legislation and Liberty', Chicago: Chicago University Press, Vol. 2, p. 69.

42. Hayek, F. (1960) 'The Constitution of Liberty' London, Routledge and Kegan Paul, p. 231.

43. Held, David (1984), The Contemporary Polarisation of Democratic Theory : The Case For A Third Way' in 'Political Theory and The Modern State' Polity Press, p. 175.

44. Hayek F.A. (1944) 'The Road to Serfdom' London : Routledge and Kegan Paul.

45. Hayek, F.A. (1976) Law, Legislation and Liberty, *op. cit.*, p. 85.

46. Spragens, Thomas, A Jr (1999) 'Civic Liberalism : Reflection and Our Democratic Ideals'. New York, Rowman and Littlefield Publishers Inc., p. 21.

47. *Ibid.*, p. 21.

48. Bankowski Zenon "Social Justice and Equality", In Theories and Concepts of Politics : An Introduction–Bellamy Richard–Manchester University Press', Manchester and New York, p. 77.

49. Held David (1984), *op. cit.*, p. 175.

50. Hayek, F.A. (1978) 'Liberalism in 'New Studies in Philosophy, Politics, Economics and The History of Ideas'–London; Routledge and Kegan Paul, p. 149.

51. Nozick, R. (1974) Asu, *op. cit.*, Preface IX.

52. *Ibid.*, p. 155.

53. Nozic, *Ibid.*, p. 160.

54. Davis, Michael (May, 1977), 'Necessity and Nozick's Theory of Entitlement', In Political Theory. Vol. 5, No. 2.

55. Nozick, *op. cit.*, p. 150.

56. *Ibid.*, p. 150.
57. *Ibid.*, p. 151.
58. *Ibid.*, p. 151.
59. *Ibid.*, p. 151.
60. *Ibid.*, p. 152.
61. *Ibid.*, p. 152.
62. *Ibid.*, p. 153.
63. *Ibid.*, p. 153.

4

Minimal State

Historical Perspective

After the First World War more and more liberal writers had followed the course of holding a plea for more and more state intervention in the interest of the society, and this had resulted in the advocacy of the doctrine of the positive state, Harold J. Laski and R.M. Maciver can be said to be the best representatives of such a trend, which eulogised the state. Waxing eloquent about the state, Laski says:

"There is no more fascinating theme in contemporary history than to follow the stages through which the laissez faire night-watchman state of the nineteenth century has been transformed into the welfare state of today–"[1]

Similarly, R.M. MacIver, writing in the same vein maintained that the modern–state has to perform all pervasive functions including upbringing of children, prevention of destitution, education, industry, scientific development, currency, regulation of marriage, etc.

In a nutshell, MacIver's modern state was an omnipotent state, interfering in all spheres of individual life.[2]

In the contemporary scenario, individual freedom is held to be of paramount importance, and in this sphere, no sort of interference can be tolerated. As a writer says :

"When the Berlin Wall fell and political régimes in eastern Europe tumbled like so many dominoes, the ideological landscape in the advanced industrial countries changed perceptibly."[3]

In today's political scenario a search is under way for new political policies, strategic and institutional arrangements–The old outlooks have given way to new ones, and there can be seen a rethinking of the relationship between the individual and the state. In the words of David Held :

"In the West the crisis of the welfare state, linked to protracted economic and political difficulties, has forced a rethinking of the relation between the economy and the state, and private initiative and public regulation, across the political spectrum. In the East there has been a growing recognition of deeply-rooted problems affecting the entire structure of state–directed rule. With it has come a fundamental questioning of the connection between planning institutions, bureaucracy, and market–relations."[4]

Contemporary liberalism has emphasised economic freedom and free market society, which involves a frank rejection of the communist system and ideology, contemporary liberals firmly believe that communism and political freedom do not go together–The totalitarian state of communist regimes can grant neither economic freedom nor political freedom. In this context, Milton Friedman, reiterated that competitive capitalism is a necessary condition of political freedom.

Defining the scope of state activity, he says :

"A government which maintained law and order, defined property rights, served as a means whereby we could modify property rights and other rules of the economic game, ...and which supplemented private charity and the private family in protecting the irresponsible, whether madman or child– such a government would clearly have important functions to perform."[5]

It was in much the same vein that Herbert Spencer also wrote in his famous book 'The Man Versus The State'.

It was with a great sense of shock that he viewed the demand of some of the liberals to extend the functions of government. In his day, the welfare state and modern liberalism were already making their presence felt. Defending laissez faire based on individual freedom, he asked in vehement tones :

"How is it that Liberalism getting more and more into power has grown more and more coercive in its legislation? How is it ... Liberalism, has to an increasing extent adopted the policy of dictating the actions of its citizens, and, by consequence diminishing the range throughout which their actions remain free."[6]

Liberalism with its emphasis on more and more state power was, in the bargain becoming its opposite.

In the words of a writer :

"New public policies of aiding the weak, regulating business, and providing certain services were condemned by Spencer. Liberalism in his eyes was horribly becoming its opposite."[7]

The revised premises of liberalism according to C.B. MacPherson, have three cardinal characteristics–

1. The individual is the absolute natural proprietor of his own capacities, owing nothing to society for them. Everyone is free, for everyone possesses atleast his own capacities.

2. The market relation is the fundamental relation of society. Society is not a system of relations of domination and subordination between men and classes held together by reciprocal rights and duties, but as a collection of free equal individuals, related to each other through their possessions, i.e., related as owners of their own capacities.

3. Finally, political society is seen as a rational device for the protection of property, including capacities.

Different people have different objectives, and governments become coercive if they interfere with people's own capacity to determine their objectives. It is highly presumptious of the government to believe that it can act in a manner as if it knew what people want/desire.

"The value of individual's services can however only justly be determined by their fellows in and through a decision-making system which does not interfere with their knowledge, choices and decisions, and there is only one sufficiently sensitive mechanism for determining collective choice on an individual basis–the free market. When protected by a constitutional state, no system provides a mechanism for collective choice as dynamic, innovative and responsive as the operations of the free market."[8]

Similarly James M Buchanan also pleads for the dismantling of the welfare state, because it has given rise to certain consequences, which, however, were 'unintended and undesired'. He says :

"During the middle years of this century the welfare state has emerged full grown in all Western nations. There is widespread agreement that many of the consequences were unintended and undesired when viewed from the perspective of the 1980s, we can agree that, things 'might have been' better had the course of history been different from what it was."[9]

The Libertarian Scenario

The political minimalism of Nozick can said to have its roots in classic liberalism, which believed that liberty and authority do not go together–the authority of the state is inimical to the liberty of the individual.

The individualists of the nineteenth century like Bentham, J.S. Mill, Locke and Herbert Spencer, as mentioned earlier, viewed the enlarged state activity with grave distaste and apprehension.

In the economic sphere, the classical economists like, David Ricardo, Alfred Marshall and Adam Smith held a plea for the doctrine of the laissez faire in the name of non-interference in the initiative of the individual.

In the present century, be it Hayek, Berlin, Friedman or Nozick all have viewed the restraints imposed by the state in the name of public welfare as utterly wrong–as such restrictions violate individual initiative and enterprise. As Friedman says :

"As in the simple matters, so in the complex enterprise and money-exchange economy, cooperation is strictly individual and voluntary provided : (a) Enterprises are private, so that the ultimate contracting parties are individuals and, (b) individuals are effectively free to enter into any particular exchange, so that every transaction is strictly voluntary."[10]

MacPherson says that Friedman has endeavoured to present a 'classic defense of free-market liberalism'.[11]

He believed that, society is quite inconsistent in political freedom, because (a) Competitive capitalism, which is negated by socialism, is a necessary condition of political freedom. (b) A socialist society is so constructed that it cannot guarantee political freedom. In his words :

"The market removes the organisation of economic activity from the control of political authority. It thus reduces the concentration of power which enables economic strength to be a check to political power ..."[12]

Thus, we see that in liberal thought and action two viewpoints have emerged lately, earlier, liberty and welfare had gone together–in fact, they were considered complementary–but, of late, "there is a disposition to devalue the latter. This tendency, which vitiates much of socialist thought, is seen at its logical extreme in communism. 'Libertarians', on the other hand, are apt to deny that the new freedoms are freedoms at all, to dwell on the restrictions their establishment has involved, and to use 'Welfare State' as a term of disparagement."[13]

Many are the allegations levelled against the welfare state–

It is alleged that all the spoon-feeding involved saps the character of the nation, because when the state does so much for the citizen, it obviously follows, that the citizen loses the desire and the enthusiasm to do things for himself. He becomes too dependent on these welfare measures. In the long run, they become like crutches without which they simply cannot walk. Thus, it is alleged that such an all-pervasive and rampant influence of the state, is fatal to initiative and enterprise.

In order to implement the all-pervasive welfare measures–a lot of restrictions, which are naturally resented by the individuals come into effect. "A not unimportant liberty is the liberty to get and spend one's income as one likes, this is seriously curtailed by the heavy taxation required to finance the social services and the contributions required from 'insured persons' ......"[14]

Thus, we see that such a system, with the advance of years, started making more and more inroads into the sphere of individual rights, thus curtailing them to an extent. Thus gradually "it has become evident that a state monopoly in welfare has certain illiberal consequences."[15]

Individual freedom, initiative, a free-market have thus become the hall-marks of the present libertarian scenario.

Hayek, one of the leading advocates of these ideas is unequivocal about this–namely, a government can only legitimately intervene in society to enforce rules which broadly protect–life, liberty and estate. He believes that a free liberal order is incompatible with the enactment of rules which specify how people should use the means at their disposal.[16]

In the words of a writer :

"The New Right (or neo-liberalism as it is sometimes called) is, in general, of the view that political life, like economic life, is–or ought to be–a matter of individual freedom and initiative (Hayek, Nozick). Accordingly a laissez faire or free-market society is the key objective along with a 'Minimal State'. The political programme of the new right includes the extension of the market to more and more areas of life and reduction of state's involvement in the economy and in the provision of opportunities"[17] They insist that individual freedom and individual responsibility have been diminished in recent times as a result of the proliferation of bureaucratic state agencies which try to regulate and control individuals. Thus they commit themselves to the classic liberal doctrine that the collective good (or the good of all individuals) can be properly realised in most cases only by people acting in complete isolation with Minimal–State intervention."[17]

Similarly, another writer states that the partisans of the libertarian school "see the crowning purpose of liberal democracy to be maximizing individual freedom. Individual liberty is championed in part for its instrumental value–in producing material prosperity and social stability, for example. But freedom should in the libertarian view also be venerated as the most important intrinsic good that politics can safeguard."[18]

Spragens, very succinctly puts forth the libertarian argument in one of his essays:

"It is neither necessary nor proper to campaign for the sacrifice of personal autonomy on the altar of community and rectitude. Such an agenda is not only wrong in principle but self-defeating in practice. For it is one of liberalism's defining insights that genuine social solidarity and human virtue cannot be produced by coercion or manipulation, however well intentioned."[19]

He further states that in the name of general welfare, no one can be allowed to bully recalcitrant members into professions of faith they do not hold or by authorising jurists to impose their judgments about the humanly good life upon a community that harbours other convictions or prioritises goods differently."[20]

The need of the hour is the maximisation of individual liberty, by the absence of restraints because such restraints, block an individual's thought and action.

"Individual liberty must be maximized and the chief threat to it comes from the state. The sense is clear that when government authority expands (rules, regulations, interventions) beyond a certain necessary minimum, individual freedom contracts."[21]

Contemporary liberalism, like classic liberalism believes in the absence of restraints and in the inviolability of the rights of an individual–and this can be possible only in a state which interferes the least in the sphere of individual freedom. As Coker says :

"The constant concern has been with pleas for deliverance from restraints, which, although perhaps widely regarded at a given time as a normal part of life have come to be regarded by some in the community as unnatural and intolerable."[22]

The basic presumptions of the welfare state were severely criticised during the 1970s in Britain. Margaret Thatcher's Conservative Government went hammer and tongs at the welfare state, which, it believed was responsible for the "combined stagnation, unemployment and inflation that plagued Britain and much of the world economy at that time, as well as a decline in patriotism and, in general the traditional moral values of the national community."[23]

Against the evils perpetrated by the welfare state, they talked of a revolution "that would install neoliberal economic policies, such as tight money to reduce budget deficits, an end to state subsidies or ownership of industry, and free trade along with a neo-conservative politico-moral agenda to restore traditional national values. The latter consisted of promoting individual self-reliance against welfare 'hand-outs' by the state and of increasing its police powers."[24]

During the 1990s, the major political parties in core European states widely accepted the neo-liberal agenda, and later it spread to the world order itself.

"In so called newly industrialising states such as Singapore, South Korea and Chile, similar programmes of neoliberal economics .... have been promoted as the way to develop the state economically. Neoliberal economic programmes have been promoted more generally as a way for poorer states to get out from under their enormous debts to western banks and the IMF..... Neoliberalism gained credibility after the collapse of the Soviet Union, as did the acceptance of 'Shock therapy' to turn post-Soviet Russia and other Eastern European states quickly into advanced capitalist ones."[25]

In America, after the 1994 elections, the version of liberalism which emerged triumphant was the 'classical, eighteenth century free-market capitalism and individual rights', thus ringing the death knell of 'Welfare State Liberalism'.

The Republicans favoured a "dismantling of remnants of the New Deal, a return to rugged individualism, minimal government ..."[26] and they strongly maintained that the welfare state has aggravated the problems of the poor by making generations of poor people so dependent upon welfare that crime, illegitimacy, drugs on so on, have increased significantly in the last twenty years."[27]

In the contemporary scene where more and more states are dismantling the welfare model, and questions are being asked about the relevance of welfare measures, Nozick's views on political minimalism need to be taken seriously.

The thrust of the libertarian argument is that the welfare state, with its all-pervasive power is an assault on individual rights, and has certain illiberal consequences. In no case, can individual autonomy be sacrificed at the altar of general welfare. Hence the libertarians want the extension of the market to more and more areas of life, and the reduction of the state's involvement in the economy and the provision of opportunities.

Towards the end of the nineteenth century, there were many changes in the American society–which were, primarily the renewed emphasis on economic freedom in a free-market society, the curtailment of the state's power.

In the words of a writer:

"The modernisation of America, which began in the 1890s, transformed the country in a variety of ways. Upheaval would not be too strong a term to use in this connection"[28], resulting in an emphasis on political individualism and the Minimal State.

A true libertarian, Nozick believing in a very strong doctrine of individual rights–upholds and justifies a Minimal State–which is 'inspiring' and 'right' and does not overstep its boundaries of protection against force, theft, fraud, enforcement of contracts, any more excessive state–like the welfare state, with its gigantic proportions, and all-pervasive power tends to violate people's rights and is unjustified. Whereas the Minimal State, does not violate either the moral side constraints or the libertarian side constraints. The moral side constraints constitute moral prohibitions, and as Nozick says:

"They reflect the fact that no moral balancing act can take place among us, ... This root idea, namely that there are different individuals with separate lives and so no one may be sacrificed for others, underlies the existence of moral side constraints."[29]

Besides the moral side constraints, there are also the libertarian side constraints, which prohibit aggression against one another.

The Anarchists claim that the state is 'Intrinsically Immoral' as it violates moral side constraints–Being an unmitigated evil, the sooner it is abolished, the better it is for all concerned. The compulsive authority of the state mars the development of human personality and is an assault on human dignity:

"The state is the enemy; every moment longer it lasts is a standing affront to human dignity and freedom. The state has arisen from violence and conquest. It is ever the tool of a clique of exploiters against the rest of society."[30]

The Anarchists believed in the 'Absolute Cult of The Free Individual'. Any sort of authority for them was an anathema, and it desired an emancipated individual free from all sorts of shackles–whether political or economic or religious.

This philosophy, as developed by Bakunin, Kroptokin and Proudon desired to save man from the yokes of the state, capitalist and God in his capacities respectively as a citizen, a producer, and a man.[31]

Bakunin vehemently denies that the state is "a natural human society which supports and reinforces the life of every one by the life of all–quite the contrary, it is the immolation of every individual as well as of local associations .... it is the limitation, or rather the complete negation, of the life and of the rights of all the parts of the whole society."[32] Hagopian succinctly summing up says: The state is a blood sucker drawing its vitality from the society of victims."

In the words of Nozick:

"When the state monopolises the use of force in a territory and punishes others who violate its monopoly, and when the state provides protection for everyone by forcing someone to purchase protection for others, it violates moral side constraints on how individuals may be treated."[33]

Refuting this claim of the anarchists, Nozick maintains that the Minimal State is 'uniquely right', just and moral because it violates no side constraints–either moral or libertarian.

There are four stages in the evolution of the Minimal State, and in these stages, no 'morally illegitimate steps' have been taken, hence such a state is morally justified. It is not 'intrinsically immoral', it is not a 'blood-sucker', it is not 'a standing affront to human dignity and freedom', as the anarchists believe, but the Nozickean state, not being an extensive state, does not violate person's rights, hence is 'inspiring as well as right', being based, as it is, on voluntarism.

Minimal State

Nozick's theory of the Minimal State is a logical outburst against the all-intrusive nature of the welfare state, which, due to its omnipotence trespassed in the sphere of individual freedom.

Following in the footsteps of John Locke, he maintains, that there are inalienable rights of the individual, possessed independent of society and any state which tries to intrude into the sphere of these inalienable rights is unjust.

In the words of Nozick:

"Our main conclusions about the state are that a Minimal State limited to the narrow functions of protection against force, theft, fraud, enforcement of contracts, and so on, is justified, that any more extensive state will violate person's rights not to be forced to do certain things and is unjustified; and that the Minimal State is inspiring as well as right."[34]

Two implications that follow from these conclusions are:

(a) The state may not use its coercive apparatus for the purpose of getting some citizens to aid others.

(b) It may also not use its coercive apparatus to prohibit activities to people for their own good or protection.

Nozick admits that people might reject these conclusions outright, because 'they don't want to believe anything so apparently callous toward the needs and suffering of others'[35], and, he also maintains that he might also be guilty of a double offence : 'for the position expounded, and for the fact that I produce reasons to support this position'[36], but nonetheless, intellectual honesty, compels him to expound the position he believes in, and to produce elaborate arguments in support of his position.

The Minimal State as opposed to any more extensive state is 'inspiring as well as right' because :

1. It treats individuals as inviolate individuals, who may not be used by others as mere tools.
2. It treats individuals as persons having individual rights–hence dignified.
3. It does not intrude in our rights, or does not transgress our individuality–on the contrary it allows us to choose our lives, individually or with whom we may choose, and in so doing it helps us realise our ends, and keeps our dignity intact.

True to his libertarian leanings, Nozick, also in the spirit of Locke, upholds an extremely strong doctrine of individual rights specially the right of property, and these rights, Nozick firmly believes, cannot be secured by an interventionist welfare state, because any form of intervention is a blatant assault on individual rights.

Nozick is so passionate about individual rights, that the very preface of 'Anarchy, State and Utopia', begins with the words :

"Individuals have rights, and there are things no person or group may do to them (without violating their rights) so strong and far-reaching are these rights that they raise the question of what, if anything the state and its officials may do. How much room do individual rights leave for the state?"[37]

Nozick, being a strong believer in individual rights gives serious consideration to the claim of the anarchists, that the state is immoral, because it has the monopoly of the use of force, and its use may result in the violation of individual rights.

Against this claim of the anarchists that the state is 'intrinsically immoral', Nozick argues "that a state would arise from anarchy (as represented by Locke's state of nature) even though no one intended this or tried to bring it about, by a process which need not violate anyone's rights."[38]

He strongly criticizes the welfare notion which believes that it is the society which allocates the resources. He says that such a notion is wrong and illegitimate because there is no such thing as society, except in the minimal sense of being an aggregate of individuals–There are only individual people with their own individual lives, and society is no more than the sum of its individual components. State intervention amounts to the appropriation of both "one's resources and one's self."

The libertarian concept of rights, specially property rights is so strong, that welfarism stands outright rejected. The welfare state is an extensive state, because it violates people's, inalienable rights, by going beyond the narrow functions of protection against force, theft, fraud, enforcement of contracts.

Such an extensive state, being a threat to liberty, is unjustified, because the individual is the sole owner of himself and his talents, whereas the all-intrusive welfare state, by interfering in all phases of the individual's life, renders the notion of self-ownership null and void. As a writer puts it :

"There is no such thing as benevolent government. Government is an unfortunate necessity .... It is always and by definition liable to encroach upon the individual liberties ....."[39]

Locke's State of Nature

Nozick begins by reviving the state-of-nature of Locke, because he feels that "this state-of-nature situation is the best anarchic situation one reasonably could hope for. Hence investigating its nature and defects is of crucial importance to deciding whether there should be a state rather than anarchy."[40]

Nozick maintains that Locke's state of nature is the 'most favoured situation of anarchy, the best that can realistically be hoped for.'[41]

He further states that if one could show that the state is superior even to this most favoured situation of anarchy–if it would arise by a process involving 'no morally impermissible steps or would be an improvement if it arose'[42]–this would provide a rationale for the state's existence–and also its justification.

Referring to Locke's State of Nature, Ivor Brown says :

"For Locke the state of nature was a state of liberty, not of license, still, however satisfactory the state of nature may have been, it contained three inevitable defects. 'First, the want of an established, settled known law. Secondly, there is no 'known and indifferent judge'; and thirdly, there is no executive power to back up a just decision. Hence men form societies, and this formation by contract is a guarantee and not a destruction of liberties."[43]

Chapter 2nd of 'Anarchy, State and Utopia' is entitled 'The State of Nature' and begins by quoting extensively from John Locke's 'Two Treatises of Government'.

In Locke's state-of-nature, individuals are "in a state of perfect freedom to order their actions and dispose of their possessions and persons as they think fit, within the bounds of the law of nature, without asking leave or dependency upon the will of any other man. (Section 4)

The bounds of the law of nature require that "no one ought to harm another in his life, health, liberty or possessions (Section 6). Some persons transgress these bounds, invading others rights and ..... doing hurt to one another", and in response,people may defend themselves or others against such invaders of rights (Chapter 3). The injured party and his agents may recover from the offender 'so much as may make satisfaction for the harm he has suffered." (Section 10), "everyone has a right to punish the transgressors of that law to such a degree as may hinder its violation" (Section 7), each person may and may only 'retribute to (a criminal) so far as calm reason and conscience dictate, what is proportional to his transgression which is so much as they serve for reparation and restraint." (Section 8)

Despite the fact that this Lockean state of nature is a state of 'perfect freedom' there are certain inconveniences here.

In the words of Nozick :

"There are inconveniences of the state of nature" for which says Locke, "I easily grant that civil government is the proper remedy." (Section 13) To understand precisely what civil government remedies, we must do more than repeat Locke's list of the inconveniences of the state of nature. We also must consider what arrangements might be made within a state of nature to deal with these inconveniences....... Only after the full resources of the state of nature are brought into play, namely, all those voluntary arrangements and agreements persons might reach acting within their rights, and only after the effects of these are estimated, will we be in a position to see how serious are the inconveniences that yet remain to be remedied by the state and to estimate whether the remedy is worse than the disease."[44]

Sometimes, Nozick admits, that the remedy can prove worse than the disease, in other words, governing and government might aggravate the inconveniences, and not remedy them. In this context he extensively quotes Proudhon, who says :

"To be governed is to be watched, inspected, spied upon, directed, law-driven, numbered, regulated, enrolled, valued, ensured, commanded, by creatures who have neither the right nor the wisdom nor the virtue to do so......."[45]

To make a long story short, the government, while trying to remedy the inconveniences, might prove to be worse than the disease–a curse rather than a blessing–because in the name of general interest and public utility, it might completely obliterate and choke the individuality and identity of an individual :

In the Lockean State of Nature, the natural law may not be in a position to provide for every contingency in a proper fashion. Moreover, the men who are judging in their own cases, will naturally be biased in their favour, and will "always give themselves the benefit of the doubt and assume that they are in the right. They will overestimate the amount of harm or damage they have suffered, and passions will lead them to attempt to punish others more than proportionately and to exact excessive compensation" (Sections, 13, 124, 125). Thus private and personal enforcement of one's rights leads to feuds, to an endless series of acts of retaliation and exaction of compensation and there is no firm way to settle such a dispute, to end it and to have both parties know it is ended.

"Any method a single individual might use in an attempt irrevocably to bind himself into ending his part in a feud would offer insufficient assurance to the other party; tacit agreements to stop also would be unstable. Such feelings of being mutually wronged can occur even with the clearest right and with joint agreement on the facts of each person's conduct; all the more is there opportunity for such retaliatory battle when the facts or the rights are to some extent unclear. Also, in a state of nature a person may lack the power to enforce his rights; he may be unable to punish or exact compensation from a stronger adversary who has violated them (Sections 123,126)."[46]

Nozick asks, "How might one deal with these troubles within a state of nature."[47]

He goes on to say that in order to tackle the problems arising in the SN, "an individual may himself enforce his rights, defend himself, exact compensation and punish. Others may join with him in his defense at his call."[48] They may cooperate with him to repulse an attacker, or go after an aggressor. They might do so due to various reasons, for example :

(a) Because they are public-spirited

(b) They are his friends.

(c) He has helped them in the past.

(d) They wish him to help them in the future.

(e) In exchange for something.

Mutual Protection Associations

Realising that in union there is strength, mutual protection associations might be formed by groups of individuals: all will answer the call of any member for defense or for the enforcement of his rights.

But however, such simple MPAs are beset with two inconveniences:

1. Everyone is always on call to serve a protective function (and how shall it be decided who shall answer the call for those protective functions that do not require the service of all members)

2. Any member may call out his associates by saying his rights are being or have been violated.

"Protective associations will not want to be at the beck and call of their cantankerous or paranoid members, not to mention those of their members who might attempt, under the guise of self-defense to use the association to violate the rights of others. Difficulties will also arise if two different members of the same association are in dispute each calling upon his fellow members to come to his aid."[49]

To deal with so many difficulties, many solutions could be resorted to, but because of these solutions being beset with certain complications, it would not be feasible to follow such policies or solutions.

One such policy, which Nozick refers to, is a policy of non-intervention, but because of its inherent complications, Nozick believes, it would be futile to follow this policy. Some of the complications could be :

(a) It would lead to the break-up of the association. There would be discord within the association, leading to the formations of sub-groups, which might be involved in mutual bickering, thus leading to the break-up.

(b) Such a policy would also lead potential aggressors to join as many MPAs as possible, in order to immunise oneself against retaliatory or defensive action.

In the face of these complications, a policy of non-intervention appears to be impractical.

Instead, the MPAs might resort to some arbitrary measures, (like act on the side of the member who complains first) in order to deal with the conflicts among its members.

In the words of Nozick "the inconvenience of everyone being on call, whatever their activity can be handled in the usual manner by division of labour and exchange. Some people will be hired to perform protective functions, and some entrepreneurs will go into business of selling protective services. Different sorts of protective policies would be offered at different prices, for those who may desire more extensive or elaborate protection."[50]

At the individual level, the individual might also resort to certain arrangements. "Short of turning over to a private protective agency, all functions of detection, apprehension, judicial determination of guilt, punishment and exaction of compensation. Mindful of the danger of being the judge in his own case, he might turn the decision as to whether he has indeed been wronged, and to what extent, to some other neutral or less involved party.

In order for the occurrence of the social effect of justice's being seen to be done, such a party would have to be generally respected and thought to be neutral and upright ....[51]

Drawing similarities between a state and a Mutual Protection Agency, Nozick states that sometimes, certain individuals are repelled by the state and its legal system, as a result of which, "they might agree to forms of arbitration or judgment outside the apparatus of the state; They might develop diverse forms of judicial adjudication–but, in the ultimate analysis, they find, that it is only the state that can enforce a judgment against the will of one of the parties, or, in other words, the issue of ultimate enforcement lies with the state. So those persons opposed to a given state system will be left with particularly "poignant and painful choices." Those parties who wish their claims put into effect will have no recourse permitted by the state's legal system other than to use the very legal system."[52]

After resuscitating, what Nozick calls the 'Archaic notion of the state of nature', he goes on to maintain that from this SN will arise MPAs, if some persons do not act morally and violate other's rights.

As Robert L. Holmes says :

"Nozick's contention is that from a state of nature in which people possess natural rights and generally act morally (making this a 'most favoured situation of anarchy'), there will, if some persons do not act morally and violate the rights of others, evolve first mutual protection associations, in which individuals purchase protection against others like a market–governed economic good, and eventually a dominant protective association, an MPA of preeminent power in a territory, the DPA will, in turn eventually evolve into an Ultra Minimal State (UMS), a DPA in which protection is purchased as an economic good but which, in addition has a monopoly of force. The latter will finally evolve into a Minimal State (MS) which, in addition to possessing the two features of the UMS, will make a redistribution of protection to certain independents (nonclients of the UMS) at costs to the clients.[53]

In the words of Nozick :

"Out of anarchy, pressed by spontaneous grouping, mutual protection associations, division of labour, market pressures, economies of scale-interest there arises something very much resembling a Minimal State or a group of geographically distinct Minimal States."[54]

In this context, he refers to the invisible hand explanation ("every individual intends only his own gain and he is in this, as in so many other cases, led by an invisible hand to promote an end which was not part of his intention") in other words :

He believes that there is a certain "lovely quality" to explanations of this sort. They show how some overall pattern or design, which one would have thought had to be produced by an individual's or group's successful attempt to realize the pattern, instead was produced and maintained by a process that in no way had the overall pattern or design in mind."[55]

Borrowing the notion of the (IHE) from Adam Smith, he mentions some characteristics of this notion.

(a) IHEs minimise the use of notions constituting the phenomena to be explained.

(b) They don't explain complicated patterns by including the full-blown pattern-notion as objects of people's desires or beliefs.

(c) They yield greater understanding than do explanations of them as brought about by design as the object of people's intentions, hence Nozick believes that such explanations have a "Specially Satisfying Quality."

Here it would not be out of place to give a brief sketch of Adam Smith's concept of the invisible hand.

Invisible Hand

In 'The Theory of Moral Sentiments' Smith outlines the invisible hand thus :

"The produce of the soil maintains at all times nearly that number of inhabitants which its capable of maintaining, the rich only select from the heap what is most precious and agreeable. They consume little more than the poor, and in spite of their natural selfishness and rapacity, though they mean only their own conveniency, though the sole end which they propose from the labours of all the thousands whom they employ, be the gratification of their own vain and insatiable desires, they divide with the poor the produce of all their improvements. They are led by an invisible hand to make nearly the same distribution of the necessaries of life, which would have been made, had the earth been divided into equal portions among all its inhabitants, and thus without intending it, without knowing it, advance the interest of the society......"[56]

Similarly, in 'The Wealth of Nations' he writes that an individual :

"Neither intends to promote the public interest, nor knows how much he is promoting it. By preferring the support of 'domestic to that of foreign industry' he intends only his own security and by directing that industry in such a manner as its produce may be of the greatest value, he intends only his own gain, and he is in this, as in many other cases, led by an invisible hand to promote an end which was no part of his intention."[57]

Talking about the invisible hand, J. Cropsey says :

"The invisible hand is a metaphor that certainly presupposes that men are compelled to respond in act to their natural selfishness and rapacity. It presupposes that men may be described as being in bondage to the compulsions of nature. But in contradistinction to what it presupposes, what it says is that something called nature transforms the ugliness and bondage of man into a true human good."[58]

The invisible hand, Cropsey maintain is a way of extricating 'humanity from a desperate slavery that, in destroying freedom, threatens morality.'

In a similar strain, Overton H. Taylor paraphrases Smith thus:-

"The goal of his selfish ambition is a chimera with which cunning 'nature' lures him into serving others better than he serves himself."[59]

Similarly, Wilhelm Hasbach has this to say about the invisible hand:

"Man produces and saves, in order to acquire wealth for himself but without his knowledge or will he indirectly advances the material condition of the whole society. He is a tool in God's hand."[60]

Throwing some more light on the invisible hand, L. Schneider maintains:

"The invisible hand thus intervenes or mediates between limited self-interest and general welfare. It effects a balancing or smoothing out.

But Rosenberg believes that Smith's invisible hand has nothing to do with divine guidance. On the contrary, "the invisible hand is the hard hand of competition, which places immense pressure upon individuals to behave in a way that simultaneously promotes the public interest as well as the private interest............The hand that guides individual behaviour is invisible in the sense that no government official dictates the behaviour of individual market forces do."[61]

Variously described as a 'Conversion Mechanism', an institutional system, for disciplining the business community', 'the hand of divine providence', 'a mysterious term that refers to a somewhat miraculous process', the invisible hand was used by Smith to solve the problem of morality .... the distinction between right and wrong, virtue and vice.

After having dealt at length with the invisible hand explanation, Nozick maintains that the individuals are goaded into forming mutual protection agencies without any 'intelligent design' or without any conscious attempt on their part to realise this pattern. It was not their 'intentional design' or their desire/want/belief to form such protective agencies, but they were 'led by an invisible hand to promote an end which was not part of his intention'.

Outlaw Agencies

Once the MPAs are established through an invisible hand, many types of complications might arise.

In the words of Nozick :

"Initially, several different protective associations or companies will offer their services in the same geographical area. What will occur when there is a conflict between clients of different agencies? Things are relatively simple if the agencies reach the same decision about the disposition of the case. But what happens if they reach different decisions as to the merits of the case, and one agency attempts to protect its client while the other is attempting to punish him or make him pay compensation."[62]

Thus, Nozick reiterates that different protective agencies provide different protective services to its customers, thus bringing them into violent conflict with each other, because all the protective agencies compete for customer's patronage and no customer, the agency realizes will settle for the lesser good. So the competing companies are 'caught in a declining spiral', but still, each of the agencies attempts in good faith to act within the limits of Lock's law of nature, but there is the possibility that "One protective association might aggress against other persons. Relative to Locke's law of nature it would be an outlaw agency. What actual counterweights would there be to its power?"[63]

Nozick believes that such an 'outlaw agency', which is an openly aggressive agency 'pillaging, plundering and extorting under no plausible claim of justice—will have a harder time than states."[64]

Its clients will consider it illegitimate and will have no faith in it, refusing to give their voluntary cooperation to it.

As Nozick maintains :

"For the state's claim to legitimacy induces its citizens to believe they have some duty to obey its edicts, pay its taxes, fight its battles, and so on, and so some persons cooperate with it voluntarily. An openly aggressive agency could not depend upon, and would not receive any such voluntary cooperation, since persons would view themselves simply as its victims rather than its citizens."[65]

Dominant Protective Agency

Because of the conflicting claims of various protective agencies, and because of the need of a counterweight against the various protective agencies which might aggress against each other, and also because of the need to tackle 'outlaw agencies', an MPA of 'preeminent power' emerges, naturally through the invisible hand process–this is the dominant protective agency but it falls short of being a state, because the state has a monopoly of force, which the DPA lacks. To quote Nozick :

"A state claims a monopoly on deciding who may use force when; it says that only it may decide who may use force and under what conditions; it reserves to itself the sole right to pass on the legitimacy and permissibility of any use of force within its boundaries; furthermore it claims the right to punish all those who violate its monopoly."[66]

The DPA despite being a preeminent power in a territory lacks such a monopoly of power which the state can rightly claim. As Nozick says, that the DPA "appears to lack any monopoly element and so appears not to constitute or contain a state."[67]

Another reason which he puts forth is that the DPA fails to provide protection to all within the territory–"The second reason for thinking the system described is not a state is that under it (apart from spillover effects) only those paying for protection get protected, furthermore differing degrees of protection may be purchased."[68]

In the DPA, unlike the state, protection services and enforcement of people's rights "is treated as an economic good to be provided by the market, as are other important goods such as food and clothing. However, under the usual conception of a state, each person living without (or even sometimes travelling outside) its geographical boundaries gets (or at least, is entitled to get) its protection."[69]

Thus, we see that the DPA falls short of being a state due to two reasons :

It "not only lacks the requisite monopoly over the use of force, but also fails to provide protection for all its territory, and so the dominant agency appears to fall short of being a state."[70]

Ultra Minimal State

Thus, without deliberately intending to do so, an Ultra Minimal State is produced by the people which is a "social arrangement intermediate between the scheme of private protective associations and night-watchman state. Since the night-watchman state is often called a Minimal State, we shall call this other arrangement the Ultra Minimal State. An Ultra Minimal State maintains a monopoly over all use of force except that necessary in immediate self-defence, and so excluded private (or agency) retaliation for wrong and exaction of compensation."[71]

Its greatest shortcoming is that "it provides protection and enforcement services only to those who purchase its protection and enforcement policies. People who don't buy a protection contract from the monopoly don't get protected."[72] Hence, Nozick believes that the transition to the Minimal State is inevitable.

"The transition from an Ultra Minimal State to a Minimal State morally must occur. It would be morally impermissible for persons to maintain the monopoly in the Ultra Minimal State without providing services for all even if this requires specific 'redistribution'. The operators of the Ultra Minimal State are morally obligated to produce the Minimal State."[73]

Nozick, so far has tried to explain "how, without anyone having this in mind, the self-interested and rational actions of persons in a Lockean state of nature will lead to single protective agencies dominant over geographical territories, each territory will have either one dominant agency or a number of agencies federally affiliated so as to constitute, in essence one. And—how, without claiming to possess any rights uniquely, a protective agency dominant in a territory will occupy a unique position. Though each person has a right to act correctly to prohibit others from violating rights (including the right not to be punished unless shown to deserve it) only the dominant protective association will be able, without sanction, to enforce correctness as it sees it, its power makes it the arbiter of correctness; it determines what, for purposes of punishment counts as a breach of correctness.[74] Our explanation does not assume or claim that might makes right. But might does make enforced prohibitions, even if no one thinks the might have a special entitlement to have realised in the world their own view of which prohibitions are correctly enforced."[74]

The DPA, Nozick claims is the 'Arbiter of Correctness' its unique position empowers it with the authority to determine what constitutes a 'Breach of Correctness', and then to punish the erring individual accordingly.

In the words of Robert L Holmes :

"Nozick's burden is two fold here. He must show not only that it is plausible to suppose that the monopoly of force would in fact arise within the DPA, but also that it would be morally legitimate that it did so."[75]

The anarchist's objection to the state is that the state is 'intrinsically immoral' because it 'monopolises force', and provides protection for everyone within its territory by requiring some to finance protection for others, and in so doing, violates certain moral 'side constraints' in the form of natural rights.

Referring to the 'moral side constraints', Nozick says :

"This root idea, namely that there are different individuals with separate lives and so no one may be sacrificed for others, underlies the existence of moral side constraints, but it also, I believe leads to a libertarian side constraint that prohibits aggression against another."[76]

The anarchist's argument is that 'Monopolising the use of force—is itself immoral, as is redistribution through the compulsory tax apparatus of the state—By what right, then can the state and its officials claim a unique right (a privilege) with regard to force and enforce this monopoly?"[77]

Nozick tries to prove that the Minimal State that gradually evolves through the state of nature violates neither (a) Moral Side Constraints nor (b) Libertarian Side Constraints.

In his words :

"To get to something recognisable as a state we must show 1. how an Ultra Minimal State arises out of the system of private protective associations; and 2. how the Ultra Minimal State is transformed into the Minimal State. To show that the Minimal State is morally legitimate, to show it is not immoral itself, we must show also that these transitions in 1. and 2. each are morally legitimate—We argue that the first transition from a system of private protective agencies to an Ultra Minimal State, will occur by an invisible-hand process in a morally-permissible way that violates no one's rights. Secondly, we argue that the transition from an Ultra Minimal State to a Minimal State morally must occur."[78]

Dominant Protective Agency Vis a Vis The Independents

In chapter IV entitled "Prohibition, Compensation and Risk", Nozick addresses himself to the colossal task of the role of the dominant protective agency vis a vis the independents.

He begins the chapter with the following words :

"Let us suppose that interspersed among a large group of persons who deal with one protective agency lives some miniscule group who do not. These few independents (perhaps even only one) jointly or individually enforce their own rights against one and all, including clients of the agency."[79]

Nozick admits that for the DPAs it is indeed a Herculean task to deal with the independents. What should be the policy/strategy/attitude to be followed towards this miniscule group? He asks :

"How might the protective association and its members deal with this? They might try to isolate themselves from the independent in their midst by forbidding anyone permission to enter their property who hadn't agreed to forgo exercising rights of retaliation and punishment. The geographical territory covered by the protective association then might resemble a slice of Swiss cheese, with internal as well as external boundaries."[80]

Nozick says that it is quite possible that some wealthy independents might have private helicopters to retaliate/ travel, without trespassing upon anyone's land-what then?

In his words :

"But this would leave acute problems of relations with independents who had devices enabling them to retaliate across the boundaries, or who had helicopters to travel directly to wrongdoers without trespassing upon anyone else's land."[81]

Nozick further says that there is still another way of dealing with recalcitrant independents.

"Instead of (or in addition to) attempts at geographically isolating independents, one might punish them for their misenforcements of their rights of retaliation, punishment and exaction of compensation. An independent would be allowed to proceed to enforce his rights as he sees them and as he sees the facts of his situation, afterwards the members of the protective association would check to see whether he had acted wrongly or overacted. If and only if he had done so, would they punish him or exact compensation from him."[82]

But, in such a possibility, Nozick concedes, the victim may be fatally injured. So is it feasible to wait to check to see whether the independent had acted wrongly?

"But the victim of the independent's, wrongful and unjust retaliation may be not only damaged but seriously injured and perhaps killed. Must one wait to act until afterwards?"[83]

He further asks:

"Is it not within a person's rights to announce that he will not allow himself to be punished without its first being established that he has wronged someone? May he not appoint a protective association as his agent to make and carry out this announcement and to oversee any process used to try to establish his guilt?"[84]

Nozick admits that there are other possibilities–

"And if the protective agency tries to punish an independent who punished a client, independently of whether their client did violate the independent's rights, isn't the independent within his rights to defend himself against the agency?"[85]

Nozick states that in order to answer these various questions, and to decide how a DPA may act towards independents, two issues need to be investigated :

(a) The moral status within a SN of procedural rights

(b) Prohibitions upon risky activities.

Referring to these complex issues he talks of a circumscribed area of an individual.

"A line (or hype plane) circumscribes an area in moral space around an individual. Locke holds that this line is determined by an individual's natural rights, which limit the action of others—"

Much of Chapter IV is devoted to unravelling this crucial question. He says :

"Let us say that a system forbids an action to a person if it imposes (is geared to impose) some penalty upon him for doing the act, in addition to exacting compensation from him for the act's victims. Something fully compensates a person for a loss if and only if it makes him no worse off than he otherwise would have been."[86]

Addressing himself to the question "Why Ever Prohibit", he delimits this concern by stating two contrasting questions:

1. Why is any action ever prohibited rather than allowed, provided its victims are compensated?
2. Why not prohibit all crossings of the moral boundary that the party impinged upon did not first consent to? Why ever permit any one to cross another's boundary without prior consent?

A truncated form of these questions would read as :

1. Allow actions and compensate victims.
2. Disallow all boundary crossing not consented to.

If full compensation is paid, in such a manner that both are able to strike a mutually advantageous bargain, the problem of distribution of benefits of voluntary exchange in an unfair and arbitrary manner can be solved.

"Consider further how such a system allocates goods. Anyone can seize a good, thereby coming to own it, provided he compensates its owner. If several people want a good, the first to seize it, gets it, until another takes it, paying him full compensation (why should this sort of middlemen receive anything). What amount would compensate the original owner if several persons wanted a particular good? An owner who knew of this demand might well come to value his goods by its market price. Where markets exist, isn't the market price the least price a seller would accept?"[87] "......... and so on and so forth. There can be many complicated combinations which Nozick says might 'succeed in disentangling an owner's preferences from his knowledge of the desires of others and the prices they are willing to pay."[88]

But so far, no one has actually succeeded in providing the requisite combinations. But how to discover the price then?

In that case, Nozick concedes, "The best method to discover this price, of course, is to let the negotiations actually take place and see what their upshot is. Any other procedure would be highly inaccurate as well as incredibly cumbersome."[89]

Thus from the foregoing arguments two features follow:

(a) The free allowing of all acts, provided compensation is paid.

(b) The fairness of the exchange price.

But besides this, Nozick maintains that there are certain acts which give rise to an atmosphere of general apprehension and fear, and in order to avoid such apprehension, these acts are prohibited and made punishable. As Nozick puts it "even some acts that can be compensated for may be prohibited. Among those acts that can be compensated for, some arouse fear. We fear these acts happening to us, even if we know that we shall be compensated fully for them."[90]

Nozick further states that "Not every kind of border crossing creates such fear. If told that my automobile may be taken during the next month, and I will be compensated fully afterwards for the taking and for any inconvenience being without the car causes me, I do not spend the month nervous, apprehensive and fearful."[91]

Distinguishing between private wrongs and public wrongs, Nozick says :

"Private wrongs are those where only the injured party need be compensated; persons who know they will be compensated fully do not fear them.

Public wrongs are those people are fearful of, even though they know they will be compensated fully if, and when the wrongs occur."[92]

Moreover, there is a strong possibility that "even under the strongest compensation proposal which compensates victims for their fear, some people (the non-victims) will not be compensated for their fear. Therefore, there is a legitimate public interest in eliminating these border crossing acts especially because their commission raises everyone's fear of its happening to them."[93]

Nozick reiterates that despite knowing that if harmed, they will be adequately compensated, individuals are still victims of fear. It is not just 'physical injury' that is feared, but individuals are afraid of being a humiliated, shamed, disgraced, embarrassed, and so on'–hence the argument that all acts producing general fear should be prohibited is justified.

This brings him to the second question, "Why not prohibit all boundary crossing to which the victim has not consented in advance." Answering this, he states :

"The penalisation of all impingements not consented to, including accidental ones and those done unintentionally, would incorporate large amount of risk and insecurity into people's lives. People couldn't be sure that despite the best of intentions they wouldn't end up being punished for accidental happenings."[94]

Apart from being unfair, there is a practical complication involved in getting prior consent–Even if it is known who the victim is going to be, it might be temporarily impossible to contact him, moreover, 'it might be known that some person or other will be the victim of an act, but it might be impossible to find which person'.

In each of these cases, Nozick maintains, 'that no agreement gaining the victim's permission to do the act can be negotiated in advance'–Apart from the cost involved, it might be difficult to get in touch with the victim–"The known victim can be communicated with, but only by first performing a brain operation on him, or finding him in an African jungle, or getting him to cut short his six-month sojourn in a monastery where he has taken a vow of silence and abstinence from business affairs ...... all very costly."[95]

Thus, Nozick concludes by saying that "the three considerations of fear, divisions of the benefits of exchange, and transaction costs delimit our area."[96] Hence they do not provide us with a solution.

"An independent might be prohibited from privately enforcing justice because his procedure is known to be too risky and dangerous–that is, it involves a higher risk (than another procedure) of punishing an innocent person or overpunishing a guilty one–or because his procedure isn't known not to be risky."[97]

Since he is being prohibited from doing a particular 'risky activity, those who benefit from the reduction in risks to themselves have to 'make it up' to those who are restricted.'[98] But then, Nozick asks:

"Must I really compensate someone, when in self-defense, I stop him from playing Russian roulette on me? If some person wishes to use a very risky but-efficient (and if things go well harmless) process in manufacturing a product, must the residents near the factory compensate him for the economic loss he suffers from not being allowed to use the possibly dangerous process? Surely not."[99]

'Anarchy, State and Utopia' is replete with many such examples which he uses to try to arrive at an acceptable principle of compensation but unable to reach a precise principle of compensation, he concludes by saying "that it is all right as a beginning to leave a principle in a somewhat fuzzy state;"[100] despite the possibility that it might meet a 'frosty reception' from many critics. Suffice it to say that such a principle is needed requiring those imposing a 'prohibition on risky activities to compensate those disadvantaged through having their risky activities prohibited to them."[101]

Nozick further states that procedures of justice differ from person to person. "Suppose now that you have no reliable knowledge about another's procedure of justice. May you stop him in self-defense and may your protective agency act for you, solely because you or it does not know whether his procedure is reliable? .... One may think of the state as the authoritative settler of doubts about reliability and fairness. But of course there is no guarantee that it will settle them and there is no reason to suppose it will manage to do so more effectively than another scheme?"[102]

Nozick further asks:

"What then may a dominant protective association forbid other individuals to do? The dominant protective association may reserve for itself the right to judge any procedure of justice to be applied to its clients. It may announce, and act on the announcement that it will punish anyone who uses on one of its clients a procedure that it finds to be unreliable or unfair. It will punish anyone who uses on one of its clients a procedure that it already knows to be unreliable or unfair, and it will defend its clients against the application of such a procedure."[103]

He further states:

"By what right could the protective agency announce that it will punish anyone using an unreliable procedure who punishes its clients independently of the guilt or innocence of the clients."[104]

Trying to answer these questions, Nozick says, that a person who is using an 'unreliable procedure' is imposing a risk, irrespective of the fact whether his procedure misfires or not–Reverting to the example of Russian roulette, he states, "Someone playing Russian roulette upon another does the same thing if when he pulls the trigger the gun does not fire. The protective agency may treat the unreliable enforcer of justice as it treats any performer of a risky action."[105]

The DPA is the most powerful applier of principles, hence will act on its discretion 'since the dominant protective association judges its own procedures to be both reliable and fair, and believes this to be generally known, it will not allow anyone to defend against them; that is it will punish anyone who does so. The dominant protective association will act freely on its own understanding of the situation whereas no one else will be able to do so with impunity. Although no monopoly is proclaimed, the dominant agency does occupy a unique position by virtue of its power. It, and it alone enforces prohibitions on other's procedures of justices as it sees fit. It does not claim the right to prohibit others arbitrarily; it claims only the right to prohibit anyone's using actually defective procedures on its clients .... As the most powerful applier of principles which it grants everyone the right to apply correctly, it enforces its will, which from the inside it thinks is correct. From its strength stems its actual position as the ultimate enforcer and the ultimate judge with regard to its own clients. Claiming only the universal right to act correctly, it acts correctly by its own lights, it alone is in a position to act solely by its own lights."[106]

Thus, the DPA, Nozick believes embodies the universal right to act correctly, it being the 'Ultimate Enforcer and the Ultimate Judge' with regard to its clients. It being dominant, no one else will be able to exercise this exclusive right with impunity.

'Does this unique position constitute a monopoly? There is no right the dominant protective association claims uniquely to possess. But its strength leads it to be the unique agent acting across the board to enforce particular right. It is not merely that it happens to be the only exerciser of a right it grants that all possess, the nature of the right is such that once a dominant power emerges, it alone will actually exercise that right, for the right includes the right to stop others from wrongfully exercising the right, and only the dominant power will be able to exercise this right against all others. Here if anywhere, is the place for applying some notion of a de facto monopoly: a monopoly that is not dejure because it is not the result of some unique grant of exclusive right while others are excluded from exercising a similar privilege."[107]

Nozick tries to maintain that the unique position of the DPA constitutes a de facto monopoly, and not a dejure one because this position of the DPA does not stem from the granting of some exclusive right to it. Yet the fact of its monopoly cannot be glossed over, it does have a unique position, in the sense that 'it, and it, alone enforces prohibitions on other's procedure of justice, as it sees fit'. It is the ultimate enforcer and the 'Ultimate Judge' with regard to its own clients. Its procedures are both 'Reliable and Fair', which, by implication means that all other procedures are 'Unreliable' and 'Unfair'

That the DPA has preeminent power in a particular territory cannot be denied, but it naturally follows that other protective agencies might not be too happy with such a situation. In the words of Nozick:

"Other protective agencies, to be sure, can enter the market and attempt to wean away customers from the dominant protective agency. They can attempt to replace it as the dominant one. But being the already dominant protective agency gives an agency a significant market advantage in the competition for clients. The dominant agency can offer its customers a guarantee that no other agencies can match: only procedures we deem appropriate will be used on our customers."[108]

He further says:

"Thus, the dominant protective agency must supply the independents–that is, everyone it prohibits from self-help enforcement against its client on the ground that their procedures of enforcement are unreliable–with protective services against its clients."[109]

This raises a pertinent question: "if the dominant protective agency provides protective services in this way for independents, won't this lead people to leave the agency in order to receive its services without paying?"[110]

"Not to any great extent", Nozick reiterates, "since compensation is paid only to those who would be disadvantaged by purchasing protection for themselves".[111]

The DPA within a territory satisfies two crucial necessary conditions for being a state.

(a) It has the requisite sort of monopoly over the use of force in the territory.

(b) It protects the right of everyone in the territory, even if this universal protection could be provided only in a redistributive fashion.

The DPA is the 'only generally effective enforcer of a prohibition on other's using unreliable enforcement procedures and it oversees these procedures. The agency also protects those non-clients in its territory whom it prohibits from using 'self-help enforcement procedures' on its clients, in their dealing with its clients, even if such protection must be financed in apparent redistributive fashion by its clients.

It is here that the principle of compensation comes in, because "it is morally required to do this by the principle of compensation, which requires those who act in self-protection in order to increase their own security to compensate those they prohibit from doing risky acts which might out to be harmless for the disadvantages imposed upon them."[112]

Nozick has stated that whether the provision of protective services for some by others was 'redistributive' would depend upon the reasons for it. He further states that such provision need not be redistributive since it can be justified on the ground of compensation.

To sharpen this point he imagines two types of protective policies offered by the protective agencies.

(a) Those protecting clients against risky private enforcement of justice.

(b) Those protecting only against theft, assault etc.

"Since it is only with regard to those with the first type of policy that others are prohibited from privately enforcing justice, only they will be required to compensate the person prohibited private enforcement for the disadvantages imposed upon them."[113]

On the other hand, the policy-holders of the second variety will not have to pay for the protection of others, since there is nothing they have to compensate these others for.

Thus, it follows that 'since the reasons for wanting to be protected against private enforcement of justice are compelling, almost all who purchase protection will purchase this type of protection, despite its extra costs, and therefore will be involved in providing protection for the independents."[114]

Thus, we see that there is no unjust imposition of monopoly but this monopoly grows by an invisible hand process and by morally permissible means, without any violation of rights involved, and without any claims being made to a special right that others do not possess.

"And requiring the clients of the de facto monopoly to pay for the protection of those that they prohibit from self-help enforcement against them, far from being immoral, is morally required by the principle of compensation."[115]

Nozick refers to a discursive description by an anthropologist–Lawrence Krader,[116] wherein he lists some necessary features of the state :

"The concentration of all physical force in the hands of the central authority is the primary function of the state and is its decisive characteristic—no one in the society governed by the state may take another's life, do him physical harm, touch his property or damage his reputation save, by permission of the state. The officers of the state have powers to take life, inflict corporal punishment, seize property as fine or by expropriation—"

The state has means for the suppression of what the society considers to be wrongs or crimes police, courts of law, prisons,—-

No one person or group can stand in place of the state; the states acts can only be performed directly or by delegation.[117]

On the basis of these features Nozick states:

"Clearly the dominant agency has almost all the features specified; and its enduring administrative structures, with full time specialised personnel, make it diverge greatly--in the direction of the state–from what anthropologists call a stateless society."[118]

Nozick believes it would be a futile exercise to specify conditions on the size of population and territory necessary for a state to exist. Moreover, he admits that although it might be interesting to know:

(a) What is the percentage of clients.

(b) How subordinate the power position of the independents must be, yet, he concedes that he has nothing interesting to say regarding these questions.

Earlier, he had extracted one more necessary condition from the Weberian tradition. To quote him :

"Writers in the tradition of Max Weber treat having a monopoly on the use of force in a geographical area, a monopoly incompatible with private enforcement of rights, as crucial to the existence of a state."[119]

In other words, the state claims to be the sole authorizer of violence, but the DPA makes no such claim.

Nozick tries to weaken the Weberian necessary condition to include a "de facto monopoly which is the territory's sole effective judge over the permissibility of violence, having a right to make judgments on the matter and to act on correct ones,—we therefore conclude that the protective association dominant in a territory, as described is a state."[120]

However, reminding the reader of the slight weakening of the Weberian condition, he maintains that, occasionally the DPA will be referred to as 'a state-like entity', instead of simply as 'a state'.

The Minimal State : A Framework for Utopia

In the final chapter of 'Anarchy State and Utopia', 'A Framework For Utopia', Nozick concedes that utopian theorists might find the ideal of the Minimal State 'pale and feeble'. He asks:

"But doesn't the idea, or ideal, of the Minimal State lack luster. Can it thrill the heart or inspire people to struggle or sacrifice?

Would anyone man barricades under its banner?–Whatever its virtues, it appears clear that the Minimal State is no utopia.[121]

Since it is no utopia, Nozick ventures into an investigation of utopian theory which would highlight the defects and shortcomings of the Minimal State, besides promising to be 'intrinsically interesting'.

He admits that it is quite incredible that there can be just one best society for everyone to live in. There are different kinds of people with different inclinations and mindsets and 'there is a wide range of very different kinds of life that tie as best', there are 'many different strands of aspiration' and many different paths leading to it–for example :

Picasso, Einstein, Socrates, Thomas Jefferson, Elizabeth Taylor, Freud, Bertrand Russell–to name just a few of the individuals mentioned by Nozick–all belonged to different fields–Art, science, politics, the performing arts, psychoanalysis, philosophy.

Nozick asks:

"Is there really one kind of life which is best for each of these people? Imagine all of them living in any utopia you've ever seen described in detail."[122]

All of them cannot be imagined living in one utopia, because of their differing interests, natural inclinations and so on.

"Utopia is the focus of so many different strands of aspiration that there must be many theoretical paths leading to it."[123]

Therefore, he believes it would be feasible to sketch some of these alternative, mutually supporting theoretical routes. The theoretical routes which he sketches are:

1. People are Different
2. No System of Trade-offs can Command Universal Assent
3. People are Complex.

1. People are Different

The first route begins with the fact that people are different. People differ in temperament, interests, intellectual ability, aspirations, natural bent, spiritual quests and the kind of life they wish to lead hence no one community can be ideally suited them.

Nozick concedes that despite being quite confident of the virtues and correctness of the visions presented by utopian authors, 'No utopian author has everyone in his society, leading exactly the same life', "Don't the reasons also count against just one kind of community," he queries. Hence, he concludes that all these different people cannot live ideally in one Utopia, because it cannot cater to their different ambitions/desires/fields. So:

"There will not be one kind of community existing and one kind of life led in utopia. Utopia will consist of divergent communities in which people lead different kinds of lives under different institutions."[124]

This utopia, he believes is actually an environment, wherein utopian experiments may be tried out. It is an environment where everyone is left free to pursue his own life in the manner which he deems fit.

Thus, this utopia which Nozick envisages is a "framework for utopias, a place where people are at liberty to join together voluntarily to pursue and attempt to realise their own vision of the good life in the ideal community, but where no one can impose his own utopian vision upon others."[125]

So, we see that the hall-mark of the Nozickean Utopia is voluntarism,-the people join the communities on their own accord, they leave the communities at their will, they cannot be browbeaten into joining one community or leaving another. They have a vision of the good life, and they join the community, which they think will help them in realizing that vision. If some people do not join a particular community in the initial stages. They may join it later, when all the ambiguities regarding its working have been sorted out.

2. No System of Trade-offs Can Command Universal Assent

Nozick laments the fact that all social and political goods can not be realised simultaneously. As he puts it:

"That it is impossible simultaneously and continually to realise all social and political goods is a regrettable fact about the human condition worth investigating and bemoaning."[126] Hence it follows that trade-offs will have to be resorted to, but there is no system of trade-offs, that can be universally accepted.

"Different communities, each with a slightly different mix, will provide a range from which each individual can choose that community which best approximates his balance among competing values."[127]

3. People and their Webs of Possible Relationships are Complex

Nozick asks us to suppose that one kind of society is best for all–but how are we to find out what this society is? For finding this out, he suggests two possible methods:

1. Design Devices
2. Filter Devices

Through the design device, a description of one society is obtained by people, who sit together and think of the best possible society, and then proceed to pattern everything on this one model.

But Nozick is apprehensive of such a device, because of the complexity of man. As he says:

"Given the enormous complexity of man—it is enormously unlikely that even if there were one ideal pattern for society it could be arrived at this a priori fashion."[128]

In the face of such enormous human complexitities, it is not possible to dream up a description of the perfect society, and then setting out to institute it. Hence, another method–the filter devices can be used. "In which the people planning out ideal society consider many different kinds of societies and criticise some, eliminate some modify the descriptions of other's until they come to the one they consider best."[129]

Nozick says that the filtering process which the utopian framework involves is very simple.

"People try out living in various communities, and they leave or slightly modify the ones they don't like. Some communities will be abandoned others will struggle along, others will split, others will flourish, gain members and be duplicated elsewhere. Each community must win and hold the voluntary adherence of its members. No pattern is imposed on everyone, and the result will be one pattern if and only if everyone voluntarily chooses to live in accordance with that pattern of community."[130]

Thus, we see that the keyword here is voluntarism and not imposition.

Referring to the design devices, Nozick says that "The design devices comes in at the stage of generating specific communities to be lived in and tried out. Any group of people may devise a pattern and attempt to persuade others to participate in the adventure of a community in that pattern."[131]

Hence, it follows, that people of all hues and shades can have a try at building their vision.

"Visionaries and crackpots, maniacs and saints, monks and libertines, capitalists and communists and participatory democrats, proponents of phalanxes (Fourier) palaces of labour (Tristan), villages of unity and cooperation (Owen), mutualistic communities (Proudhon), time stores (Josiah Warren) Bruderhof, Kibbutzim Kundalini, yoga ashrams and so forth, may all have their try at building their vision, and setting an alluring example."[132]

Nozick, however concedes that one should not hastily conclude that every pattern will be explicitly designed, on the contrary.

"Some will be planned modifications and others will be built up spontaneously........and as the communities which people live in improve, ideas for new communities often will improve as well."[133]

Thus, we see, that the operation of this framework for utopia realizes the advantages of a filtering process in which there is 'mutually improving interaction between the filter and the surviving products of the generating process. So that the quality of generated and nonrejected products improves'.[134]

In other words–

1. Through the design device specific communities are generated.

2. Through the filter process there is qualitative improvement of the generated and non-rejected products.

Now with an almost triumphant air, Nozick maintains that, 'any utopian will agree that our framework is an appropriate one for a society of good men',—for each thinks his own particular vision would be realised under it.[135]

Thus, the two added advantages of this framework can be stated thus:

(a) It will be acceptable to almost every utopian at some future point in time, whatever his particular vision.

(b) It is compatible with the realisation of almost all particular visions.

Nozick distinguishes between three utopian positions.

1. **Imperialistic :** This position can force everyone into one pattern of community.

2. **Missionary Utopianism :** Without using force, it will try to convince everyone to live in one particular kind of community.

3. **Existential Utopianism :** This utopianism hopes that a particular pattern of community will exist, though not universally, so that those who wish to do so, may live in accordance with it. These are the types of utopians who will whole-heartedly support the framework.

Without any particular admiration for the additional virtue of the framework of allowing the 'simultaneous realization of many possibilities,-their aspirations being universal, the Missionary Utopians will also join them in supporting the framework.

But, on the other hand, the Imperialistic Utopians will oppose the framework.

Thus, we see that such a utopian framework has the virtue of compatibility with all utopian visions.

"Since any particular community may be established within the framework, it is compatible with all particular visions, while guaranteeing none."[136]

Nozick, however maintains that, this framework is laissez faire and libertarian, in the sense that everyone is at liberty to choose among various communities–but this is not denying the fact that there are no restrictions among various communities.

"For though there is great liberty to choose among communities, many particular communities internally may have many restrictions unjustifiable on libertarian grounds: that is restrictions, which libertarians would condemn if they were enforced by a central state apparatus. For example, paternalistic intervention into peoples lives, restrictions on the range of books etc ..."[137]

In other words, though this framework is libertarian, the characteristics of the framework need not pervade the individual communities–

Nozick further says that some persons might want to 'unite kindred spirits', but despite their yearning and desires, no one has the right to "impose their vision of unity upon the rest."

Nozick says that all sorts of criticisms can be applied to utopian writers, but there are two criticisms which particularly seem to apply to all of them.

1. Firstly, their object is a perfect society, and in their vision of a perfect state/society, there can be no

opportunity or expectation of change, and no opportunity for the inhabitants to choose new patterns.

2. All utopians are over-optimistic about the working of their society.

But, Nozick says that his framework of utopia cannot stand guilty to the charge of these two criticisms. As he says:

"We do not detail the character of each particular community within the society, and we imagine the nature and composition of these constituent communities changing over time."[138]

Nozick says that he does not want to fix in advance all of the important social details, nor does he want a framework which is 'fixed in character and unchanging' on the contrary, he wants a framework which 'leaves liberty for experimentation of various sorts'.

Moreover, regarding the second criticism, he opines that he does not naively believe, with the rest of the utopian visionaries, that his framework will not be beset with problems. Far from it,

One major problem, according to Nozick is :

(a) The role of the central authority (or protective association)–How will this authority be selected, and how will it be ensured that it does not go beyond its jurisdiction.

However, Nozick says that "The major role, as I see it, would be to enforce the operation of the framework–for example, to prevent some communities from invading and seizing others, their persons or assets. Furthermore, it will adjudicate in some reasonable fashion conflicts between communities which cannot be settled by peaceful means."[139]

Nozick does not want to investigate the best form of such a central authority, because he wishes to leave room for improvement. Moreover, regarding some powerful control on the central authority he does not want to say anything because this does not 'fit easily into one's hopes for a sleek, simple utopian scheme.'

The persistent strand in Nozick's views regarding the framework for utopia is that 'nothing can be fixed permanently', but there is one point, regarding which Nozick has no second thought or misgiving,-and that is the 'voluntarism' of the framework–as, he maintains emphatically–'yes, the framework should be fixed as voluntary'–

"Some things individuals may choose for themselves, no one may choose for another—But remember that any individual may contract into any particular constraints over himself and so may use the voluntary framework to contract himself out of it."[140]

Nozick maintains that the conception of utopia that he has presented has a Dual Nature:

1. The Framework of Utopia.
2. The Particular Communities within the Framework.

He asks:

"Well, what exactly will it all turn out to be like? In what direction will people flower? How large will the communities be? Will there be some large cities? How will economies of scale operate to fix the size of the communities? Will all the communities be geographical, or will there be many important secondary associations and so on."[141]

Regarding the nature of the communities within the framework, Nozick, does not want 'planning in detail', nor does he want to make any guesses, because he says that he is neither a fool nor a prophet.

"Only a fool, or a prophet would try to prophesy the range and limits, and characters of the communities after, for example, 150 years of the operation of this framework."[142]

Lauding his framework, Nozick says : "Conjoined with many person's particular visions the framework enables us to get the best of all possible worlds—one community in which everyone is to live yet sympathises with voluntary utopian experimentation, and provides it with the background in which it can flower."[143]

Finally, he maintains that this framework for utopia that he has envisaged is 'equivalent to the Minimal State', although "the argument of this chapter starts (and stands) independently of the argument of Parts I and II, and converges to their result, the Minimal State, from another direction."[144]

He further says:

"We need not mesh our discussion here with our earlier one of dominant protective agencies beyond noting that whatever conclusions people reach about the role of a central authority (the controls on it, and so forth) will shape the (internal) form and structure of the protective agencies they choose to be client of."[145]

In Part I of ASU, Nozick argued that the Minimal State was 'Morally Legitimate'. In Part II he argued that no more extensive state could be morally justified, that any more extensive state would violate the individual rights.

Now, in the concluding paragraphs of his magnum opus, he reiterates with a sense of satisfaction, that the Minimal State also realise the ideals of dreamers and visionaries. He says:

"This morally legitimate state, the only morally tolerable one, we now see is the one that best realises the utopian aspirations of untold dreamers and visionaries—Is not the Minimal State, the framework for utopia, an inspiring vision?"[146]

The Minimal State, leaves the individual unfettered, his individuality and dignity intact, hence it is tolerable, favoured and legitimate. It is the least intrusive form of political power, based as it is, on voluntarism, and hence is 'Inspiring As Well As Right'.

"The Minimal State treats us as inviolate individuals, who may not be used in certain ways by others as means or tools or instruments or resources; it treats us as persons having individual rights with the dignity this constitutes. Treating us with respect by respecting our rights, it allows us, individually or with whom we choose, to choose our life and to realise our ends and our conception of ourselves, insofar as we can, aided by the voluntary cooperation of other individuals possessing the same dignity. How dare any state or group of individuals do more or less."[147]

Conclusion

In a nutshell, Nozick's theory of the Minimal State can be stated thus–

His concern for individual liberty is so strong, that he cannot tolerate any Excessive State, for such a state would violate the rights of the individual, which are inalienable. Nozick's libertarianism advocates the least intrusive form of political power which is commensurate with the defence of individual liberty

(a) Strongly convinced that individuals are autonomous beings with capabilities, capacities and initiatives hence what is needed is the least intrusion of the state. In fact, the less the state interferes in the autonomous sphere of the individual, the better it is, both for the state and the individual.

(b) The state being minimal, it should not try to step beyond its legitimate functions–because then it becomes uninspiring and wrong.

(c) The individual rights are 'so strong and far-reaching' that they leave very little room for the state.

(d) It is merely a protective agency and therefore protects people against force, theft, fraud and the violation of contracts.

(e) Trying to promote equality does not fall under its jurisdiction.

(f) In order to protect the rights of the people, it has to sustain a monopoly of force, through which it can adjudicate conflicts.

(g) Voluntarism is the hall-mark of the Minimal State.

(h) The Minimal State is the framework for utopia, wherein every individual can choose his life according to his desires/aspirations.

(i) It arises from the state of nature via only legitimate steps, without violating anyone's rights.

(j) It is based on an invisible hand explanation.

Notes and References

1. Laski, H.A., (1925) 'A Grammar of Politics', London, George Allen and Unwin.
2. Maciver, R.M. (1966) 'The Modern State' London, Oup, pp. 185-86.
3. Spragens Thomas, A. Jr. : (1999) 'Civic Liberalism : Reflections On Our Democratic Ideals', New York, p. xi.
4. Held David (1984) 'The Contemporary Polarisation of Democratic Theory : The Case For A Third Way' In David Held Eg. 'Political Theory and The Modern State'– Polity Press, p. 174.
5. Friedman Milton : (1962) 'Capitalism and Freedom, Chicago : University of Chicago Press, p. 34.
6. Spencer, Herbert (1969) 'The Man Versus The State' Baltimore : Penguin Books, p. 67.

7. Hagopian, Mark N., (1985) 'Ideas and Ideologies of Modern Politics', New York, London, p. 176.

8. Held, David, *op. cit.*, p. 175.

9. Buchanan, James M. (1985). 'Liberty Market, and State–Political Economy in the 1980's', New York, N.Y. University Press, p. 178.

10. Friedman Milton, *op. cit.*, p. 14.

11. Macpherson C.B. (1973) 'Democratic Theory : Essays in Retrieval', Oxford, Clarendon Press, p. 143.

12. Friedman, M., *op. cit.*, p. 15.

13. Watson, George, Ed. 'The Unservile State : Essays In Liberty and Welfare'–London, Ruskin House, George Allen and Unwin Ltd., p. 17.

14. *Ibid.*, p. 17.

15. *Ibid.*, p. 20.

16. Hayek, F.A. (1960) 'The Constitution of Liberty', London, Routledge and Kegan Paul, pp. 231-32.

17. Held David, (1984), *op. cit.*, p. 175.

18. Spragens, Thomas A., (1999), p. xiv–Introduction.

19. *Ibid.*, p. 137.

20. *Ibid.*, p. 137.

21. Opello Walter A., Jr. and Rostow Stephen J. (1999) 'The Nation State and Global Order–A Historical Introduction to Contemporary Politics, Lynne Rienner Publishers, p. 245.

22. *Ibid.*, p. 245.

23. *Ibid.*, p. 245.

24. Hollinger, R., (1996) 'On Liberalism, Democracy and Elitism Today'–In 'The Dark Side of Liberalism : Elitism Vs Democracy', London, Praeger, p. 110.

25. *Ibid.*, p. 110.
26. Hollinger, Robert (1996) 'American Liberalism' in 'The Dark Side of Liberalism : Elitism Vs Democracy', London, p. 27.
27. Nozick, R., Anarchy, State and Utopia, *op. cit.*, p. 33.
28. Hagopian, Mark, N., (1985), *op. cit.*, p. 108.
29. Joad, C.E.M., (1946) 'Modern Political Theory', London, Oxford University Press, p. 102.
30. Bakunin, Michael, 'The Political Philosophy of Bakunin', Ed. G.P. Maximoff–New York, The Free Press, p. 206.
31. Nozick, Anarchy, State and Utopia, *op. cit.*, p. 51.
32. Nozick, *Ibid.*, Preface–ix.
33. Nozick, *Ibid.*, Preface–ix.
34. Nozick, *Ibid.*, Preface–ix–x.
35. *Ibid.*, p. ix.
36. *Ibid.*, p. xi.
37. Dahenrendrof, R., (1984), Quoted In Anthony Arblaster, 'Rise and Decline of Western Liberalism', Oxford–Blackwell, p. 5.
38. Nozick, *op. cit.*, p. 5.
39. *Ibid.*
40. *Ibid.*
41. Brown, Ivor : (1929) English Political Theory : London, Methuen and Co. Ltd., p. 63.
42. Nozick, *op. cit.*, p. 11.
43. Proudhon, P. (1923) 'General Idea of The Revolution In The Nineteenth Century' Translation John Beverley Robinson–London, Freedom Press, pp. 293-94, Quoted in Asu, p. 11.

44. Nozick, *op. cit.*, p. 12.
45. *Ibid.*, p. 12.
46. *Ibid.*, p. 12.
47. *Ibid.*, p. 13.
48. *Ibid.*, p. 13.
49. *Ibid.*, p. 14.
50. *Ibid.*, p. 15.
51. Holmes, Robert, L. (May 1977) 'Nozick On Anarchism', Political Theory, Vol. 5, No. 2, May 1977.
52. Nozick, *op. cit.*, pp. 16-17.
53. *Ibid.*, p. 18.
54. Smith, Adam, (1869) 'The Theory of Morals'.
55. Sentiments, London, Alex Murray, p. 163.
56. Smith, Adam, 'The Wealth of Nations', p. 423.
57. Cropsey, Joseph (1979), 'The Invisible Hand : Moral and Political Considerations' in 'Adam, Smith and Modern Political Economy' Ed. Gerald O'Driscoll, Iowa, Iowa University Press, p. 171.
58. Overton. H. Taylor, (1960), 'A History of Economic Thought' New York : Mcgraw Hill, p. 70.
59. Wilhelm, Hasbach (1890) Leipzig, Duncker and Humboldt, Quoted In Adam Smith and Modern Political Economy, *op. cit.*, p. 51.
60. Rosenberg N. (1979) 'Laissez–Faire Revisited', In Adam Smith and Modern Political Economy, *Ibid.*, p. 24.
61. Nozick, p. 16.
62. *Ibid.*, p. 17.
63. *Ibid.*, p. 17.

64. *Ibid.*, p. 17.

65. *Ibid.*, p. 23.

66. *Ibid.*, p. 24.

67. *Ibid.*, p. 24.

68. *Ibid.*, p. 25.

69. *Ibid.*, p. 25.

70. *Ibid.*, p. 26.

71. *Ibid.*, p. 26.

72. *Ibid.*, p. 52.

73. *Ibid.*, pp. 118-19.

74. Holmes, Robert L., *op. cit*, p. 247.

75. Nozick, *op. cit.*, p. 33.

76. *Ibid.*, p. 52.

77. *Ibid.*, p. 52.

78. *Ibid.*, p. 54.

79. *Ibid.*, pp. 54-55.

80. *Ibid.*, p. 55.

81. *Ibid.*, p. 55.

82. *Ibid.*, p. 56.

83. *Ibid.*, p. 56.

84. *Ibid.*, p. 56.

85. *Ibid.*, p. 57.

86. *Ibid.*, p. 64.

87. *Ibid.*, p. 64.

88. *Ibid.*, p. 65.

89. *Ibid.*, p. 66.
90. *Ibid.*, pp. 66-67.
91. *Ibid.*, p. 67.
92. *Ibid.*, p. 67.
93. *Ibid.*, p. 71.
94. *Ibid.*, p. 72.
95. *Ibid.*, p. 73.
96. *Ibid.*, p. 88.
97. *Ibid.*, p. 79.
98. *Ibid.*, p. 79.
99. *Ibid.*, p. 87.
100. *Ibid.*, p. 87.
101. *Ibid.*, p. 101.
102. *Ibid.*, p. 101.
103. *Ibid.*, p. 105.
104. *Ibid.*, p. 105.
105. *Ibid.*, p. 109.
106. *Ibid.*, p. 109.
107. *Ibid.*, p. 109.
108. *Ibid.*, pp. 112-113.
109. *Ibid.*, p. 113.
110. *Ibid.*, p. 113.
111. *Ibid.*, p. 114.
112. *Ibid.*, p. 114.
113. *Ibid.*, p. 114.

114. *Ibid.*, p. 115.

115. Krader, Lawrence, (1968) 'Formation of The State'. Englewood Cliffs, NJ. Prentice Hall, pp. 21-22, quoted in ASU, pp. 116-17.

116. Nozick, *op. cit.*, p. 117.

117. *Ibid.*, p. 117.

118. *Ibid.*, p. 23.

119. *Ibid.*, p. 118.

120. *Ibid.*, p. 297.

121. *Ibid.*, p. 310.

122. *Ibid.*, p. 309.

123. *Ibid.*, p. 312.

124. *Ibid.*, p. 312.

125. *Ibid.*, p. 297.

126. *Ibid.*, p. 127.

127. *Ibid.*, p. 313.

128. *Ibid.*, p. 315.

129. *Ibid.*, p. 316.

130. *Ibid.*, p. 316.

131. *Ibid.*, p. 316.

132. *Ibid.*, pp. 316-17.

133. *Ibid.*, p. 317.

134. *Ibid.*, p. 319.

135. *Ibid.*, p. 320.

136. *Ibid.*, p. 320.

137. *Ibid.*, p. 329.

138. *Ibid.*, p. 330.

139. *Ibid.*, p. 331.

140. *Ibid.*, pp. 331-32.

141. *Ibid.*, p. 332.

142. *Ibid.*, p. 333.

143. *Ibid.*, p. 333.

144. *Ibid.*, p. 333.

145. *Ibid.*, p. 333.

146. *Ibid.*, pp. 333-34.

5

The Great Debate : Rawls and Nozick

This chapter will be a comparative study of the political theories of John Rawls and Robert Nozick–the two dominant souls of our time. While Rawls represents the Keynesian tradition of liberal egalitarianism, Nozick epitomises the classic liberal view of the free market and the minimal state. Before I venture into a comparison of these two political theorists, I would like to give a brief summary of their views.

After the Second World War, there was a renewed defence of liberal ideas, while earlier, with the rise of fascist and communist regimes in the 1920s and 1930s, there had been many gloomy predictions regarding the demise of liberal values. The Second World War saw liberal thinking ranging across a fairly wide ideological spectrum–resulting in its becoming the only legitimate form of political discourse. Now all major groupings seem to be employing the liberal language of rights, freedom and equality to express and legitimise their views. From new right conservatives to democratic socialists, it seems all are liberals now.

This vigorous revival of liberal political theory specially in the USA, also represents the diverse and contradictory strands of liberal ideology–thus, we find Rawls and Nozick, two intellectual giants of our time–speaking the liberal language but with differing accents.

Speaking from the diverse angles of liberal thought, 'Nozick appeals to the more libertarian individual liberals, whereas Rawls is rapidly becoming the patron saint of the social liberal persuasion.'[1]

John Rawls

John Rawls can be credited with the revival of political theory in recent times; his path-breaking book. 'A Theory of Justice' (1971) laying a novel foundation of moral political theory. For about one hundred years J.S. Mill's utilitarian argument of liberalism had been the basis of moral philosophy and he justified a welfare state, catering to the majority of the people. For Mill, the basis of liberalism was utility, understood in terms of the 'greatest good of the greatest number', and not liberty. Challenging this notion of utility, Rawls argued that justice, and not utility should be the basis of a liberal state. Rendering a major blow to the moral appeal of socialism, he maintained that his liberal state can provide equality without sacrificing liberty, and it can be just and caring for the least advantaged person.

After having dealt at length with the shortcomings of utilitarianism, he proceeds to establish his own conception of justice–based on the contract method, which he believes is not unfair, partial or selfish, and does not maximise anything.

Like the contract theorists, Rawls begins from the assumption of original and social equality and assumes that individuals in their 'original position' would choose to construct society on the basis of these two principles."[2]

To quote Rawls :

'I then present the main idea of justice as fairness a Theory of Justice that generalises and carries to a higher level of abstraction the traditional conception of social contract."[3]

In the Original Position, men try to promote their own personal interests, since they are rational beings, but they are not able to use their rationality for the sake of individual ends because they do not know their own personal and particular interests. But despite this, they have enough knowledge to choose the 'two principles of justice' from among the different alternatives present in the original position. They being the best pair on which one can depend for the just distribution of benefits and burdens of the society.

The twin principles of justice which the individuals choose in the original position are :

1. Each person is to have an equal right to the most extensive basic liberty compatible with a similar liberty for others.

2. Social and economic inequalities are to be arranged so that they are both (a) reasonably accepted to be the everyone's advantage (b) attached to positions and offices open to all."[4]

His first principle is the principle of equality–which deals with the basic liberties of individuals Rawls' second principle is the principle of distribution, having both the provisions–of equal distribution and unequal distribution and on the basis of the distribution principles, he insists that if there is to be any inequality, in the distribution, it must be for the benefit of the poor class.

He emphasises the fact that when these two principles are applied to the 'basic structure of the society–a just social order results'. Practically speaking, it is in a democratic society that such a social order can be found, and this democratic society is based on the provisions of the constitution, which is enacted by a constitutional convention. This constitutional convention, theoretically speaking, comes into effect after the 'two principles of justice have been agreed upon in the original position.

Thus, in his just social order, the interests of all and specially the interests of the least advantaged persons are safeguarded.

As mentioned earlier, his 'A Theory of Justice' was the culmination of the intellectual churning that had been going on in his mind since the 1950s, and in the preface of the book he says, "In presenting a Theory of Justice, I have tried to bring together, into one coherent view the ideas expressed in the papers I have written over the past dozen years or so."

His second major book, 'Political Pluralism' was published in 1992–and is considered to be more mature and covers the thought experiments that were undertaken by him after the publication of 'A Theory of Justice' in 1971.

In this book, he addresses himself to the task of answering the question : How can a stable and just society of free and equal citizens live in concord when confronted with the plurality of incompatible and irreconcilable doctrines–religious philosophical and moral, which coexist within the framework of a pluralistic democratic society?

In order to answer this question, he redefines a 'well-ordered society'–which is no longer a society united in its basic moral beliefs but in its political conception of justice–which is the focus of an overlapping consensus.

As the front flap of 'Political Liberalism' proclaims :

'Political liberalism represents the distinctive form of liberalism resting on an idea of free public reason that yields new insights into the questions of justice facing us today in our pluralistic society.'

In the introduction of 'Political Liberalism' he concedes that in 'A Theory of Justice', 'the idea of a well-ordered society of justice as fairness is unrealistic.'

In 'A Theory of Justice', he had tried to find an alternative to utilitarianism, and in so doing, he adopted some unrealistic conceptions which, he self-admittedly tried to rectify in 'Political Liberalism.'

Robert Nozick

Robert Nozick was one of the twentieth century's most influential thinkers, who was known for his wide-ranging intellect. Hailed as a 'brilliant and fearless thinker', his controversial and challenging views gained him considerable attention and influence in the entire world. He was the recipient of many awards and honours. The presidential citation from the American psychological association in 1998 described him as 'one of the most brilliant and original living philosophers.'

When he died on 23rd January 2002, he left behind a massive intellectual legacy in the form of unique books and ideas, which have influenced generations of readers and will continue to influence people for generations to come.

His first book "Anarchy, State and Utopia" (1974) transformed him from a young philosophy professor, known only within his profession to a theoretician of a national political movement. As mentioned earlier, this book was written as a critique of 'A Theory of Justice' (1971) by his Harvard colleague John Rawls. This book, as we have already seen, provided a philosophical underpinning for the bureaucratic welfare state, a methodically reasoned argument in defense of a redistributive state, which would rightly and legitimately redistribute wealth in order to help the poor and the disadvantaged.

'Anarchy, State and Utopia' (1974) argued that the rights of the individual are primary ('individuals have rights, and there are things no person or group may do to them'– Nozick ASU, 54, p. ix).

Minimal State

Beginning from this premise, he went on to argue that only a minimal state, limited to the narrow functions of protection against force, theft, fraud, enforcement of contracts' is justified, and any more extensive state which interferes in the moral sphere of an individual is unjust, illegitimate and unfair.

His minimal state arises voluntarily from the Lockean state of nature which he is credited with having revived.

After reviving the Lockean state of nature in the II chapter of 'Anarchy State and Utopia' Nozick contends, that from this state of nature, will arise mutual protection agencies, if some persons do not act morally and violate the rights of others.

"From a state of nature (SN) in which people possess natural rights and generally act morally (making this a 'most favoured' situation of anarchy), there will, if some persons do not act morally and violate the rights of others, evolve first Mutual Protection Associations (MPAs) in which individuals purchase protection against others like a market–governed economic goods and eventually a dominant protective association (DPA) an MPA of preeminent power in a territory. The DPA will in turn eventually evolve into an ultra minimal state (UMS) a DPA in which protection is purchased as an economic goods but which in addition has a monopoly of force. The latter, finally will evolve into a Minimal State (MS), which in addition to possessing the two features of the UMS, will make a 'redistribution' of protection to certain independents (non-clients of the UMS) at costs to the clients."[5]

Thus, from the above we gather, that the process of the evolution of the MS is a long drawn-out one. There are four stages in this process:

(a) From state of nature to mutual protection associations.

(b) From MPAs to DPA.

(c) From DPA to a UMS.

(d) From a UMS to an MS.

$$SN \rightarrow MPAs\ DPA \rightarrow UMS \rightarrow MS$$

In this context he talks of the 'invisible hand explanations' ("every individual intends only his own gain, and he is in this, as in so many other cases, led by an invisible hand to promote an end which was no part of his intention"). In other words, the state arises from anarchy even though no one intends this. Such invisible-hand explanations. 'Show how some overall pattern or design, which one would have thought had to be produced by an individuals' or group's successful attempt to realise the pattern, instead was produced and maintained by a process that in no way had the overall pattern or design "in mind".[6]

The DPA, no doubt has preeminent power in a territory, but it falls short of being a state due to two reasons :

(a) It lacks the requisite monopoly over the use of force in a territory.

(b) It cannot provide protection for all in its territory.

To quote Nozick again :

"Thus it appears that the dominant protective agency in a territory not only lacks the requisite monopoly over the use of force, but also fails to provide protection for all in its territory, and so the dominant agency appears to fall short of being a state."[7]

So, without deliberately intending to do so (IHE), an ultra minimal state is produced by the people which is a 'social arrangement intermediate between the scheme of private protective association and the night-watchman state.... An ultra minimal state maintains a monopoly over all use of force except that necessary in immediate self-defense....'[8]

It provides protection and enforcement services only to those who purchase its protection and enforcement policies and those people who don't buy a protection contract don't get protected.

The UMS's shortcoming lies in the fact that it cannot provide services for all. Hence : "the transition from an ultra minimal state to a minimal state must occur. It would be morally impermissible for persons to maintain the monopoly in the ultra minimal state without providing protective services for all, even if this requires specific "redistribution". The operators of the ultra minimal state are morally obligated to produce the minimal state.'[9]

Thus, the minimal state arises out of the shortcomings of the stage preceding it. Because of the shortcomings of the SN, the MPA emerges and eventually a DPA–which has pre-eminent power in a territory–The DPA arises out of the need of a counterweight against the various protective associations which might aggress against each other. The DPA gives rise to the UMS which lacks the all-pervasive service-providing capacity–hence–the minimal state, which provides services to all–and is morally justified.

Entitlement Theory of Justice

In Part II 'Beyond the minimal state?' Nozick advocates the entitlement Theory of Justice (Chapter 7th) (149-231).

Libertarians, as we know, relate justice with the market and this is best expressed in Nozick's theory of entitlement. Libertarianism defends market freedom and demand limitations on the use of state for social welfare policies. Redistributive taxation schemes to implement liberal welfare theory of socio-economic equality are considered inherently wrong by libertarians. The rights of the people are sacrosanct, and they cannot be violated. According to Nozick the most important right is the right over oneself–the right of self-ownership–in other words, 'what one owns and what is owned are one and the same and the whole person', i.e., if I own myself, then I own my talents and also what proceeds from my talents–what proceeds from my talents cannot be transferred to the disadvantaged because it violates the principle of self-ownership–which is an important right.

As Nozick says in the preface of ASU "Individuals have rights, and there are things no person or group may do to them (without violating their rights) so strong and far reaching are these rights that they raise the question of what, if anything the state and its officials may do"[10]–

Since the minimal state is limited to the narrow function of protection against force, theft, fraud, enforcement of contracts, and so on is justified, any more extensive state will violate persons rights not to be forced to do certain things, and is unjustified. Some people cannot be coercively taxed by the state in order to rectify the inequalities rampant in society. As Nozick puts it :

"However, we are not in the position of children who have been given portions of pie by someone who now makes last minute adjustments to rectify careless cutting."[11]

It thus follows that in the minimal state there is no public education, transportation, roads or parks–because it involves coercive taxation of some people against their will, and is a blatant violation of the principle. From each as they choose to each as they are chosen.

According to Nozick, the entitlement Theory of Justice is based on three principles:

1. The original acquisition of holdings or the principle of justice in acquisition.
2. The transfer of holdings from one person to another.
3. The principle of rectification of injustice, i.e., how to deal with acquisitions which are unjustly acquired or transferred.

The need for the third principle arises, because "Not all actual situations are generated in accordance with the two principles of justice in holdings : the principle of justice in acquisition and the principle of justice in transfer.

The existence of past injustice (previous violations of the two principles of justice in holdings) raises the third major topic under justice in holdings : the rectification of injustice in holdings."[12]

The gist of the entitlement theory can be stated thus, in Nozick's words :

"From each according to what he chooses to do, to each according to what he makes for himself (perhaps with the contracted aid of others) and what others choose to do for him and choose to give him of what they have been given previously (under this maxim) and haven't yet expended or transferred."[13]

This gist can be further simplified as a slogan :

"From each as they choose, to each as they are chosen."

We see that the essence of Nozick's Entitlement theory is self-ownership–'no one else owns me, and that includes my whole self, thick with particular traits'. In other words, I am my own master–my fads, my foibles, my idiosyncrasies belong to me, as do my good traits–and no one can claim to be my owner because I own myself. In short "We are 'entitled' in his view to anything that we have acquired without violating anyone else's rights .... our natural assets, our various talents and attributes, and to whatever of value our deployment of these talents and attributes can manufacture."[14]

Rawls and Nozick : A Comparison

A comparison of the views of Robert Nozick and John Rawls is essential because both are two prominent liberals of our time.

When Robert Nozick gave a critique of Rawls' 'A Theory of Justice', the whole debate surrounding liberalism–the welfare of the poor ... the role of the state, redistribution taxation divided the movement into liberals and libertarians.

Lending his vehement voice to the torrent of criticism that Rawls'. 'A Theory of Justice' faced, Robert Nozick, criticised it from the libertarian perspective, which emphasised the fact that force is to be confined to dealing with aggression, and may not be used to any other end, however noble it may seem–that includes the welfare of others such as the poor.

Advancing the Lockean notion of the inalienable right to life, liberty and property, Nozick criticised Rawls on the ground, that the Rawlsian state, with its redistributive policies is an assault on the sovereign individual, who has the right to live in any way he pleases. He argues that the redistribution programmes of a welfare state are unjust, because they are non-consensual limitations on individual freedom.

There are many parameters to the Rawls/Nozick debate, and many facets of it to consider–like–justice, rights, contract, state, welfare, redistribution, liberty, etc. In the following pages I will attempt a comparative and critical evaluation of the Rawls/Nozick debate, incorporating these facets.

A strong believer in social justice, Rawls upholds redistribution, while Nozick is vehemently hostile to it. For Rawls, it is an interventionist state, which can be instrumental in bringing about redistribution, whereas Nozick believes that an interventionist or all-pervasive state undermines individual liberty.

The welfare of the least-advantaged is uppermost in the Rawlsian scheme, whereas as Fraser King, maintains, in the Nozickean scheme, 'the poor and the needy do not have any right to welfare...."[15]

For Nozick, liberty is the only meaningful value, and all other values are low in priority, whereas for Rawls, it is equality that gets the upper berth.

Nozick waxes eloquent about self-ownership, emphasising that an individual is his own master and whatever rights he has, impose 'moral constraints' on what governments and other individuals may do to them.

While Nozick suggests a return to classical liberal principles of laissez faire, emphasising that governments have no legitimate grounds for meddling with capitalistic acts between consenting adults, Rawls introduces principles of distributive justice into liberal theory, which is denounced by Nozick, who counters it with a libertarian theory of social equity based preeminently on individual rights. Taking his cue from Locke, Nozick believes that individual rights are of prime importance, and that there is no procedure to preserve or enhance the greater good that justifies the infringement of individual rights.

Both resort to a contract, but while Nozick has revived the Lockean state of nature, Rawls has tried to build on the work of Rousseau and specially Kant.

Contract : Traditionally understood, the contract theory, tried to justify a political order, on the basis of a state of nature, which was a conception of a pre-political human existence–coupled with a social contract. For Hobbes, the state of nature was a state of war, where life was 'nasty, brutish and short'. For Locke, the state of nature was relatively placid and prosperous, where people discover morality through reason, Rousseau envisages amoral, entirely independent individuals who are noble savages, who form pre-moral associations, resulting from familial and filial interdependence—and because of their natural freedom–(man is born free, yet is everywhere in chains), they cannot be ruled legitimately unless they consent to be ruled by an artificial authority–so a social contract comes into existence.

As a writer puts it :

"Hobbes' state of nature is intolerable and must give way to the state; Locke's moral relations are hobbled by uncertainty without state enforcement of natural rights. Rousseau's state of nature is bound to degenerate initially into philistine civilisation but is populated by individuals whose most exalted capability, their potential for moral interaction will be stunted unless they embrace political relations."[16]

When we look at the Contract method, of Rawls and Nozick, we come across certain differences.

In the words of an analyst :

"Rawls employs a hypothetical contract like Nozick but its structure and explanatory status are very different. Nozick's appeal was to a modified version of Locke's state of nature, but Rawls sees himself as building on the work of Rousseau and especially Kant who sought to give a philosophical foundation to Rousseau's idea of the general will" (Rawls, 1971 : 264).[17]

After having revived the Lockean state of nature, Nozick reiterates in the concluding paragraph of the first chapter : "We shall begin with individuals in something sufficiently similar to Locke's state of nature"[18]–as he believes, that this 'state of nature situation is the best anarchic situation one reasonably could hope for"[19] because, in this situation people generally 'satisfy moral constrants'.

While Nozick takes his cue from John Locke, the Rawlsian contract is closer to Kant's conception of contract. Without talking directly of any contract, the conception of the contract sneaks into the Kantian vocabulary when he talks of universal state, and when he refers to the state as 'a necessary good.'

Although Rawls' envisages a state of affairs, very similar to the contractualists, he calls it the Original Position, wherein the principles of justice are chosen behind a veil of ignorance, by rational people, who however, have no particular knowledge about their real selves, hence they cannot use their rationality for the purpose of satisfying their individual ends.

While, his theory of Justice 'generalises and carries to a higher level of abstraction the traditional conception of social contract,' the fact and which he himself concedes is, that he has resorted to the contract, simply for the reasons of theoretical convenience, he does not trace the origin of the state as developing from that situation.

Whereas, for Nozick, the Lockean state of nature, is the starting point from which the minimal state voluntarily emerges.

Nozick's Minimal Libertarian State Vs Rawls' Liberal Egalitarian State

As mentioned earlier, both Rawls and Nozick were two prominent liberals of the 1970s–who talked the liberal language but with differing accents and intonations.

For both, liberty was sacrosanct, but for Rawls, the danger to liberty came from a distributively unjust society–and, he believed that a distributively just and equal society could be possible only on the basis of an extensive state–'one that reflects and implements the will of the people who own it, that strives to end poverty and secure equal opportunities for all ...... and that strives to create not only a democratic polity but also a democratic social structure."[20]

To Nozick, the danger to liberty comes from an all-pervasive egalitarian state, because it interferes in the realm of individual rights.

In this context, an analyst talks of two prominent types of liberalism, in terms of how they conceive of liberty. In the first category, she includes libertarians like Nozick, who, she believes are 'Locke's descendants', who are "invariably committed to markets and market based solutions .... because........ these Lockeans say, markets best realise freedom ...... The Lockeans focus on the danger to liberty coming from the power of the state and thus advocate minimal government."[21]

In the second category she includes liberals like Rawls; who, being opponents of the Lockeans, "have their source in ideas first put forward by Rousseau."[22]

These liberals believe that the remedy of the social ills is not a limited but an active state, which tries to ameliorate the condition of the 'least advantaged' on the basis of its redistribution programmes, on the other hand, Nozick believes that such an extensive state is unjust, because it interferes in the 'Moral Space' of an individual.

As a writer says :

"Robert Nozick's widely admired book, 'Anarchy, State and Utopia' (1974) took as a postulate the view that human beings have rights which impose moral constraints on what governments and other individuals may do to them."[23]

As Nozick says in the concluding paragraph of 'Anarchy, State and Utopia' :

"The minimal state treats us as inviolate individuals, who may not be used in certain ways by others as means or tools or instruments or resources, it treats us as persons having rights with the dignity this constitutes ..... How dare any state or group of individuals do more or less."[24]

In the words of Fraser King and Mike Mills :

"Rawls argues in favour of positive state action to promote the individual pursuit of the good life and as such relies upon the state doing more than simply guaranteeing to individuals choices in how they want to live. So there is likely to be some redistribution of resources by the state to allow for a greater equality of opportunity to pursue the good life than would be possible under a predominantly market led system."[25]

On the other hand, Nozick, as we have seen, "takes a much more minimal view of the freedoms necessary for liberalism to work and would happily rest with the state doing little more than, for example, facilitating the free market and preserving law and order. This is a very limited, minimalist state which keeps us free from coercion but does not promote positive freedoms to do what we want."[26]

Primarily, the Rawls/Nozick debate revolves "around the extent to which individuals can be defined without reference to their social attachments and the degree to which the state should facilitate greater equality of opportunity than markets would ordinarily allow."[27]

In the Western democracies, most apparently in Britain and the United States, there has been a debate about the relative virtues of the market order as the allocator of resources, as opposed to state intervention.

Libertarians like Nozick, hold that the state, which pursues a variety of goals, is solely responsible for a variety of socio-economic ills, and that 'more markets therefore ought to lead to less state'–They believe that the welfare activities, and redistribution that a more than minimal state resorts to, saps the character of a nation.

There are many questions, bristling with difficulty–questions that are raised by the Rawls/Nozick debate. Does spoon feeding resorted to by a Rawlsian state really sap the character of a nation, or as George Watson puts it: "Are the social services to be regarded as crutches, necessary while so many are unable to walk freely as they would like but to be discarded as soon as they are able to use their own legs? Or are they, to be considered a permanent feature...."[28]

This has indeed been a major issue of political conflict in the last two decades. While Nozick argues against what, he calls patterned principles of justice, which require interference with consensual economic interaction, thus making it unjust and wrong, Rawls justifies these principles on the basis of social justice-which an extensive state is expected to provide.

In the words of a writer : "Nozick's is a theory that gives primacy to liberty over any attempts to undermine distributive inequality; Rawls seeks to construct a theory in which commitment to liberty and equality are compatible."[29]

In the major debate, "Rawls supplied the philosophical framework for the side of the debate, that advocates public policies directed at improving the relative distributions of the least advantaged, Robert Nozick's, 'Anarchy, State and Utopia' (1974) supplied a framework for the other."[30]

Both Rawls and Nozick, however, believe in the neutrality of the state. In the words of a writer :

".... the liberal state is presented as a neutral arbiter or aggregator of different individual interests. Even in Rawls' liberal corporatist account, the state's *raison d'etre* is to enable individuals to pursue their individual conceptions of the good. He differs from Nozick only in his account of how this is to be achieved and what it entails in practice. Both writers view the (legitimate) state as neutral among citizens, performing essentially regulative functions."[31]

Nozick's Entitlement Theory of Justice/Rawls' Theory of Justice

Part II Chapter VII of 'Anarchy State and Utopia', entitled 'Beyond the minimal state' deals with his Entitlement theory in Section I, and Section II of this chapter is devoted to Rawls' theory of distributive justice.

Nozick's Theory of Justice, which is elaborately dealt with, in this section of the book stands opposed to that of Rawls which he has outlined in 'A Theory of Justice' 1971 and which to quote Nozick is a 'powerful deep, subtle, wide-ranging systematic work in moral and political philosophy', which has not seen its like since the writings of John Stuart Mill. It is a fountain of illuminating ideas integrated together into a lovely whole.'[32]

Although Nozick sings paeans in favour of 'A Theory of Justice', he goes on to refute his theory, which, no doubt, is deep and elegant,' but not without 'deep-lying inadequacies'. For Rawls, justice is synonymous with fairness–it is seen as a particular pattern of social arrangements, adjusting entitlements and resources in as neutral and fair a manner as possible, whereas Nozick believes that: "the term 'distributive justice' is not a neutral one. Hearing the term 'distribution', most people presume that some thing or mechanism uses some principles or criterion to give out a supply of things.... However, we are not in the position of children who have been given portions of pie by someone and who now makes last minute adjustments to rectify careless cutting."[33]

The rectification of 'careless cutting' would involve redistribution, which, in Nozick's view is a patterned device which is incompatible with a minimal state–and such redistribution would violate peoples' rights–which are inalienable, and have to be respected at all costs. For him, individuals rights are so fundamental, and the constraints upon others' actions so strong that only the minimal state can be justified. As Nozick says in the preface :

"Individuals have rights and there are things no person or group may do to them (without violating their rights). So strong and far-reaching are these rights....."[34]

He further states :

'A minimal state, limited to the narrow functions of protection against force, theft, fraud, enforcement of contracts, and so on, is justified; that any more extensive state will violate persons' rights."[35]

The implications that follow from this are :

(a) The state may not use its coercive apparatus for the purpose of getting some citizens to aid others.

(b) It may not prohibit or order activities of people for their own good or protection.

If the state does something against the individual for which he is entitled, it is a case of sheer injustice, if the state takes away the inalienable rights to which the individual is entitled the state is guilty of an unjust act.

Nozick's theory is based on the assumption that an individual's rights are prior to the state–they inhere in an individual because he is an individual. No state has ever given these rights to him, and no state can take away these rights from him through any arrangement. There are certain entitlements that rights yield, and justice for Nozick, lies in not disrupting individual entitlements through any patterned device–and this can be possible only in a minimal state–not in any more extensive state. The minimal state, conversely means, where there are the minimum of laws and the maximum of liberty. His passion for individual's basic rights– makes him a defender of Locke's natural rights theory in the present century.

Nozick believes that almost every principle of distributive justice is patterned.

'To each according to his moral merit or needs or marginal product or how hard he tries, ... and so on.'

The entitlement theory, on the other hand is not patterned, and a theory is 'patterned if it specifies that a distribution is to vary along with some natural dimension.'[36]

Rawls emphasised the fact that the essence of common good or justice lies in the distribution of primary–goods which are of two types :

Social goods (income, wealth, opportunities, power, rights liberties) and natural goods (health, intelligence, imagination, natural talent).

Rawlsian justice demands that these goods should be distributed equally, unless inequalities in the distribution of goods are so arranged as to the advantage of the least favoured. As a writer puts it, "common good lies in the redistribution of primary goods. Ideally, they should be distributed equally, But if some inequalities benefit everyone....... then they must be accepted by everyone.'

On the other hand, Nozick's entitlement Theory of Justice is opposed to the very idea making talents and natural assets as the Common Pool, to be distributed according to the principles of social justice.

As he so succinctly puts it :

"No one has a right to something whose realisation requires certain uses of things and activities that other people have rights and entitlements over."[38]

This is a reflection of the underlying Kantian principle that 'individuals are ends and not merely means, they may not be sacrificed or used for the achieving of others ends without their consent. Individuals are inviolable.'[39]

Quoting Kant, he says, "Act in such a way that you always treat humanity, whether in your own person or in the person of any other, never simply as a means, but always at the same time as an end."[40]

Nozick believes that since an individual and his rights are sacrosanct, no individual can be used for the benefit of others, or, for the benefit of a so called 'social entity'–As he says :

"But there is no social entity with a good that undergoes some sacrifice for its own good. There are only individual people, different individual people, with their own individual lives."[41]

Justice and an overall social good is merely an eye wash. It befools individuals into sacrificing themselves for an imaginary social good. He further says :

"He does not get some overbalancing good from his sacrifice, and no one is entitled to force this upon him–least of all a state or government that claims his allegiance and that therefore scrupulously must be neutral between its citizens."[42]

While Rawls believed that a state can intervene in order to benefit the least advantaged, for Nozick such an idea is atrocious.

For him, individual rights are so strong that only a minimal state or a night-watchman state which is limited to the narrow functions of protection against force, theft, fraud, enforcement of contracts and so on, is justified.

While Rawls sees justice as a particular pattern of social arrangements, adjusting entitlements and resources in as neutral a manner as possible (justice as fairness), for Nozick, justice is not a question of attempting to organise or reorganise society and its institutions to achieve a particular distribution, for then, it becomes a type of patterned distributive justice, which he strongly condemns, as it would involve appropriating the actions of other persons.'

Justice, for Nozick is a matter of how the distribution has come about, what one is entitled to, and last, but not the least, it is a matter of protection of one's entitlements–and such a type of justice is compatible with a minimal state.

His concept of minimal state and his intense passion for individual basic rights–specially the right to property make him a defender of Locke's theory in the present century.

In a nutshell, when we compare the two theories of justice, we reach the conclusion, that while Rawls favours distributive justice, Nozick vehemently opposes it, Nozick begins his argument with individual rights, and Rawls' starting point is social obligation while Nozick upholds and extols the virtues of a minimal state, Rawls defends a liberal democratic welfare state, the function of which is to distribute primary goods in such a manner that it benefits the least advantaged.

Social Cooperation : Views of Rawls and Nozick

Nozick doesn't see eye to eye with Rawls when Rawls says that it is social cooperation which creates the problem of distributive justice. Nozick asks :

"Would there be no problem of justice and no need for a theory of Justice, if there was no social cooperation."[43]

Holding a plea for the entitlement Theory of Justice, Nozick asks :

"Why does social cooperation create the problem of distributive justice? ...... It cannot be said that there will be conflicting claims only when there is social cooperation; that individuals who produce independently and fend for themselves will not make claims of justice on each other."[44]

Nozick states that even ten Robinson Crusoes living in separate islands can make claims of justice on each other, although they are not bound by social cooperation. To quote him:

"If there were ten Robinson Crusoes, each working alone for two years on separate islands who discovered each other and the facts of their different allotments by radio communication via transmitters left twenty years earlier, could they not make claims on each other, supposing it were possible to transfer goods from one island to the next?"[45]

The different Robinson Crusoes would make claims on different grounds. One could stake a claim on grounds of need, the other could do it on the basis of the poverty of his island, and still another could do it on the grounds of his inferior capacity.

"Mightn't he say that justice demanded he be given some more by the others, claiming it unfair that he should receive so much less and perhaps be destitute, perhaps starving? He might go on to say that the different individual non-cooperative shares stem from differential natural endowments which are not deserved, and that the task of justice is to rectify these arbitrary facts and inequities."[46]

Nozick goes on to state that its not as if these claims will not be made in the social non-cooperation state–the point is that such claims 'clearly would be without merit, because, in such a situation : Each individual deserves what he gets unaided by his own efforts or no one else can make a claim of justice against this holding.

Nozick maintains "It is pellucidly clear in this situation who is entitled to what, so no Theory of Justice is needed."[47]

Nozick maintains that the only purpose social co-operation serves is, to create ambiguity and confusion all around, with the result that it is difficult to pinpoint exactly who is entitled to what. He puts it better this way :

"On this view social cooperation introduces a muddying of the waters that makes it unclear or indeterminate who is entitled to what... Rather than saying that no Theory of Justice applies to this non-cooperate case. I would say that it is a clear case of application of the correct Theory of Justice: the entitlement theory."[48]

In other words, Nozick reiterates, that all other theories of justice are vague and confusing, and there is only one Theory of Justice that is correct-and that is the entitlement Theory of Justice.

Difference Principle

Rawls specifies the II principle as the difference principle, and this principle holds that the 'institutional structure is to be so designed that the worst-off group under it is, at least as well off as the worst-off group (not necessarily the some group) would be under any alternative institutional structure."[49]

Rawls argues that the persons in the original position will choose the difference principle, if they follow the minimax policy in making the significant choice of principles of justice.

Nozick does not see eye to eye with Rawls' difference principle and he expresses his disagreement in the following words :

"Still, we should question why individuals in the original position would choose a principle that focuses upon groups, rather than individuals."[50]

He further asks :

"Won't application of the minimax principle lead each person in the original position to favour maximising the position of the worst–off individual? To be sure, this principle would reduce questions of evaluating social institutions to the issue of how the unhappiest depressive fares .... Nor is it clear which groups are appropriately considered; why exclude the group of depressives or alcoholics or the representative paraplegic."[51]

Nozick further asserts :

"No doubt, the difference principle presents terms on the basis of which those less well endowed would be willing to co-operate. (What better terms would they propose for themselves?) But is this a fair agreement on the basis of which those worse endowed could expect the willing cooperation of others."[52]

Nozick views with suspicion Rawls' contention that in a just social order arrangements may be such that it is able to convince people–the better endowed ones–to sacrifice their personal interests for the interests of the less-endowed ones. Is this fair? Nozick wants to know.

"What does follow from the conclusion is a deep suspicion of imposing, in the name of fairness, constraints upon voluntary social cooperation (and the set of holdings that arise from it) so that those already benefitting most from this general cooperation benefit even more!"[53]

On the other hand, praising the difference principle for its fairness Rawls says :

"The difference principle, then seems to be a fair basis on which those best endowed, or more fortunate in their social circumstances, could expect others to collaborate with them when some workable arrangement is a necessary condition of the good of all."[54] Nozick finds the use of the word 'Then' in the above sentence puzzling.

He wonders, how persons in the original position, 'who do not knowingly possess, or at any rate, utilise particular moral notions,' can know what is fair and what is unfair? Nozick asks :

"Are we to understand this as : someone in the original position wonders what to say to himself as/he then thinks of the possibility that he will turn out to be one of the better endowed?

And does he then say that the difference principle then seems a fair basis for cooperation despite the fact that, and even while, he is contemplating the possibility that he is better endowed or does he say then, that even later if and when he knows he is better endowed the difference principle will seem fair to him at the later time."[55]

Nozick contends that when Rawls is talking of the fairness of the difference principle, he cannot possibly be addressing himself to individuals in the original position, because they can have no idea about fairness or unfairness. As he says :

"I see no coherent way to incorporate how Rawls treats and speaks of the issue of the terms of cooperation between the better and the worse endowed into the structure and perspective of the original position."[56]

Moreover, Nozick also believes that 'Rawls' construction is incapable of yielding an entitlement or historical conception of distributive justice ... The whole procedure of persons choosing principles in Rawls' original position presupposes that no historical–entitlement conception of justice is correct.'[57]

According to Nozick's entitlement theory, Wilt Chamberlain is entitled to the $250,000 that he earns as a result of the contract that he had signed, whereby 25 cents from the price of each ticket of admission would go to him. He is so very much in demand, that his fans have willingly chosen to part with this money in order to see him play basket–ball. Hence, Wilt Chamberlain has an exclusive right over the $250,000 that he has earned, this is what Nozick's entitlement theory would have us believe, but Rawls would say that Chamberlain's talent is sheer brute luck, and this money is not the exclusive property of Chamberlain, but should be distributed in the society in such a way that it benefits the least advantaged.

Nozick states that as a governing principle, the difference principle is inadequate. Even when applied to a family of individuals who love one another, it appears to be inappropriate. "Should a family devote its resources to maximising the position of its least well off and least talented child, holding back the other children or using resources for their education and development only if they will follow a policy through their life times of maximising the position of their least fortunate sibling? Surely not. How then can this even be considered as the appropriate policy for enforcement in the wider society?[58]

Redistribution : Rawls and Nozick

While Rawls upholds redistribution, Nozick criticses it. He says that 'maintaintaining a distributional pattern is individualism with a vengeance!" It is recipient oriented.

Patterned Principles of Distributive Justice Necessiate Redistribution

Nozick believes that redistribution is a very serious flaw of patterned principles of distributive justice. To put it in his words :

"From the point of view of an entitlement theory, redistribution is a serious matter indeed, involving, as it does, the violation of people's rights."[59]

Furthermore, he says that 'taxation of earnings from labour is on par with forced labour.'

Citing the instance of two sorts of men, and the role of the taxation system he says that one man prefers working overtime and gaining more income and the other prefers leisure activities to working overtime, in such a situation, "It would be illegitimate for a tax system to seize some of a man's leisure (forced labour) for the purpose of serving the needy, how can it be legitimate for a tax system to seize some of a man's goods for that purpose."[60]

Aiming a few barbed questions at the redistributionists, he asks : 'Why should we treat the man whose happiness requires certain material goods or services differently from the man whose preferences and desires make such goods unnecessary for his happiness?'

"Why should the man who prefers seeing a movie (and who has to earn money for a ticket) be open to the required call to aid the needy, while the person who prefers looking at a sunset (and hence needs no extra money) is not?

"Why is the person with the non-material or non-consumption desire allowed to proceed unimpeded to his most favoured feasible alternative, whereas, the man whose pleasures or desires involve material things and who must work for extra money (thereby serving whomever considers his activities valuable enough to pay him) is constrained in what he can realise?"

He asks :

"Indeed, isn't it surprising that redistributionists choose to ignore the man whose pleasures are so easily attainable without extra labour, while adding yet another burden to the poor unfortunate who must work for his pleasures. If anything, one would have expected the reverse."[61]

This amply demonstrates Nozick's disenchantment with redistribution and taxation, which he holds at par with forced labour, while, for Rawls, this is absolutely important for the upliftment of the 'least advantaged.'

On the basis of the above views the following conclusions can be deduced regarding their views.

Views About Society

For the libertarian Nozick 'humanity is composed of individuals who are autonomous rational, self-interested utility maximisers. Individuals are conceived of as 'social atoms' that is to say they are independent of any social attachments and form interests independent of any moral obligation to society or community ..... Individuals are the best judges of what those interests may be.'[62]

On the other hand, Rawls is of the opinion, that society is a cooperative venture among individuals. Rawls' individual is an individual who is governed by rational self-interest and to realise this, he seeks the cooperation of others. As Rawls puts it :

"The society ... is typically marked by a conflict as well as by identity of interests."[63]

Rawls' implication is that being egoistic, man seeks his self-interest, but being rational enough, he also thinks in terms of the general good and for this he favours a social order that is in conformity with his basic nature.

Rights : Rawls and Nozick

Rights are social claims necessary for the development of the human personality and different theorists have enunciated different theories and viewpoints regarding rights.

A great champion of individual rights, Nozick, toeing the Lockean line, declares, in the preface of 'Anarchy, State and Utopia', in very strong terms :

'Individuals have rights and there are things no person or group may do to them'. He believes that these rights are 'so strong and far-reaching' that they leave very little for the state to do. In the words of a writer, "liberal thought holds that the ultimate authority on which government should rest lies not in the divine sanction of God, but rather in the natural right of the individual to seek his own self-preservation."[64] This basic assumption is reflected both in Nozick and Locke.

The major feature of Locke's position is the firm conviction that the ultimate authority resides in the individual's inalienable right to self-preservation and he proclaims, 'Man being born ... with a title to perfect freedom and an uncontrolled enjoyment of all the rights and privileges of the law of nature equally with any other man or number of men in the world, hath by nature a power not only to preserve his property, that is, his life, liberty and estate.....'[65]

For both Locke and Nozick self-preservation is closely associated with the right to property–hence the inescapable conclusion is that once inalienable rights have been shown to be necessary, the individuals are at liberty to assert their rights–'but unless a properly constituted public authority defines the entitlements conferred by these rights ... rights assertion becomes fraught with distrust and .... conflict.'[66] Hence, a minimal state is the only state which is legitimate, morally inspiring and just, and any more extensive state, is unjust and illegitimate, because by resorting to social engineering, it violates the moral sphere of the individual.

A staunch supporter of the principle of self-ownership, unlike Rawls, Nozick believes that an individual is his own master, and no state can treat him/her as a means to an end, hence redistribution taxation which Rawls upholds, is criticised by Nozick on the grounds of the self-ownership argument, which maintains that the state cannot use its coercive machinery for the purpose of getting some citizens to aid others because that way it would be violating the inviolable rights of the individuals–which, anyway have not been conferred on them by the state, but "are already possessed by each individual in a state of nature."

Rawls, on the other hand, believes in contractual rights, which are conferred on the individuals by the contract.

After conceiving a hypothetical contract, and the notion of the veil of ignorance, which results in the formulation of the twin principles of justice, Rawls then proceeds to ensure how justice could be applied to the social institutions and to their basic structure. He emphasises the fact that when the two principles of justice are applied to the basic structure of social institutions, a just order results, which requires an obligation from individuals regarding its dictates.

While applying the first principle–the principle of equality, to the basic structure, Rawls maintains that institutions should be such that they ensure equal basic liberty–which includes general liberties and political liberties. When he applies his second principle–the difference principle–the social order becomes complex, having a combination of both equality and inequality.

Rawls uses the words 'Rights' and 'Justice' interchangeably. For him, rights are embedded in justice– and they belong to all disinterested political individuals beyond the veil of ignorance–Unlike Locke, and Nozick who talk of natural rights and inalienable rights of an individual, Rawls believes that individuals had no natural rights except those which they chose unanimously in their original position–and which were accepted because of the considered judgement of the people.

On the other hand, when Nozick revives the Lockean state of nature he is also reviving the natural rights that exist there–namely, the rights to life, liberty and estate.

A libertarian society, by respecting the individual, respects his rights, and it allows the individuals to choose their lives either individually or with whomsoever they choose, aided by the voluntary co-operation of other individuals.

Nozick holds a very strong doctrine of individualistic rights, specially the right to acquire and hold property, in which, unlike Rawls, he can tolerate no interference.

Liberty : Nozick and Rawls

Although the concept of negative liberty had been replaced by the concept of positive liberty in the twentieth century, yet writers such as Robert Nozick revived it in the twentieth century.

Nozick identifies liberty with the natural right to self-ownership, in the sphere of which there should be no interference, either from any individual or group.

Passionately espousing the cause of self-ownership, and the autonomy of the individual, Nozick restricts the idea of freedom to the individual and his person, hence only a minimal state–the night-watchman state of classical liberalism–can protect the individuals from each other and from external threat. In the words of a writer 'the attempted defence of the minimal state, of course, depends on some claims about rights which are developed throughout 'Anarchy, State and Utopia, ... These are negative rights of non-interference, not positive rights to aid or assistance from others or the state."[67]

For Nozick, liberty, like the early liberal assumption of classical liberalism implies the absence of restraints–in simple terms it is 'liberty from' as distinct from 'liberty to'.

Restraints can be multi-dimensional–political, economic, civil, personal. True to his libertarian leanings, Nozick believes that, in order to protect the individual liberty, the state must perform the minimum of functions, but provide the maximum of liberty to the individuals.

In Part III, of 'Anarchy, State and Utopia', he provides a framework for utopia, which is equivalent to the minimal state-, wherein groups of individuals may voluntarily create sub-states. "One group could create a communist village, ... whilist another group creates a perfectionist society ..... A third might try to set up a model free market."[68]

The purpose behind this thought experiment is that Nozick wants us to imagine a world where all persons are at absolute liberty to inhabit a world of their own choosing– and this, in Nozick's terminology "is the best of all possible worlds and "whatever resulted from this process of universal self-determination would be optimal outcome compatible with the basic human right, embodied in Kant's maxim, not to be used as means to another's ends."[69]

In the economic sphere, individual liberty means free trade, laissez faire capitalist economy and an unlimited right to property–in fact, Nozickean liberty in the economic sphere is virtually identified with the protection of property, whereas in Rawls' liberal egalitarianism, it is the duty of the state to rectify these economic wrongs and provide economic equality, even if it means taxing some to benefit the least advantaged.

When we compare the Nozickean view of liberty with the Rawlsian view, we find Rawls upholding the positive view of liberty–which does not mean the absence of restraints, but the providing of such an atmosphere where an individual can realise his liberty–and on this ground, he justified the extension of social and welfare legislation, by an extensive state, which as we have seen, is severely criticised by Nozick, who sees such an all-pervasive state as an assault on individual liberty.

At the core of the Rawlsian concept of liberty lies the fact that there can be no liberty unless there is some measure of economic equality, and the model of a just society that he so painstakingly outlines, is a liberal democratic capitalist welfare state which is accountable, restricted and restrained and regulates free economy in many ways.

In his concept of liberty, he rises both above the laissez faire view of classical liberalism, which Nozick upholds, and which believes in individual liberty, but leaves the individual alone, and the highly controlled communist states which call for the submerging of the individual autonomy in the interest of social equality.

Rawls believes that liberty becomes real only when it is rooted in equality. His two principles of justice say :

1. Each person is to have an equal right to the most extensive basic liberty, compatible with a similar liberty for others.

2. Social and economic inequalities are to be so arranged so that they are both (a) Reasonably accepted to be to everyone's advantage (b) Attached to position and offices open to all.

Rawls believes that citizens in a just society must have equal basic liberties–political liberties, i.e., right to vote and to be eligible for public offices freedom of speech and assembly, freedom of thought, freedom of conscience, freedom to hold property, and freedom from arbitrary arrest and seizure. These liberties are defined by the rule of law.

Distinguishing between liberty and the worth of liberty, he states that liberty is represented by the complete system of liberties of equal citizenship, and the worth of liberty to persons and groups is proportional to their capacities to advance their ends within the framework of the system defined.

The first principle is the principle of equality, which he believes should be given priority over the second, but his difference principle emphasises the fact the undeserved inequalities need to be redressed, and if in the process of promoting equality, more resources are spent on the disadvantaged–then that is also justified.

While Nozick believes that only a non-interventionist state can promote liberty, Rawls believes that an interventionist state, armed with welfare measures, redistributive taxation, can bring about equality, because equality provides the basis on which liberty comes to acquire a positive meaning. Although Nozick believes in the equal rights of self-ownership, he does not defend it by an appeal to equality.

In a nutshell, while Nozick believes in natural rights, which existed in the Lockean state of nature, Rawls believes in contractual rights, which all disinterested individuals chose unanimously in the original position, which were accepted because of the considered judgment of the people.

As far as the substance of rights is concerned, Nozick's concept of rights is very strong, specially his right to property, which excludes welfare right of individuals and their protection by the state, whereas in the Rawlsian scheme, the rights should guarantee a fair share of economic resources–he gives certain egalitarian rights to citizens, emphasising that the social and economic in equalities should be so regulated that those deprived of material goods such as income, wealth, education, get the greater share.

Unlike Nozick, he believes that the individuals' rights to social goods should not depend upon their natural endowments–in fact, he strongly asserts that the tax system should be proportionately used to redistribute goods to the worst off, on the other hand, vehemently criticising redistribution, Nozick, argues that this might involve forceable redistribution ("you've been sighted for all these years; now one–or even both–of your eyes is to be transplanted to others)."[70]

Although both reject the utilitarian theory of rights believing in the Kantian dictum that individual is an end in himself/herself–however, for Nozick, the individual has an exclusive domain which cannot be breached without his consent, while for Rawls, the most important right is the right to a certain share in the resources of society, and it is the duty of the state to rectify the unequal distribution, by redistributive taxation, which will benefit the disadvantaged.

View Regarding Welfare : Rawls/Nozick

A staunch believer in the inalienable rights of the individual, Nozick holds that every individual has an exclusive domain which must not be breached without his consent, hence he argues that property rights of the individual exclude welfare rights and their protection by the state, on the other hand, Rawls believes in social justice and social engineering, therefore he holds a plea for welfare rights.

Rawls argues in favour of positive state action to enhance the individual pursuit of the good life since he believes in a greater equality of opportunity, the state has to perform welfare functions. The welfare of the least advantaged is uppermost in the Rawlsian scheme.

Referring to the actual operation of redistributive welfare programmes in the United States, Nozick maintains that, it has been noticed quite often that the poor in the United States are not net beneficiaries of the total of government programmes and interventions in the economy. He firmly believes that the welfare programmes are geared to protect the position of established firms against competition.

Self-ownership

Rawls argues that all the natural talents of people in a well-ordered society should be regarded as assets to be held in common by everyone–or to be more specific in Rawlsian vocabulary, justice represents "an agreement to regard the distribution of natural talents as a common asset and to share in the benefits of this distribution whatever it turns out to be."[71] He invokes the basic position that morally arbitrary inequalities should be mitigated, and this can be done by appropriating the fruits of our natural talents (athletic abilities, strength, beauty, writing talent, singing, talent) as common assets and distributing them in accordance with the criteria of justice, rather than in accordance with the capriciousness of nature-because, we did nothing to deserve the bounteous gifts from nature.

This argument stands in stark contrast to the libertarian doctrine of self-ownership, which is so stoutly defended by Nozick, who, while conceding that our natural capacities are undeserved, denies that they should be appropriated from us as individuals and relegated to a common pool of resources, because, Nozick believes, that we are entitled to our natural talents, and to whatever of value our deployment of these talents and attributes can manufacture, and to justify this claim, he invokes the much debated Chamberlain argument which is supposed to show intuitively that no 'patterned' theory of just distribution is defensible–that redistributive taxation is equivalent to using people as mere means, since it uses them without their consent.

Simply put, Nozick argues that if we own ourselves, it naturally follows, that we own what we produce absolutely–

so, what Chamberlain earns ($250,000) as a result of his talent at playing basket–ball belongs to him–and to no one else.

Conclusion

With the publication of his path-breaking book 'A Theory of Justice' (1971), John Rawls not only challenged the most dominant theory–(utilitarianism) of the day, but also revived normative political theory, which had been dormant for quite some time, and about which obituaries had started being written.

'Anarchy, State and Utopia', which was written in 1974, came as a rejoinder to Rawls' 'A Theory of Justice'–Describing this brilliant book as a 'powerful, deep, subtle, wide-ranging systematic work in political and moral philosophy'. Nozick goes on to say that now 'the political philosophers must either work within Rawls or explain why not,' but this praise is followed by an in-depth criticism of Rawls' theory.

This chapter dealt at length with this Rawls/Nozick debate, which continues to rage to this day. Both Rawls and Nozick, as the chapter maintains, have been two dominant souls of our time, while Rawls represents the Keynesian tradition of liberal egalitarianism, Nozick epitomizes the classical liberal view of free market and the minimal state-which remerged after the 70s under a different name : libertarianism.

A comparative analysis of the theories of Rawls and Nozick reveals that although both talk the liberal language, their accents and tenor differ. While both held liberty to be sacrosanct, Rawls believed that this liberty was imperilled by a distributively unjust society and state, and hence a welfare state was justified, on the other hand, Nozick limits the legitimate use of the power of the state to the prevention of force, theft, fraud, excluding the power to tax or confiscate property, because he is convinced that unconsented taxation is like forced labour.

For Rawls, wealth is a cooperative enterprise, all members of a society have a claim to a share of its products. The government must treat all its citizens fairly, giving them equal economic opportunities and a minimal standard of living. All this involved redistribution of wealth, which is vociferously opposed by Nozick, who believes that redistribution is an infringement of individual rights, and it also imposes a pattern, which ignores the history of how goods have come to be distributed through trade, labour purchase, gifts, etc.

The kernel of the debate is that while the Rawlsian just society which he so painstakingly outlines is a liberal democratic capitalist welfare society–which tries to uplift the condition of the least–advantaged–through redistribution taxation, the Nozickean just society is the one where entitlements are protected by a minimal state, for, he believes that the danger to individual liberty comes from an all-pervasive egalitarian state, which is an assault on individual rights.

Thus, we see, that the theory of Justice that Nozick backs up in 'Anarchy, State and Utopia' is the libertarian belief in the free-market because, he believes, that it is the only economic order that respects individual freedom.

In conformity with his libertarian leanings, Nozick postulates absolute rights–not merely prima facie rights which might be overridden, but boundaries not to be crossed without the free consent of the persons whose rights they are.

Thus, we can safely conclude that these two intellectual giants gave a new complexion to liberalism. In 'A Theory of Justice', liberalism found a new and able defender in the economic, contractarian based system of Rawls, which upheld liberal egalitarianism and Nozick's, 'Anarchy State and Utopia', while providing an in-depth critique of Rawls' also provided the seeds for a new revival of libertarian political theory.

The State : Rawls and Nozick

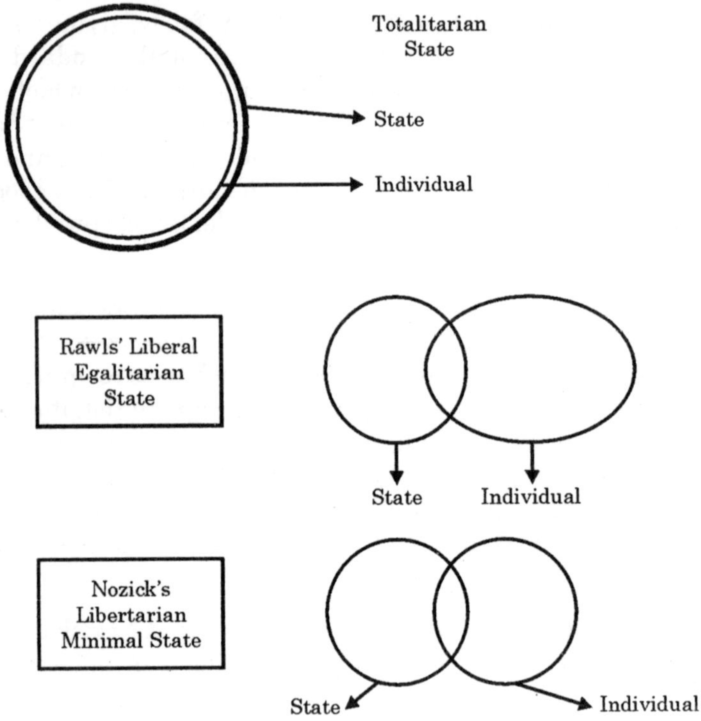

Libertarian and Egalitarian View of Individual, Society and State (Nozick and Rawls)

	Individuals	*Society*	*State*
Libertarian	Consumers/ Producers Preference Maximisers	Voluntary Association of Individuals, Market Contracts based on Self-Interest	Nightwatchman State Umpire-Minimal
Liberal Egalitarian	Equally Deserving Rational Actors who possess, a Sense of Justice, and divergent Conceptions of the Good	Advantaged and Disadvantaged Groups who (a) Cooperate Economically (b) Compete Over allocation of Societal benefits and burdens	Welfare State Enforcer of of Distributive Justice Grantor of Goods and Services

Notes and References

1. Vincent Andrew, *op. cit.*, p. 54.
2. Koerner, Kirk F Liberalism and Its Critics', 'London Sydney : Croom Helm, p. 3.
3. Rawls, John, *op. cit.*, p. 3.
4. *Ibid.*, p. 60.
5. Holmes, Robert L ; 'Nozick On Anarchism' Political Theory, Vol. 5, No. 2, May, 1977.
6. Nozick, Robert, *op. cit.*, p. 19.
7. *Ibid.*, p. 25.
8. *Ibid.*, p. 26.
9. *Ibid.*, p. 52.
10. *Ibid.*, p. IX.
11. *Ibid.*, p. 149.
12. *Ibid.*, p. 152.
13. *Ibid.*, p. 160.
14. Spragens, Thomas A Jr (1999), 'The Appeals and Limits of Liberalism' In 'Civic Liberalism : Reflections on our Democratic Ideals', New York, Rowman and Little Field Publishers Inc.
15. King, Fraser, *op. cit.*
16. Meyers, Diana, T (1985) 'Inalienable Rights : A Defense'– New York, Columbia University Press, pp. 188-89.
17. Shapiro Ian 'The Evolution of Rights in Liberal Theory', Cambridge, Cambridge University Press.
18. Nozick, *op. cit.*, p. 9.
19. *Ibid.*, p. 5.
20. Hampton, Jean (1998) 'Political Philosophy, Oxford, Oup, p. 170.

21. *Ibid.*, p. 170.

22. *Ibid.*, p. 171.

23. Langan, John S.J 'Defining Human Rights : A Revision of the Liberal Tradition In Langan and Hennelly (Eds) Human Rights in the Americas : The Struggle for Consensus.' Washington D.C., Georgetown University Press.

24. Nozick, *op. cit.*, p. 334.

25. Mills and King (1995), 'The Promise of Liberalism : Comparative Analysis of Consensual Politics'. p. 3 (Introduction)

26. *Ibid.*, p. 3.

27. *Ibid.*, p. 7.

28. Watson, George (Ed) 'The Unservile State : Essays in Liberty and Welfare'–London, Ruskin House, George Allen and Unwin Ltd. Museum Street, p. 18.

29. Young, Iris Marion (1996) 'Political Theory : An Overview' In A New Handbook of Political Science Goodin and Klingemann (Eds), Oxford, Oup, p. 482.

30. *Ibid.*, p. 482.

31. Shaprio, Ian, *op. cit.*, p. 285.

32. Nozick. *op. cit.*, p. 183.

33. *Ibid.*, p. 149.

34. *Ibid.*, p. ix.

35. *Ibid.*

36. Nozick, *Ibid.*, p. 156.

37. Kymilicka, Will, *op. cit.*, pp. 633-64.

38. Nozick, *op. cit.*, pp. 25-38.

39. *Ibid.*, p. 31.

40. *Ibid.*, p. 32.

41. *Ibid.*, p. 33.
42. *Ibid.*, p. 33.
43. *Ibid.*, p. 185.
44. *Ibid.*, p. 185.
45. *Ibid.*, p. 185.
46. *Ibid.*, p. 185.
47. *Ibid.*, p. 185.
48. *Ibid.*, p. 185.
49. Nozick, *op. cit.*, p. 190.
50. *Ibid.*, p. 190.
51. *Ibid.*, p. 190.
52. *Ibid.*, p. 193.
53. *Ibid.*, p. 195.
54. Rawls John, Atoj, *op. cit.*, p. 103.
55. Nozick, *op. cit*, p. 197.
56. *Ibid.*, p. 197.
57. *Ibid.*, p. 202.
58. *Ibid.*, p. 167.
59. *Ibid.*, p. 169.
60. *Ibid.*, p. 170.
61. *Ibid.*, p. 170.
62. King Fraser, *op. cit.*, p. 19.
63. Rawls, John, *op. cit.*, p. 4.
64. Bayes, Jane, H (1982) 'Ideologies and Interest Group Politics' Novato, California : Chandler and Sharp Publishers Inc., pp. 41-42.
65. Locke, J (1690) Essay Concerning the True Original Extent and End of Civil Government, Part vii, 87.

66. Meyers, Diana, *op. cit.*, p. 190.

67. Wolff, Jonathan (1991) 'Robert Nozick: Property, Justice and the Minimal State', Cambridge Polity Press.

68. *Ibid.*

69. Spragens Thomas A Jr (1999) *op cit.*, p. 33.

70. Nozick, *op. cit.*, p. 206.

71. Rawls, John, *op. cit.*, p. 101.

6

Conclusion

Before I draw conclusions about the political theory of Robert Nozick, a brief resume of the earlier five chapters would not be out of place here.

After giving a brief outline of Robert Nozick's political theory, and his relevance in the post-communism scenario, the book attempted a historical and analytical explanation of the liberal milieu from Locke to Nozick which included

1. Classical Liberalism (Locke and Adam Smith)
2. Revisionist Liberalism (Bentham and Mill)
3. Modern Liberalism (John Dewey, Milton Friedman, Hayek I, Berlin and C. B. MacPherson.)
4. Contemporary Liberalism (John Rawls and Nozick)

It also threw light on the communitarian liberals and the libertarians–Prominent among the communitarian liberals were : Michael Walzer (Spheres Of Justice) Alasdair MacIntyre, Charles Taylor, Michael Sandel

A synoptic survey of liberalism and the liberal milieu outlined reveals that it has been the most complex and intricate of ideologies. It has had many diverse strands, shooting out in the social-political, moral and economic sphere.

Right from the natural rights liberalism of Locke, to the libertarianism of Nozick, despite undergoing many changes–

there has been one resilient strand, which has surfaced as the common strand among all the liberal strands–and that strand has been the principle of individual liberty.

Some believe that liberalism has been a problematic and inconsistent phenomenon, sometimes being referred to as the programme of a particular political party, sometimes as an 'umbrella that can include a variety of particular liberal philosophies, sometimes, an 'overarching secular political faith,' sometimes it becomes synonymous with fairness sometimes with idealism, sometimes with pragmatism and sometimes with utility.

Contemporary Liberalism

In the post-Second World War period liberalism reappeared in a number of forms. In the 1950s, it was bracketed in cold war 'end of ideology' group, which had a considerable impact in America and Europe. Liberalism, stood, against the ideological mind, which always seemed to be either partially or totally totalitarian. Out of this anti-totalitarian sphere, another strand of liberal thought emerged, which attacked the end of ideology mindset. During this period the fortunes of classical liberalism, as represented by laissez faire, suffered a setback due to the Great Depression, but then in the 1970s, the libertarians, as represented by Nozick, revived the tenets of classic liberalism–by their emphasis on inalienable rights of individuals, and a minimal state, as opposed to the views of John Rawls, who in 'A Theory of Justice', favoured a social democratic welfare state for the establishment of social justice.

John Rawls

John Rawls', 'A Theory of Justice' gave us the most compelling and insistent arguments on behalf of conceiving the democratic society as a cooperative venture committed to an egalitarian ideal of social justice.

Although he has been the subject of voluminous criticism, he emphatically maintains, that his theory of justice captures the 'basic intuitive ideas that are embedded in the political institutions of a constitutional democratic regime'.

Beginning from the Original Position, which is a state of perfect fairness, where rational parties, covered as they are by the veil of ignorance, agree to certain terms of association govern their cooperative endeavours–and because these terms emerge from a condition of perfect fairness, they are called the principles of justice and they are 'the most appropriate', moral basis for a democratic society.

These principle of justice, Rawls maintains, can be expressed as follows : "all social values–liberty and opportunity, income and wealth, and the basis of self-respect-are to be distributed equally unless an unequal distribution of any or all of these values is to everyone's advantage." 'everyone's advantage' as we have seen, does not imply the average or aggregate advantage but the greatest benefit of the least advantaged.

In a nutshell, the Rawlsian scheme emphasises that the regulative principles of a well-ordered democratic society, must be absolutely committed to maximising the absolute welfare of its least well-off members.

On the basis of his arguments, it was concluded that Rawls' liberalism is heavily egalitarian in its substantive imperatives.

Robert Nozick

One enduring strand of the liberal tradition is what today goes under the label of 'libertarianism', and Nozick, whose book, 'Anarchy, State and Utopia' (1974) was a rejoinder to the Rawlsian scheme of liberal egalitarianism, is a libertarian, who, while criticising the all-intrusive social welfare state of Rawls, holds a plea for the minimal state, which is confined to the task of protecting the individual against force, theft, fraud, and enforcement of contracts.

Passionately believing in individual rights and self-ownership, he maintains that if any state infringes upon the rights of an individual, it is immoral and illegitimate. It follows that any state which indulges in redistributive activities–like the Rawlsian state, which is entrusted with the task of providing social justice to the individuals–is unjust, because it violates the inalienable rights of the individual.

Apart from seeking a diminished role for the state, Nozick's emphasis is also on a free market, where there is a heavy reliance on market transactions, unhindered by the dictates of an extensive state.

The book also undertook a comparative study of communitarianism and libertarianism.

Communitarianism has become the focus of some debate and interest and some representative communitarians mentioned were Michael Walzer, Alasdair MacIntyre, Charles Taylor and Michael Sandel.

As against the libertarian view of the atomistic individual, they emphasised the social embeddedness of individuals, pointing out that the individuals can take shape only within the context of communities.

The book also dealt with Nozick's 'Entitlement Theory of Justice', and threw light on the meaning and etymology of justice, the various dimensions of justice, comparing it with the different theories of justice—the Platonic justices, Anarchist, Marxist, Democratic, socialistic theories of justice.

Nozick Entitlement Theory of Justice

Nozick's theory of entitlement is based on his theory of rights, which, he believes no 'state' can deprive him of. According to him, there are certain entitlements that these rights yield, and justice for Nozick lies in not disrupting individual entitlements through any patterned device–and this can be possible only in a minimal state–not in any more extensive state.

Strongly upholding his entitlement theory, he emphasises that the entitlement theory is not patterned.

The salient features of Nozick's entitlement theory were:

(a) Nozick's argument begins with individual rights.

(b) These rights are 'so strong and far-reaching' that they put constraints upon actions.

(c) No citizen can be sacrificed for the other, because all citizens have separate lives.

(d) This theory is historical, and it did not emerge through any formula or pattern–which implies that 'past circumstances can create differential entitlements.'

(e) It is the task of justice to protect individuals rights to which they are entitled.

(f) Any type of interference in the rights or entitlements of an individual is unjust–property right is an entitlement, and it cannot be violated.

(g) Following in the Lockean footsteps, he believes in the inviolability of individual rights, including the right to property.

(h) The slogan of the Entitlement theory is 'from each as they choose, to each as they are chosen.'

The three different parts of the Entitlement theory sketched by Nozick are :

1. A principle of justice in original acquisition of holdings.

2. The transfer of holdings from one person to another.

3. The rectification of unjust holdings.

The first principle enlightens us as to how. 'Unheld things may come to be held' the second principle is concerned with the processes by which a person may transfer holdings to another, and the third principle tells us how unjust holdings can be rectified.

In other words, this principle will tell us that if 'past injustice has shaped present holdings', how it can be corrected– these past injustices include, stealing, defrauding, enslaving and forcibly excluding others from competing in exchange.

Although Nozick, concedes that it is quite difficult to find out about the past injustice, yet on the basis of historical information, the principle of rectification can reach some conclusions regarding these injustices and then it can go about rectifying the historical wrongs.

In short, Nozick's theory of entitlement emphasises the fact that the holdings of a person are just if he is entitled to them by the principle of acquisition and transfer, or by rectification.

After dealing with Nozick's theory of entitlement, a comparative evaluation of the different theories of justice was attempted namely :

1. Platonic Justice.
2. Anarchist Justice.
3. Marxist Justice.
4. Justice as Viewed by Democratic Socialism.
5. Libertarian Justice : Hayek and Nozick.

While Platonic justice was a meta-physical-ethical justice, which emphasised division of labour and specialisation of functions–'the anarchist justice believed that justice can result only when the state, which is an unnecessary evil is abolished and replaced by a completely free organisation of society'. For them, as mentioned earlier, justice is not to be found in the presence of the government but in its absence–not in the submission to an overarching political authority, but in the existence of free and unfettered individuals arriving independently at agreements.

The Marxist justice, as opposed to the Nozickean justice, wants a stateless–classless society based on equality, while

Nozick does not want to do away with the state altogether, but wants a minimal state, Marx wants to do away with property, but for Nozick it is an inviolable right which has to be protected at any cost.

In the democratic socialist view of justice, the state performs a positive role, in rectifying the societal wrongs, reflected in the form of economic inequalities, while in Nozick's justice, if the state performs such tasks, it is not just. The minimal state of Nozick, unlike the democratic socialist state performs only the task of protection of an individual against force, theft, fraud and enforcement of contracts.

The book also dealt at length with the minimal state of Robert Nozick, which had its roots in classic liberalism–it emphasised that fact that Nozick's theory of the minimal state was an outburst against the all-intrusive nature of the welfare state, which had started making inroads into the sphere of individual freedom.

Speaking the language of John Locke, he maintains that there are inalienable rights of the individual which are possessed, independent of society and any state which tries to intrude into this sphere of inalienable rights is unjust.

Nozick tries to limit the state to the minimum of functions, which are–protection against theft, fraud, force, and the enforcement of contracts, and any state which tries to go beyond this functional sphere, is unjust, uninspiring and wrong.

Seriously considering the anarchist claim that the state is immoral, Nozick maintains that his state cannot be immoral because it has arisen through a process which need not violate anyone's rights–and that process is voluntarism.

In the minimal state, Nozick has revived the Lockean state of nature, because as he says it is the 'most favoured situation of anarchy':

(a) A strong believer in individual rights and self-ownership, Nozick believed in the least intrusive form of the state, because an excessive state would be an assault on individual rights.

(b) The state, being minimal, it should not step beyond its legitimate functions.

(c) The 'strong and far-reaching' rights of the individual leave very little room for the state.

(d) Being merely a protective agency, it is entrusted with the task of protecting people against force, theft and fraud.

(e) Its jurisdiction does not include the task of trying to promote equality.

(f) In order to protect the rights of people, it has to sustain a monopoly of force–it is on this basis that it can try to resolve conflicts.

(g) The hall-mark of the minimal state is voluntarism.

(h) This inspiring 'morally legitimate' and 'right state is the framework for utopia, wherein, sub-utopias also exist–and the individuals can choose the sub-utopia of his/her choice–based on his/her aptitudes/ aspirations.

(i) It arises from the Lockean state of nature via only legitimate steps, without violating anyone's rights.

(j) It is based on an invisible hand explanation.

(k) This minimal state thus surpasses anarchism which believes, that all states are evil–the implication being that the Nozickean minimal state is not evil, because its emergence is legitimate and voluntary.

A comparative study of the views of John Rawls and Nozick–both two dominant souls of our time, revealed that while John Rawls represented the Keynesian tradition of liberal egalitarianism, Nozick represented the classical liberal view of free market and minimal state.

The comparative study of the two intellectual giants revealed that there is much that separates Rawls from Nozick. We saw that Rawls' argument began, with social obligation, while Nozick's argument began with individual rights. A passionate believer in individual rights, Nozick held a plea for the minimal state, which did not transgress the domain of the inviolable individual rights, and, based, as it was on voluntarism, it was just, moral, inspiring and legitimate, while Rawls state was relatively more than minimal, because it was entrusted with the task of social engineering or establishing social justice, which could be possible only on the basis of a distributive scheme, which is strongly opposed by Nozick. For Rawls, justice can never be anything but distributive, while for Nozick, if it is distributive it can never be categorised as justice but, as injustice.

Theory of Justice : Rawls and Nozick

Rawls, who formulated and reformulated his theory of Justice for about four decades, gave the final and most elaborate and comprehensive argument of his theory in 'A Theory of Justice' 1971, and in 1974, Robert Nozick launched an attack on Rawls, in his controversial and influential book 'Anarchy, State and Utopia' (1974).

After elaborating and criticising the concept of classical utilitarianism, Rawls asserts that persons in the original position reject the principle of utility and settle for the twin principles of Rawls.

Justice, for Rawls, is equivalent to fairness--It demands– due care for the least advantaged members of society, as well.

The twin principles of justice, are principles of social justice, and provide a way of assigning rights and duties in the basic institutions of society, and define the appropriate distribution of benefits and burdens of social cooperation.

Justice, for Rawls is the distribution of benefits among all the members of the society not in proportion to what he does, but in such a manner that the weakest of the weak is duly benefitted. Such a distribution is not only fair, but also in accordance with the norms of justice.

In a nutshell, Rawls' theory of Justice can be summed as :

(a) Justice, for Rawls is fairness.

(b) He views society as a fair system of cooperation between free and equal persons.

(c) The object of justice is to find out appropriate principles which help in the realisation of liberty and equality.

(d) These principles, attempting to seek liberty and equality are the result of an agreement among the people concerned in the light of their mutual advantage.

(e) As free and equal people, they soon realise that they need the same primary goods in order to pursue their own conception of good.

(f) Justice, thus, would imply that all primary goods are to be distributed equally unless an unequal distribution is to the advantage of the least favoured.

In short, justice exists to the greatest benefit of the least advantaged. Within the framework of established inequalities.

Nozick's theory of justice, stands in stark contrast to the Rawlsian justice.

While Rawls sees justice as a particular pattern of social arrangements adjusting resources and entitlements in as fair a manner as possible, Nozick, refutes this Rawlsian argument emphasising the inalienable rights of an individual, which have to be respected at all costs. For him, justice does not mean attempting to organise or reorganise society to achieve some distributive pattern, but it means respecting the basic individual rights, which limit what may be done to someone without his/her consent.

A staunch supporter of individual rights, in the tradition of John Locke, Nozick believed that rights are so fundamental, and the constraints upon them so strong, that only a minimal state is justified, which provides justice by non-intervention in individual rights. He argued that if the State tampered with individual rights, it was unjust.

Justice, for Nozick lies not in disrupting individual entitlements, but in their protection.

While Rawls believes in social justice, Nozick scoffs at it, believing that there are different individuals with separate lives–and none can be sacrificed for the other under any distributive scheme. While arguing for absolute property rights on the basis of the fact that people are ends in themselves, Nozick maintains distributive schemes such as Rawls', which allow people the products of their talents, provided they benefit the less talented, treats people as mere means to the enhancement of the less talented.

The State : Rawls/Nozick

As far as their views regarding the state are concerned, we found that while Rawls is a defender of liberal democratic, and to some extent, a welfare state, Nozick on the other hand, holds a plea for the night-watchman or minimal state, which arises voluntarily from the Lockean state of nature, without violating anyone's rights.

Out of the inconveniences of the Lockean state of nature, mutual protection agencies emerge and out of the inconveniences of these MPAs, a dominant protection agency emerges, which results in the emergence of the ultra minimal state and ultimately the minimal state–which is entrusted with the task of protecting the individuals against force, theft and fraud and enforcement of contracts–and this minimal state, Nozick believes is justified.

By implication, the Rawlsian state, is a more than minimal state–it is an extensive state, hence it is unjust because by its redistribution schemes, it violates the rights of the individual, while Nozick, believes that 'the state may not use its coercive apparatus for the purpose of getting some citizens to aid others'

Thus, a summation of the Rawls/Nozick debate on the state can be stated thus :

(a) While Nozick held that the less the state interferes in the lives of the individuals, the better it is for the society, Rawls believed that social justice could be established only on the basis of an extensive state.

(b) Nozick believed that if the state attempts to promote equality, it crosses its legitimate boundaries, and Rawls maintained, that it was the state's function to end poverty and secure equal opportunities for all.

(c) It follows that Nozick's state cannot pursue the function of redistribution of resources, because that would be beyond its function of 'protection against theft, force, fraud and enforcement of contracts ; while the Rawlsian state, being a positive state, does more than simply guaranteeing to individuals choices in how they want to live–so, it naturally follows, that there is redistribution of resources by the state, which allows for greater equality of opportunity .... than there would be under a predominantly market-led system which is upheld by Nozick.

(d) A true libertarian, Nozick tried to revive the liberal–individualistic theory of the state, following in the footsteps of John Locke, who gave the individual maximum autonomy and the state minimum functions.

Rights : Rawls and Nozick

While comparing the views of Rawls and Nozick regarding rights, we find that, Nozick, toes the line of Locke and declares :

'Individuals have rights, and there are things no person or group may do to them'–

He reiterates that these rights are 'so strong and far-reaching', that they put constraints on the state and on the individuals–hence, Nozick maintains that the state cannot use its coercive machinery for the purpose of getting some citizens to aid others, because that way, it would be violating the inviolable rights of the individuals–which, anyway have not been conferred on them by the state, but they "are already possessed by each individual in a state of nature."

Rawls, on the other hand, believes in contractual rights, which are conferred on the individuals by the contract.

After conceiving a hypothetical contract, and the notion of the veil of ignorance, which results in the formulation of the twin principles of justice, Rawls then proceeds to ensure how justice could be applied to the social institutions and to their basic structure. He emphasises the fact that when the two principles of justice are applied to the basic structure of social institutions, a just order results, which requires an obligation from individuals regarding its dictates.

While applying the first principle–the principle of equality to the basic structure, Rawls maintains that institutions should be such that they ensure equal basic liberty–which include general liberties and political liberties. When he applies his second principle–the difference principle–the social order becomes complex, having a combination of both equality and inequality.

Rawls uses the words 'Rights' and 'Justice' interchangeably. For him, rights are embedded in justice–and they belong to all disinterested political individuals beyond the veil of ignorance. Unlike Locke and Nozick who talk of natural rights and inalienable rights of an individual, Rawls believes that individuals had no natural rights except those which they chose unanimously in their original position–and which were accepted because of the considered judgment of the people.

On the other hand, when Nozick revives the Lockean state of nature, he is also reviving the natural rights that exist there–namely the rights to life, liberty and estate.

A libertarian society, by respecting the individual, respects his rights, and it allows the individuals to choose their lives either individually or with whomsoever they choose, aided by the voluntary co-operation of other individuals.

Nozick holds a very strong doctrine of individualistic rights, specially the right to acquire and hold property.

A staunch supporter of the principle of self-ownership, he believes that an individual is his own master and no state can treat him/her as a means to an end–hence redistributive taxation, which Rawls upholds, is criticised by Nozick on the grounds of the self-ownership argument.

Regarding welfare, we see that a staunch believer in the inalienable rights of the individual, Nozick holds that every individual has an exclusive domain which must not be breached without his consent, hence he argues that property rights of the individual exclude welfare rights and their protection by the state, on the other hand, Rawls believes in social justice and social engineering, therefore he holds a plea for welfare rights–through which he hopes to ameliorate the condition of the least advantaged.

Critique of Robert Nozick

When 'Anarchy, State and Utopia' was published in 1974, it received an extraordinary reception, it was hailed as original, remarkable and strikingly intelligent–'a dazzling technical achievement', which had a needle-sharp analysis. The stimulating commentary that it received stirred the curiosity of both scholars and laymen, it was subjected to devastating criticism and also praised to the skies.

One critic says : 'I believe the book to be politically naïve, philosophically deficient and historically irrelevant.'[1] While another calls his political theory a 'haunted concrete bridge', and a 'Magnificient Abstraction'–the edifice Nozick constructs is indeed a utopia : an argument which stands, quite literally nowhere—and like those haunted concrete bridges that can be found at abandoned highway projects–soars from mid-air chasm to mid-air chasm as magnificent abstractions going from nowhere to nowhere ...."[2]

In order to find out, whether Nozick's political theory is merely an abstract wordy warfare, a critique of the following topics needs to be undertaken:

1. The Critique of The Minimal State.
2. The Critique of The Entitlement Theory.
3. Individual Rights and Self-Ownership.
4. Nozick's Utopia.

Minimal State : Although Nozick calls the minimal state "morally legitimate" a 'morally favoured state'–'the only morally tolerable one–it epitomises the utopian aspirations of untold dreamers and visionaries' criticisms of all hues and shades have been levelled against it.

For Ian Shapiro, 'the idea of the minimal state has always been a myth.'[3] Jonathan Wolff finds the minimal state 'grotesquely wrong' 'not so much a dream as a nightmare.'[4]

Another analyst poses a few questions regarding the minimal state:

1. In the course of the evolution of the minimal state from the state of nature it is not at all clear why only one DPA will emerge–'By what reason–historical or logical–dare Nozick presume the inevitable outcome will be a single DPA."[5]

2. If there is only one DPA, the obvious implication is that he believes in the dictum might is right.
3. Will the DPA protect the rights of its clients–and who–or what will control the conrollers of power.
4. Will the minimal state respect the claims of the poorer classes as much as the claims of the wealthier class.
5. The invisible–hand explanation is also inadequate, because it may lead individuals to promote an evil end which was not part of their intention.
6. Although Nozick argues that the thirst for domination is inconsequential in the minimal state, yet, the fact is that power once acquired gives rise to innumerable temptations–and this, Nozick, fails to come to grips with. Thus, "Nozick's state, his morally legitimate state, appears to be no more than a variant of Marx's state: an instrument through which the ruling class secures its domination."[6]

Still another critic feels that Nozick is merely indulging in 'foolish heroics', when he states that any state more extensive than the minimal state is uninspiring and wrong. He feels that the 'eradication of politics will guarantee, not an increase in individual liberties but the expansion of corporate power."[7] He goes on to say that Nozick's vocabulary is a 'quixotic bourgeois vocabulary' which reflects his ignorance of an understanding of the economic processes in America.

Similarly, another critic opines that 'Anarchy State and Utopia' is to be criticised .... for the absence of a relevant politics altogether .... for its inadequate conception of the political."[8]

In short, Nozick's minimal state is criticised on many grounds, but the one strand that emerges as the common strand is that it is unrealistic–it can be realised only in one's fantasies, because unlike the minimal state, which does not interfere in individual freedom, some sort of interference is needed. As J.S.Mill says, 'There are matters in which the interference of the law is required, not to overrule the judgment of individuals ... but to give effect to that judgment...."[9]

Right from the days of Aristotle, the importance of the state for the sake of the good life of man, has been emphasised, but Nozick's political minimalism relegates the state to the role of an agency performing the minimum of functions.

Nozicks Entitlement Theory

Nozick's Entitlement Theory has been criticsed on many grounds–Jan Narveson, calls it a 'scrooge-like principle' and Douglas J Den Ulyl pleads for a resurrection of charity and virtues, which have been lost in the Nozickean claims of self-ownership.

Favourably citing a passage from John Locke, he maintains that a person cannot allow another to perish while he himself leads an ostentatious life.

"But we know God hath not left one man, so to the mercy of another, that he may starve ..... He has given his needy brother a right to the surplusage of his goods...."[10]

Similarly, another critic argues that unlike the Nozickean argument, a person in dire circumstances has a residual claim to the surplus of the others, and he would have respect for a regime of rights, only when it protected him.

"Individuals have reasons to value the maintenance of a regime of rights because they value their own ability to pursue projects."[11]

In short, in the Nozickean scheme of things, critics believe that words like benevolence, charity are conspicuous by their absence and that libertarianism has no distinct moral identity, and at best, it is a free market tendency, where the poor may starve, and the rich lead an ostentatious life.

Criticising Nozick's theory, another critic claims that 'under the guise of entitlement all kinds of fraudulent claims may be advanced' and that his theory holds a plea for the dictum, 'might is right'. 'In the free market it is not right but power that prevails, and in the absence of public-counter coercion, there is nothing to prevent private coercion from running amok."[12]

Another allegation that he levels against Nozick is that he fails to realise that even citizens acting in a private capacity can have public consequences and in this context, he finds fault with Nozick's Chamberlain argument.

In a similar vein, another critic believes that this argument is cut-off from reality and is 'indefensible in a world deeply scarred by illegitimate domination.'[13]

He believes that Chamberlain's rights can only be taken as absolute in an ideal world. 'Why should he be dominant over his fellow-citizens', he asks.

"Nor can his athletic abilities give him genetic dominance over any of his fellow citizens, nor may the educational system enshrine basketball in the holy of holiest of public values; nor may Chamberlain begin adult life with more material assets than the next person."[14]

Following the same thrust, David Spitz argues :

"But in the real and unequal world, many do not have sufficient earnings, or any earnings, to buy the things they need or would like–say a ticket to a basketball game, with or without the added tax for Wilt Chamberlain....."

It is surely a strange notion of justice that exempts the rich and the better off from responsibility to the less fortunate.[15]

Barber argues that Nozick seems to have lost sight of the goal of political theory, while elaborating his theory of entitlement. Historical men, according to Barber, have, from times immemorial, been 'victims of illegitimate coercion'–

Nozick's entitlement theory should have tried to 'render coercion less illegitimate, force less blind, power less blind'[16]– which he fails to do.

In a nutshell, Barber's allegations against Nozick's entitlement theory are :

(a) He holds a plea for 'raw power'.

(b) He is not clear which Entitlement theory he subscribes to, although there are allusions to Locke.

(c) He ignores the fact that individuals have a private as well as a public aspect.

(d) He fails to develop a coherent political theory of entitlement.

It is from the plurality of our nature that politics emerges, and Barber believes, that Nozick is trying to wish this plurality away, whereas, the fact is that 'dependence is intrinsic to the human condition' and it cannot be shrugged away like Nozick seems to do.

David Spitz says that for Nozick 'to mind your own business is the primary moral law; to interfere with another's business is the primary crime.'[17] But he says that Nozick seems to forget that 'rectification requires a society of persons held together by a sense of common identity–which Nozick ignores. War is not something to be left to a dominant association— Since all are affected, all must share.'[18]

For Nozick, the individuals appear to be more important than the community 'liberty is important, but at what cost?' The rich can hardly be entrusted with the rights of the poor; who, then, will take care of the widows, the orphans, the infirm, the less powerful, the poor."[19]

The first and foremost duty of the state is to provide everyone the necessities of life, and from this standpoint 'taxation is not extortion, but a necessary device to insure the welfare of the community ..... and from this standpoint, the ludicrousness of the Wilt Chamberlain episode becomes patent.'[20]

Spitz clinches his arguments by maintaining that in the Nozickean scheme,—"rights are up for grabs, for sale, and by any standard of justice other than Nozick's, this is sheer madness .... a moral theory that leads to immoral results is not a theory of Justice at all.

Justice is not and cannot be for sale .... the test of a decent Theory of Justice, ... is what it does to individuals....."[21]

It is a 'mark of its moral deficiency' that Nozick's theory is, at best, good only for some individuals.

Richard Bellamy criticises Nozick on the grounds that he holds property right to be of paramount importance and in so doing he 'seeks to avoid' the chief difficulty confronting natural-rights theorists, namely how to adjudicate between conflicting yet equally fundamental rights....'[22]

The foregoing analysis reveals that Nozick's Entitlement Theory of Justice has been criticised on many grounds, and the common strand appears to be that it suffers from moral deficiency.

Rights and Self-ownership

A great champion of individual rights, Nozick claims in the preface of 'Anarchy, State and Utopia'–

"Individuals have rights and there are things no person or group may do to them. So strong and far reaching are these rights..."[23]

Thus, Nozick believes, that individuals are ends not merely means and they cannot be sacrificed for the achieving of others' ends. Hence, only a minimal state 'limited to the narrow functions of protection against force, theft, fraud and enforcement of contracts' is justified. It follows that taxation, being based on coercion, is wrong and 'on a par with forced labour'.

Although, this is a stout defense of the integrity and autonomy of individuals against state coerciveness, and a 'morally proper admonition worthy of our respect,' however, it is 'highly contestable, not even fully coherent, and morally and socially perverse in some of its applications.'[24]

Moreover, the weaknesses of the self-ownership argument are compounded when he tries to deploy it to try to establish absolute individual rights to the possession of external goods. In the context, an analyst, says that the problem with 'libertarianism can be seen once we recognise the limitations that negative rights (libertarian constraints) themselves place on individual liberty.'[25]

He believes that the arguments of the libertarians are 'blatantly inconsistent' because, on the one hand, they argue against the restrictions on individual freedom, and, on the other hand, they cannot deny that the very presence of others is a restriction on their freedom. Citing an example, he says that the nineteenth century American slaveholders were legally coerced into freeing their slaves–which they were already morally required to do. "Morally, they didn't have to consent; it was a remedy long overdue. Even the libertarian would agree. The slave-owner's freedom was justifiably restricted by the presence of other people."[26]–But this is exactly what the libertarian denies. Citing another example, he says "Suppose ... that I am the biggest and strongest guy on the block. My size is a natural asset I inherited and then developed. But can I use my strength and size any way I please? No, atleast not morally."[27]

In short, the libertarian argument is that there can be no legitimate–consensual limitations on freedom, yet this very theory involves such limitations.

Another critic maintains that Nozick is unable to argue:

(a) Why the right of self-ownership exists at all.

(b) What is the relationship between self-ownership and other rights.

"How for example can one decide the relative merit of freedom of speech and freedom of privacy."[28]

Nozick's Libertarian Utopia

Many and varied are the criticisms levelled against the Nozickean utopia, in which he envisages voluntary associations existing within the framework of the minimal state, and which he calls an 'inspiring' vision, and 'the best of all possible worlds'.

When the concrete content of the model in the real world is juxtaposed against the abstract form in the imagination, various problematic features appear in stark relief.

Although Nozick's rhetorical allusions paint an idyllic scene of a utopia where diverse people, motivated by their different aptitudes and interests find a fitting habitat–yet, as a writer puts it, 'the real-world results of implementing Nozick's libertarian model might be considerably less inspiring than his rhetoric suggests.'[29]

He asks certain questions :

1. What if the Nozickean utopia generates more and more 'hordes of self-centered, driveling consumerist idiots.'
2. How would the constituent associations of the libertarian utopia relate to each other?
3. What would be the likely consequences of the criteria for admission into various associations?

Spragens admits that the 'internal cohesion and external diversity of the association in the real world would very probably produce racial, religious and ethnic enclaves'[30]– which would result in groups of winners and losers–on the basis of their wealth and talent, and there, would be some who would possibly 'perish between the cracks', for lack of either wealth or talent.

Moreover, the different people that Nozick refers to, cannot possibly move around, like a detached group of hermits. His thought experiment gives us the impression that these groups could float around unrelated in abstract space .... But in the actual world it cannot be denied that they would have common spaces to inhabit.

In short, the Nozickean utopia can be 'inspiring', only when it is depicted as operating in a disembodied and imaginary world–It cannot be a 'good or even a viable basis for the cooperative endeavours necessitated by living together–even under the loose umbrella of the minimal state.'[31]

In this context, another critic says that in the Nozickean utopia, rights surpass even morality.

"Indigent lepers .. may find it difficult to contract into a sub-utopia ... (their leprosy is not exactly a bargaining strength)."[32]

Still another analyst considers it a 'most peculiar utopian vision, for it justifies evil systems and practices .... Nozick would permit anyone to do anything as long as it is done voluntarily .... As a matter of moral right."[33]

Moreover, he emphasises that Nozick's utopia has 'little to do with reality'. In his words :

"Nozick's true ideal, a combination of minimal states cannot be realised. To achieve the kind of world Nozick wants, we would have to reverse history .... This would entail precisely the massive state interference ..... he rails against."[34]

Thus, he maintains that "Nozick's utopianism is not a utopia any more than his idea of entitlements is a theory of justice. Together they constitute a vision of hell."[35]

Utopia literally means 'no where' and was the title of a renowned work of the early sixteenth century statesman and humanist Sir Thomas Moore (1465-1535).

In this context, a writer says that 'the utopian vision disposes itself into explicit utopias and implicit utopias– Implicit utopias lack the detailed blueprint of explicit utopias. They parry our thrust for more information with the disclaimer that it would be idle or arrogant to legislate for the future.'[36]

On the basis, of this, we can say that the utopia that Nozick talks of, is an implicit utopia, because he does not want to make any guesses about the future of the utopian framework that he has envisaged. In his words :

"I do not think its nature can be settled finally now either."[37]

He further says :

"Well, what exactly will it all turn out to be like? In what direction will people flower? How large will the communities be? Will there be some large cities? .... Will most communities follow particular (though diverse) utopian visions? ....

I do not know and you should not be interested in my guesses about what would occur under the framework in the near future."[38]

Despite the fact that Nozick's views have been subjected to a devastating criticism, we cannot ignore his massive contribution to political theory.

Contribution of Nozick

When Nozick died on 23rd January, 2002 at the age of 63, after fighting a brave battle with stomach cancer, he left behind a very rich legacy in the form of books and ideas.

This brilliant, provocative and fearless thinker was known for his wide-ranging intellect, and he never stayed within the confines of any traditional field, but fearlessly ventured into many other areas of philosophy which have influenced generations of readers and will definitely continue to influence people for generations to come.

He was a man who was always on the move intellectually, and he once quipped to an interviewer, I didn't want to spend my life writing 'The son of Anarchy, State and Utopia'!

The introductory chapter of this book has thrown ample light on his intellectual output, which was, by no stretch of imagination, a meagre contribution.

Despite the notoriety and influence that his first book 'Anarchy, State and Utopia' brought him, Nozick explored an altogether different territory in 'Philosophical Explanations' (1981)–his next book, 'The Examined life' (1989), was an exploration of the individuals' relation to reality 'The Nature of Rationality' (1995) focussed on the functions that principles serve in our daily life and why we simply don't act on our whims or out of self-interest.

'Socratic Puzzles' (1997) was a collection of essays, articles and reviews and also short philosophical fiction of Nozick.

'Invariances' (2001), his last published book before his death, won rave reviews. It was hailed as 'an engaging book,' "an ambitious and stimulating effort to revitalise the notions of truth and objectivity."

When John Rawls' intellectually stimulating book 'A Theory of Justice' was published in 1971, two things were clear to political theorists and philosophers.

First, that liberalism had found a new and able defender in the economic–Contractarianism that Rawls had continued to improve and modify since 1971.

Second, criticism of, and reaction against 'A Theory of Justice' was both diverse and scathing–one such criticism, as we have seen, coming in the form of Nozick's influential book 'Anarchy, State and Utopia' (1974) in which he provides the seeds for a new revival of libertarian political theory, which has been described in detail in an earlier chapter.

So, one of the contributions of Nozick can be stated as :

The Revival of Libertarian Political Theory

Libertarianism, as mentioned earlier, represents the most radical form of individualism, short of outright anarchism, exalting the pure capitalist economy as the surest expression and defense of individuality.

In short, the emphasis of libertarianism is on individualism, limited government and unfettered market capitalism.

It advances the Lockean notion of the inalienable right to life, liberty and property, and believes that the state, if it exists at all, should be no more than a 'night-watchman state'.

Nozick has revived all these features of libertarianism in 'Anarchy, State and Utopia', and his argument begins with individual rights, when he proclaims :

'Individuals have rights, and there are things no person or group may do to them.'

These rights are so 'strong and far-reaching' that they put constraints on other individuals and also the state, so, it follows that only a minimal state, limited to the narrow functions of protection against force, theft, fraud, enforcements of contracts is just, and any more extensive state will definitely violate persons rights.

In the post-communism scenario, enormous socio-economic changes have been taking place at a dizzying pace. More and more nations are adopting the capitalist mode of development, and the welfare shetoric has also begun to waver, hence it is being dismantled in a number of developed as well as developing countries, because of its failure in many spheres–

It is against this backdrop that Nozick's contribution becomes very important.

With the publication of 'Anarchy, State and Utopia', in 1974, the libertarian movement received large scale academic attention. Through this book, for the first time, in at least a century, someone made a serious, sustained and forceful attempt to refute philosophical anarchism and defended the libertarian doctrine that the minimal or night-watchman state is the most powerful state morally justifiable, inspiring as well as right.

Although this minimal state, arises from anarchism, it is based on voluntarism, and does not infringe individual freedom.

As we have seen, in an earlier chapter, Nozick justifies the minimal state in vociferous terms emphasising the fact that such a state cannot transgress the liberty of the propertied people, because it does not believe in compulsory redistribution.

The market-led minimal state of Nozick upholds the libertarian belief that only free market exchanges respect people as equals.

So, we see, that Nozick's 'Anarchy, State and Utopia' is a reflection of the theory of libertarianism that had started gaining ground in the 1970s.

The Revival of Lockean State of Nature

Nozick's second major contribution is his revival of the Lockean state of nature in political theory.

In the very first chapter of 'Anarchy, State and Utopia.' Nozick has revived the Lockean state of nature. Chapter I of 'Anarchy, State and Utopia' begins with the words :

'If the state did not exist would it be necessary to invent it? Would one be needed, and would it have to be invented? These questions arise for political philosophy and for a theory explaining political phenomena, and are answered by investigating the 'State of Nature' to use the terminology of traditional political theory.'[39]

He believes that if one starts the subject of political philosophy with state of nature theory, it can serve an explanatory purpose.

The most important question of political philosophy is whether there should be any state at all, and if one upholds anarchy, it will undercut the whole subject of political philosophy hence, Nozick believes that it is appropriate to begin political philosophy with an examination of its major theoretical alternative–and that theoretical alternative is the state of nature.

To quote Nozick :

'Archists and anarchists alike, those who spring gingerly from the starting point as well as those reluctantly argued away from it, can agree that beginning the subject of political philosophy with state of nature theory has an explanatory purpose.'[40]

The state of nature is a fundamental abstract description that would encompass all situations of interest, including 'where we would now be, if' and this fundamental abstract description, can be either pessimistic like the Hobbesian state of nature, which was so awful that the state would automatically 'come out as a preferred alternative, viewed as affectionately as a trip to the dentist.'[41] Or on optimistic assumption, like Godwin's.

Both the extremes of pessimism and optimism are not feasible, because pessimistic descriptions are awful and 'such awful descriptions rarely convince, and not merely because they fail to cheer', and on the other end of the spectrum. 'imprudent optimism also lacks conviction'.[42]

Hence, there is a middle-path between the two extremes of pessimism and optimism and that is the Lockean state of nature.

The Lockean state of nature, according to Nozick, is a non-state situation in which people generally 'satisfy moral constraints', and it is 'the best anarchic situation one reasonably could hope for',[43] hence, he makes the Lockean state of nature his starting point, and argues that the state is not 'intrinsically immoral', although it would arise from anarchy (as represented by the Lockean state of nature).

"Yet this state-of-nature situation is the best anarchic situation one reasonably could hope for. Hence investigating its nature and defects is of crucial importance to deciding whether there should be a state rather than anarchy."[44]

A state of nature theory, according to Nozick serves two purposes :

(a) Its importance in the sphere of political philosophy.

(b) The purpose of explanation.

The Lockean, state of nature, believes Nozick, is the best anarchic situation one reasonably could hope for, and moreover, it is not 'wildly optimistic'

'If one could show that the state would be superior even to this most favoured situation of anarchy, the best that realistically can be hoped for, or would arise by a process involving no morally impermissible steps, or would be an improvement if it arose, this would provide a rationale for the state's existence, it would justify the state.'[45]

This Lockean state of nature, 'though non-political, is by intention far from non-moral', based as it is, on the law of nature.

In Lockean state of nature, individuals are in 'a state of perfect freedom to order their actions and dispose of their possessions and persons as they think fit, within the bounds of the law of nature', without asking leave or dependency upon the will of any other man." (Section 4)[46]

This state is also a state of equality–wherein all men have the 'same advantages of nature.'

Though this is a state of liberty, 'yet it is not a state of licence; though men in that state have an uncontrollable liberty to dispose of his person or possessions, yet he has not liberty to destroy himself..... The state of nature has a law of nature to govern it, which obliges everyone that 'no one ought to harm another in his life, health, liberty or possessions.' (Section 6)[47]

The law of nature wills the peace and preservation of all mankind, it preserves the innocent and restrains the offender, and its execution is 'put into every man's hands, whereby everyone has a right to punish the transgressors of that law to such a degree, as may hinder its violation.' (Section 7)[48]

If a person has committed any crime against any other person in the state of nature, then the person, against whom the crime has been committed has the right to punish him single handedly or jointly with others who think that the criminal has become 'degenerate' or has 'quit the principles of human nature', thereby becoming a 'noxious creature'.

Moreover, the injured person has an important right: the right of reparation–'to retribute to him, so far as calm reason and conscience dictates, what is proportionate to his transgression, which is so much as may serve for reparation and restraint.' (Section 8)[49]

Although, the state of nature is a 'state of perfect freedom', there are certain inconveniences, which have been referred to in an earlier chapter, and for rectifying these conveniences, Locke says 'I easily grant that civil government is the proper remedy.' (Section 13)[50]

Man in the Lockean state of nature is driven into civil society because of the inconveniences, but sometimes, the civil society might aggravate the inconveniences thus choking the identity and individuality of the individual.

Making the Lockean state of nature his starting point, he argues against the claim of the anarchists that the state is 'intrinsically immoral' and resuscitates 'this archaic notion' and tries to prove that 'a state would arise from anarchy (as represented by the Lockean state of nature) even though no one intended this, or tried to bring it about, by a process which need not violate anyone's rights.'[51]

Nozick states in Chapter I 'why state of nature theory' that the investigation of the SN also serves explanatory purposes.

Referring to three possible ways of understanding the political realm–1. To fully explain it in terms of the non-political, 2. To view it as emerging from the non-political but irreducible to it, 3. To view it as a completely autonomous realm–he maintains that the first promises full understanding of the whole political alternative–and he calls it a fundamental explanation.

So, he juxtaposes the state of nature, which is non-political against the state, which is political and states :

'The more fundamental the starting point, (the more it picks out basic important and inescapable features of the human situation) and the less close it is or seems to its result (less political or statelike it looks), the better.'[52]

On the other hand, if the state were reached from an 'arbitrary and otherwise unimportant starting–point', it would not serve the explanatory purpose, hence Nozick maintains that :

'Prudence alone would recommend that we pursue the alternative of showing how a political situation would arise out of a non-political one; that is, that we begin a fundamental explanatory account with what is familiar within political philosophy as state-of-nature theory.'[53]

The state of nature theory has certain advantages : (a) It is something which is not unknown or unfamiliar within political philosophy, (b) It is important, unarbitrary and fundamental, (c) This state-of-nature theory which is fundamental, also serves the purpose of explanation. In the words of Nozick.

"A theory of a state of nature that begins with fundamental general descriptions of morally permissible and impermissible actions, and of deeply based reasons why some persons in any society would violate these moral constraints, and goes on to describe how a State would arise from that state of nature will serve our explanatory purposes, even if no actual state ever arose that way."[54]

He further maintains that "State of nature explanations of the political realm are fundamental potential explanations of the realm and pack explanatory punch and illumination even if incorrect. We learn much by seeing how the state could have arisen, even if it didn't arise that way. If it didn't arise that way, we also would learn much by determining why it didn't."[55]

Giving his explanations for having revived the Lockean state of nature, he reiterates, in the concluding paragraph of Chapter I, 'why state of nature theory', that "Since considerations both of political philosophy and of explanatory political theory coverage upon Locke's state of nature, we shall begin with that. More accurately, we shall begin with individuals in something sufficiently similar to Locke's state of nature."[56]

Notes and References

1. Spitz, David (1982) 'Justice For Sale' In 'The Real World of Liberalism,' Chicago and London, The University of Chicago Press, p. 140.

2. Barber, Benjamin, R (1982) 'Deconstituting Policies : Robert Nozick and Philosophical Reductionism' In Freeman and Roberson (Eds) 'The Frontiers of Political Theory', Heritage, p. 28.

3. Shapiro, Ian, *op. cit.*, p. 202.

4. Wolff, Jonathan (1991) 'Robert Nozick, Property Justice and The Minimal State' Cambridge Polity Press.

5. Spitz, David, *op. cit.*, p. 150.

6. *Ibid.*, p. 156.
7. Mc Grath, Michael J, (1978) 'On Radical Individualism and Social Justice : A Critique of Robert Nozick's Political Theory' In 'Liberalism and The Modern Polity' Marcell Drekker Inc., New York, p. 284.
8. Barber, Benjamin, *op. cit.*, p. 31.
9. Mill, J.S. (1970) 'Principles of Political Economy : With Some of Their Application To Social Philosophy', Books IV and V Baltimore–Penguin.
10. Locke, John (1988) 'Two Treatises of Government', Ed Peter Lanslett, Cambridge, Chapter 4, Section 42.
11. Lomasky, Loren (1987) 'Persons, Rights and The Moral Community' O'up–125-28–Quoted in Machan and Rasmussen (Eds) 'Liberty For The Twenty First Century' p. 323.
12. Barber, Benjamin, *op. cit.*, p. 38.
13. Ackerman, Bruce A (1980) 'Social Justice in the Liberal State', Yale University Press, pp. 185-86.
14. *Ibid.*, p. 185.
15. Spitz, David, *op. cit.*, p. 158.
16. Barber, Benjamin, *op. cit.*
17. Spitz, David, *op. cit.*, p. 158.
18. *Ibid.*, p. 159.
19. *Ibid.*, p. 159.
20. *Ibid.*, p. 160.
21. *Ibid.*
22. Bellamy, Richard 'Liberalism and Modern Society : An Historical Argument' Polity Press, pp. 220-21.
23. Nozick, R (1974) 'Anarchy, State and Utopia', *op. cit.*, p. ix.
24. Spragens, Thomas, A (1999) 'Civic Liberalism : Reflections On our Democratic Ideals', New York, Rowman and Littlefield Publishers, Inc., p. 36.

25. Lafollette, Hugh (1979) 'Why Libertarianism Is Mistaken' In John Arthur and William Shaw (Eds) 'Justice and Economic Distribution.' pp. 194-206.
26. *Ibid.*
27. *Ibid.*
28. Bellamy, Richard, *op. cit*, pp. 220-21.
29. Spragens, Thomas A, *op. cit*, p. 47.
30. *Ibid.*, p. 48.
31. *Ibid.*, p. 49.
32. Barber, Benjamin (1982) *op. cit.*
33. Spitz, David, *op. cit.*, p. 162.
34. *Ibid.*, p. 162.
35. *Ibid.*, p. 162.
36. Hagopian, Mark N (1985) 'Ideals and Ideologies of Modern Politics' New York, Longman Inc., p. 80.
37. Nozick, R (1974) 'Asu', *op. cit.*, p. 331.
38. *Ibid.*, p. 332.
39. Nozick, R, (1974) *op. cit.*, p. 3.
40. *Ibid.*, p. 4.
41. *Ibid.*, p. 4.
42. *Ibid.*, p. 5.
43. *Ibid.*, p. 5.
44. *Ibid.*, p. 5.
45. *Ibid.*, p. 5.
46. Locke, John, II Treatise, *op. cit.*
47. *Ibid.*
48. *Ibid.*
49. *Ibid.*
50. *Ibid.*

51. Nozick, R. (1974), *op. cit.*, p. 7.
52. *Ibid.*, p. 7.
53. *Ibid.*, p. 7.
54. *Ibid.*, pp. 8-9.
55. *Ibid.*, p. 9.
56. *Ibid.*, p. 9.

Bibliography

Primary Sources

Books by Nozick

1. Nozick, Robert (1974) 'Anarchy, State and Utopia', New York, Basic Books, Inc, Publishers.
2. Nozick, Robert (1981) 'Philosophical explanations, Harvard; Belknap/Harvard.
3. Nozick, Robert (1989) 'The examined life': Philosophical Meditation'–New York, Simon and Schuster.
4. Nozick, Robert (1993) 'The Nature of Rationality' Princeton, Princeton University Press.
5. Nozick, Robert (1997) 'Socratic puzzles' Harvard; Belknap/Harvard.
6. Nozick, Robert (2001) 'Invariances, Harvard University Press.

Articles by Nozick

1. Nozick, Robert (1973, December) Distributive Justice, Philosophy and Public Affairs.
2. Nozick, Robert (1969) "New Comb's problem and Two principles of choice in N. Rescher et al. (eds) Essays in Honour of C.G. Hempel, Holland: D, Reidel.

3. Nozick, Robert (1963) 'The normative theory of individual choice', Ph.D. Dissertation, Princeton University.

4. Nozick, Robert (1968) 'Moral complications and moral structures' Natural Law Forum 13.

5. Nozick, Robert (1969) 'Coercion' in S. Morgenbasser et al. (eds) 'Philosophy, Science and Method,' New York: St. Martin's Press.

6. Nozick, Robert (1969) 'Weighted voting and one man, one vote' in J.R., Pennock and R. Chapman (eds) Representation, New York, Atherton Press.

7. Nozick, Robert (1971) 'On the Randian argument', The Personalist' 52, Spring.

Secondary Sources

Books

1. Ackerman, Bruce (1980) 'Social Justice in the liberal state', New Haven: Yale University Press.

2. Arbalaster A (1984) 'The rise and decline of western liberalism', Oxford Oup.

3. Barker, E. (1951): 'Political thought in England', London, Oxford University Press.

4. Barry, Brian (1973): 'The liberal Theory of Justice: A critical examination of the principal doctrines in a Theory of Justice', Oxford : Clarendon Press.

5. Barry, Brian (1995): 'Justice as Impartiality', Oxford: Clarendon Press.

6. Bellamy Richard (ed) (1991) 'Victorian Liberalism : Nineteenth century, political thought and practice,' London, Routledge.

7. Bellamy, Richard (1992) 'Liberalism and Modern Society', Ambridge, Polity Press.

8. Berlin, I. (1969): 'Four essays on liberty', Oxford, Oup.

9. Boaz, David (1997): 'Libertarianism: A Primer', New York: The Free Press.

10. Boyes, Jane, H (1982) 'Ideologies and interest group politics' Novato, California. Chandler and Sharp Publishers Inc.

11. Bramstead, E. K., Melhuish E.K. (eds.) (1978) 'Western liberalism : A History of Documents from Locke to Croce', London, Longman.

12. Brecht, Arnold (1959): 'Political Theory, The foundation of twentieth century political thought', Princeton, Princeton University Press.

13. Clarke, Peter (1978): 'Liberals and Social Democrats', Cambridge, Cambridge University Press.

14. Cohen, G.A. (1995): 'Self-Ownership, Freedom and Equality', Cambridge: Cambridge University Press.

15. Cohen, M.R. (1946): 'The faith of a liberal', New York: Henry Halt and Co.

16. Crick, B. (1973): 'Political theory and practice', London, Allen Lane.

17. Daniels, Norman, ed. (1975): 'Reading Rawls: Critical Studies of a Theory of Justice', Oxford: Blackwell.

18. Delaney C.F. (Ed.) (1994): 'The liberalism communitarian debate', Maryland: Rowman and Littlefield.

19. Dodd Lawrence and Jillson Calvin (eds) (1994) 'The dynamics of American politics: Approaches and interpretations', San Francisco, Oxford: Westview Press.

20. Dunn, J, (1979): 'Western Political theory in the face of the future', Cambridge: CUP.

21. Dunn, John (1969): 'The political thought of John Locke: An Historical Account of the argument of the two treatises of government', Cambridge, CUP.

22. Dworkin, Ronald (1978): 'Taking rights seriously', Cambridge, Harvard University Press.

23. Dworkin, Ronald (1985): 'A matter of Principle', Cambridge: Harvard University Press.

24. Eccleshall, Robert (1986) 'British Liberalism : liberal thought from the 1640s to 1980s, Harlow, Longman.

25. Freeden, Michael (1978) 'The New Liberalism : An Ideology of social Reform', Oxford, Clarendon.

26. Freeman, Michael, Robertson David (ed.) (1982): 'The Frontiers of Political Theory: Essays in a revitalized discipline', Heritage Publishers.

27. Friedman, Milton (1962): 'Capitalism and Freedom', Chicago: University of Chicago Press.

28. Galston, William (1991); 'Liberal purposes', Cambridge: Cambridge University Press.

29. Galston, William, A (1991): 'Liberal purposes'; New York, Cambridge University Press.

30. Gaus, Gerald (1982): 'The Modern liberal theory of man': London, Canberra Croom Helm, St. Martin's Press, New York.

31. Gauthier, David (1986): 'Morals by Agreement', Oxford: Clarendon Press.

32. Girvetz, Harry K. (1950, Rev; 1963): 'The evolution of liberalism', New York; Collier.

33. Goldstone, Paul, N (1980) 'The collapse of the liberal empire: science and revolution in the Twentieth Century' Novato, California: Chandler and Sharp Publishers.

34. Gray and Pelczynski (eds) (1984) 'Conceptions of liberty in political philosophy', London, Athlone Press.

35. Gray, John (1989): 'Liberalisms: Essays in Political Philosophy', London and New York: Routledge.

36. Grimes, Alan Pendleton, 'American Political Thought', New York, Holt, Rinehart and Winston.

37. Hall, John, A (1987) 'Liberalism : politics, Technology and the market', London, Paladin.

38. Hampton, Jean (1998): 'Political philosophy', Delhi, Oxford University Press.

39. Hartz, Louis (1962): 'The liberal tradition in America', New York: Harcourt, Brace and World.

40. Hartz, Louis (1995): 'The liberal tradition in America', New York, Harcourt.

41. Haworth, Alan (1994): 'Anti-Libertarianism: Markets, Philosophy, and Myth', London and New York: Routledge.

42. Hobhouse, L.T. (1964): 'Liberalism'; New York, OUP.

43. Hobson, J.A. (1909) 'The Crisis of liberalism : New issues of Democracy', London, P. S. King and Son.

44. Horton, John and Mendus, Susan, eds., (1994): 'After MacIntyre: Critical Perspectives on the Work of Alasdair MacIntyre', Cambridge. Polity Press.

45. Hospers, John (1971) 'Libertarianism', Los Angles: Nash.

46. King, D (1987) 'The New Right : Politics, markets and citizenship,' London, Methuen.

47. Koerner, Kirk F (1985) 'Liberalism and its critics', London and Sydney, Croom Helm.

48. Kymlicka, Will (1990): 'Contemporary Political Philosophy: An Introduction': Oxford, Clarendon Press.

49. Laski, H, (1962): 'The rise of European liberalism', Atlantic highlands, N.J.: Hamilton Press.

50. Laski, H.J. (1962): 'Liberty in the modern state', New York, George Allen and Unwin, New York.

51. Locke, John (1963): A letter concerning toleration.

52. Locke, John (1965): 'Two treatises of Government' ed. Peter Laslett', New York: New American Library.

53. Macintyre, Alasdair (1981): 'After Virtue: A study in moral theory', London: Duckworth.

54. Macintyre, Alasdair (1988): 'Whose Justice? Which Rationality?', London: Duckworth.

55. Macintyre, Alasdair (1990): 'Three Rival Versions of Moral Enquiry:' Encyclopaedia, Genealogy, Tradition, London: Duckworth.

56. Macpherson, C.B. (1973): 'Democratic Theory: Essays in retrieval', Oxford, Clarendon Press.

57. MacPherson, C.B. (1977): 'The life and times of liberal democracy': Oxford–OUP.

58. Macridis, Roy C (1980): 'Contemporary political ideologies: Movements and Regimes:' Cambridge, Massachusetts; Winthrop Publishers.

59. Manning, D. J. (1976) 'Liberalism', London, Dent.

60. Mansfield, Harvey (1978): 'The spirit of Liberalism', Cambridge, Harvard University Press.

61. Meyers Diana T. (1985): 'Inalienable Rights: A defense', New York: Columbia University Press.

62. Michael J Gargas Mc. Grath (1978): 'Liberalism and the modern Polity: Essays in contemporary political theory', New York and Basel, Marcel Drekker Inc.

63. Mill, J.S. (1962) 'Essays on politics and culture', Gertrude Himmelfarb (ed) Anchor books, Doubleday and Company Inc, Garden City, New York.

64. Miller, David ed. (1991): 'Liberty'–Oxford, OUP.

65. Minogue, Kenneth (1963) 'The liberal mind' New York: Random House.

66. Mulhall, Stephen, Swift Adam (Eds.) (1992): 'Liberals and Communitarians' Oxford, Blackwell.

67. Murray, Charles (1997): 'What it means to be a libertarian', N.Y. Broadway Books.

68. Nathan, H.L., and Heathcote Wiliams (eds.) (1927) 'Liberal points of view', London, Ernest, Benn.

69. Neill, Thomas (1953): 'The rise and decline of liberalism', Milwaukee, Bruce Publishing Co.

70. Rawls, John (1993): 'Political Liberalism', New York: Columbia University Press.

71. Rawls, John: 'Collected Papers,' Freeman, Samuel (eds), Oxford, Oxford University Press.

72. Raz, Joseph (1986): 'The Morality of Freedom', Oxford: Clarendon Press.

73. Rose, Nikolas (1999): 'Powers of Freedom',– Refraining political thought', Cambridge, CUP.

74. Rothbard, Murray (1974) 'For a new liberty', New York.

75. Ruggiero, Guido De (1925): 'The history of European Liberalism', Oxford: Collingwood.

76. Ruggiero, Guido, de. (1927): 'The history of European liberalism', R.G. Collingwood (Trans), London, Oxford University Press.

77. Sabine, George H. (1937): 'A history of political theory', London, Harrap.

78. Samuel, H.L. (1902) 'Liberalism : an attempt to state the principles and proposals of contemporary liberalism in England', London, Grant Richards.

79. Sandel, Michael (1982): 'Liberalism and the Limits of Justice', Cambridge: Cambridge University Press.

80. Stankiewicz, W.J. 'Political thought since World War-II', London: The Free Press of Glencoe Collier Macmillan Ltd.

81. Taylor, Charles (1992): 'Multiculturalism and 'The politics of Recognition' Princeton': Princeton University Press.

82. Vincent, Andrew (1992): 'Modern Political Ideologies', Blackwell Publishers.

83. Walzer, Michael (1983): 'Spheres of Justice: A defense of pluralism and equality', New York, Basic Books.

84. Watkins, Frederick (1948): 'The political tradition of the west: A study in the development of modern

liberalism', Cambridge, Mass: Harvard University Press.

85. West Robin (1997): 'Caring for justice', New York, London: New York University Press.

86. Wintrop Norman ed. : 'Liberal Democratic theory and its critics', London and Canberra, Croom Helm.

87. Wolff, Jonathan (1991): 'Robert Nozick: Property, Justice and the Minimal State', Cambridge: Polity Press.

Articles

1. Acton, H.B. (1972): 'Distributive Justice: The individual hand and the cunning of reason', Political Studies, No. 4.

2. Arnold, Scott, N (1995): 'Capitalism, Socialism and Equity Ownership in Machan and Rasmussen (eds) 'Liberty for the twenty first century: Contemporary libertarian thought–Rowman and Little field, pp. 227-42.

3. Barber, Benjamin R (1974): 'Justifying Justice' in Norman Daniels (Ed) Reading Rawls: Critical Studies of a Theory of Justice, New York: Basic Books.

4. Bloom Allan, 'Justice: John Rawls Vs the Tradition of Political Philosophy', American Political Science Review, Lxix June, 1975, pp. 648-62.

5. Brubaker, Stanley, 'Can Liberals Punish', American Political Science Review, Vol. 82, No. 3, September, 1988.

6. Brugger, Bill (1983): 'Classical British and European Liberalism and Democracy', in Norman Wintrop (Ed) Liberal Democratic Theory and its critics– London and Canberra, Croom Helm, p. 10.

7. Davis, Michael (1977) 'Necessity and Nozick's theory of entitlement' in 'Political Theory' Vol. 5, No. 2, May 1977, Sage Publications Inc.

8. Doyle, Michael W. (1986): 'Liberalism and World Politics', American Political Science Review. Vol. 80, No. 4.

9. Dunbar Leslie (1991) 'What do liberals stand for' in Dunbar (ed) 'Reclaiming liberalism', New York, London, W.W. Norton and Co.

10. Dunn, John (1968): 'Justice and the interpretation of Locke's Political Theory', Political Studies' No. I.

11. Dworkin R. (1978): 'Liberalism', Hampshire (ed.) 'Public and Private Morality' ed. Cambridge, pp. 113-43.

12. Galston William, 'Liberal Virtues' American Political Science Review, Vol. 82, No. 4, December 1988.

13. Goldsmith, M.M. (1979): 'The entitlement Theory of Justice considered', Political Studies, No. 4.

14. Goodin Robert E (1990): 'Liberalism and the Best Judge Principle' Political Studies, Vol. 38, No. 2.

15. Gunnell, John, G (1988): 'American Political Science, Liberalism and the invention of political theory' American Political Science Review, Vol. 82, No. 1, March, 1988.

16. Gutmann, Amy (1985): 'Communitarian critics of liberalism', Philosophy and Public Affairs, 14, 3, 308-22.

17. Hanson, Russell, L (1994) 'Liberalism and the course of American social welfare policy' in Dodd and Jillson (eds) 'The dynamics of American politics: approaches and interpretations' San Francisco, Oxford: Westview Press.

18. Held, David (1984): 'Liberalism, Marxism and the future direction of public policy', in David Held (Ed) 'Political Theory and the modern state: Essays on state, power and democracy', Cambridge Polity Press, pp. 158-73.

19. Held, David (1984): 'The contemporary polarization of democratic theory: The case for a third way', in David Held, *op. cit.*, pp. 174-88.

20. Hospers, John (1995): 'what libertarianism is', 'Liberty for the twenty-first century: Contemporary Libertarian Thought' Machan, Rasmussen (eds) Rowman, Littlefield, pp. 5-17.

21. Hubin, D.C. (1979): 'The scope of justice', philosophy and public affairs, Vol. 3.

22. Johnson, Gregory R (1995): 'Against moral minimalism' in Machan and Rasmussen (Eds), *op. cit.*, pp. 335-49.

23. Lane, Robert, E (1986): 'Market, Justice, Political Justice', American Political Science Review, Vol. 80, No. 2.

24. Lomasky, Loren, E (1995): 'Liberal Obituary' in Machan and Rasmussen (Eds) 'Liberty for the twenty-first century: Contemporary libertarian thought', Rowman and Littlefield, pp. 243-58.

25. Machan, Tibor (1995): 'Business Ethics in a free society', in "Liberty for the twenty-first century: Contemporary libertarian thought" (eds.) Machan Rasmussen–Maryland Rowman Littlefield.

26. Machan, Tibor, R (1995): 'The non-existence of basic welfare rights' in Machan and Rasmussen (eds) 'Liberty for the twenty-first century: Contemporary libertarian thought'–Rowman and Littlefield, pp. 207-26.

27. Mack, Eric (1995): 'Moral Individualism and Libertarian Theory' in Machan and Rasmussen (Eds) Liberty for the twenty-first century: Contemporary Libertarian thought', pp. 41-58.

28. Michelman, Frank I (1974): 'Constitutional Welfare Rights and a Theory of Justice' in Norman Daniels (Ed) 'Reading Rawls: Critical studies of a Theory of Justice' New York, Basic Books, pp. 319-48.

29. Miller David (1990): 'Resurgence of Political Theory' Political Studies–Vol. 38, No. 3.

30. *Ibid.*

31. Narveson, Jan (1995): 'Contracting for Liberty' in Machan and Rasmussen (Eds) "Liberty for the twenty-first century: Contemporary Libertarian Thought".

32. Neal, Patrick (1993): 'Vulgar Liberalism', Political Theory, Vol. 21, No. 4.

33. Pateman C. (1985): 'The problem of political obligation: A critique of liberal theory', Cambridge: Polity Press.

34. Rasmussen, Douglas B. (1995): 'Community Versus Liberty' in Machan and Rasmussen (Eds) 'Liberty for the twenty-first century: Contemporary libertarian thought', Rowman Littlefield, pp. 259-87.

35. Shapiro, Daniel (1995): 'Liberalism and Libertarianism : Narrowing the Gap' in Machan and Rasmussen (Eds)–Liberty for the twenty-first century: Contemporary libertarian thought', Rowman Littlefield, pp. 289-304.

36. Sinopoli, Richard C. (1995): 'Thick-Skinned Liberalism; Redefining Civility': American Political Science Review, Vol. 89, No. 3, September.

37. Skoble, Aeon (1995): 'The anarchism controversy' in Machan and Rasmussen (Eds) "Liberty for the twenty-first century: contemporary libertarian thought', *op. cit.*, pp. 77-95.

38. Steiner, Hille (1981): 'Liberty and Equality' Political Studies, No. 4.

39. Stephen, James, Fitzjames (1874) 'Liberty, Equality, Fraternity' in Muller Jerry (ed) 'Conservatism: An anthology of social and political thought from David Hume to the present' (1997) Princeton, Princeton University Press.

40. Taylor Charles M. (1979): 'What's wrong with negative liberty' in 'the idea of Freedom' ed. Ryan. A, Oxford, OUP.

41. ULYL, Douglas T.D. (1995): 'The right to welfare and the value of charity' in Machan and Rasmussen (Eds), *op. cit.*, pp. 305-54.

42. Walzer, Michael, 'Liberalism and the art of separation', Political Theory, 12, No. 3 (August, 1984).

43. Williams, Bernard (1973): 'A critique of utilitarianism' in Smart J.J.C.: Williams Bernard (1973): Utilitarianism: For and Against', Cambridge: Cambridge University Press.

44. Yates, Steven (1995): 'Righting Civil Wrongs: Toward a libertarian Agenda' in Machan & Rasmussen (Eds) 'Liberty for the twenty-first century: Contemporary Libertarian Thought' Rowman Littlefield, pp. 121-42.

Index

M

N

O

P

R

S

T

U